POLITIPEDIA

NICK INMAN

Hh

Harriman House Ltd
3A Penns Road
Petersfield
Hampshire
GU32 2EW

Tel. +44 (0)1730 233870
Fax +44(0)1730 233880
Email: enquiries@harriman-house.com
Website: www.harriman-house.com

First published in Great Britain in 2007 by Harriman House Ltd.
Copyright © Harriman House Ltd

The right of Nicholas Inman to be identified as the author has
been asserted in accordance with the Copyright, Design and
Patents Act 1988.

ISBN 1-905-64133-8
ISBN13 978-1-905641-33-8

British Library Cataloguing in Publication Data
A CIP catalogue record for this book can be obtained from the
British Library.

Printed and bound by CPI Group, Antony Rowe Ltd.

POLITIPEDIA

A COMPENDIUM OF
USEFUL AND CURIOUS
FACTS ABOUT BRITISH POLITICS

NICK INMAN

About the author

Nick Inman was born in Yorkshire in 1956 and studied politics at the University of Bristol in the 1970s before becoming a travel writer specialising in Spain. He is married with two children and lives in southwest France.

Acknowledgements

If politics is by definition a social activity, writing a book is a solitary pastime but it depends on more than one person. I was given a solid base for my political thinking by my lecturers at Bristol University but it was a fellow student, John Godsall, who steered me off the course reading list to see the wider context in which politics exists. I have had a great many political arguments with a great many people since then – I probably lost the majority of them and I have forgotten most of them (the people and the arguments); in hindsight (but not at the time) I'm grateful to anyone who set me straight with the facts, upset my assumptions and prejudices, or forced me to think in a new direction.

More specifically to the project in hand, my principal sources are obvious on many pages of the book but I made particular use of the *Guardian*, the *Daily Telegraph*, BBC Radio 4 and the extraordinary Wikipedia (often the starting point for a train of thought).

Other people and organisations who responded to my questions included Neil Astley of the superb Bloodaxe Books, the staff of the Politics Studies Association, the Cabinet Office, Hansard and the House of Commons Information Office.

Friends who contributed in small or large measure are Richard Kelly, Stewart Wild (an eclectic disseminator of information), Philip Jenks (to call him merely my sympathetic editor would understate his contribution), Steve Eckett (zeitgeist monitor and indefatigable intellectual sparring partner), Michael Jacobs (for sensible advice which I largely ignored) and my wife, Clara Villanueva, who helps me filter good ideas from bad and who came up with the title.

If I have forgotten anyone, I hope they will take my gratitude as given. Any errors, of course, are all my own work.

To my dad who taught me – and continues to teach me – the infuriating truth that there are always two sides to any argument.

A note on sources

In compiling this book I have drawn from a wide range of sources; if these aren't acknowledged page by page it is only to avoid cluttering the text with footnotes. Wherever possible, I have used official and other primary sources – government departments, politicians' own websites, recorded interviews and the like – and the most important of these are either listed in the bibliography or webography, or can be reached by a link from one of the websites mentioned. All statistics are inevitably presented here out of their original context. I have selected them to suit my purpose and sometimes simplified them – but I hope not misleadingly so – in the pursuit of clarity.

Although I have made strenuous efforts to check and correctly credit all material, there may be errors of which I am unaware, particularly among the quotations. Attributions are hard to establish when they concern private conversations or throwaway remarks out of earshot of a microphone.

Contents

Introduction

"I have no consistency, except in politics; and that probably arises from my indifference on the subject altogether."

Byron in a letter 1814

"People are very interested in politics, they just don't like it labelled 'politics'."

Douglas Hurd, former Conservative cabinet minister

The stuff that governments get up to is usually studied under the category of 'political science' but it's hard to imagine a subject less scientific. You only have to look at any news bulletin to realise that politics is less an accumulation of clinically-derived data driving towards ineluctable truth and more a cocktail of personalities (with their ambitions, pretensions, ideals and foibles); inscrutable institutions; archaic traditions; national bad habits and nostalgic fantasies; theories experimental, out-of-date and yet to be tested; and above all a daily grind of messy interactions between all these ingredients of a dog's dinner that make up a modern state.

True, politics has a lot in common with some genuine scientific disciplines. It has as much drama and melodrama, sex and violence, rampant hormones, enflamed passions, competitions, cruelties, feuds, grudges and pack warfare as anthropology, zoology and even botany but it is just not susceptible to reasoned analysis in the same way. You can count all the election returns you can get hold of and crunch them statistically until the end of eternity but you still won't know for sure why those floating voters in that unstable ward of that marginal constituency acted the way they did when they were behind the closed curtain of the polling booth.

If politics is not termed science how then are we to make sense of it? And make sense of it we must; for politics is not a thing of marginal importance, a spectacle to entertain us and invite our derision; it is the vital process by which human beings decide who gets what and how they treat each other in the meantime. On it hangs the present and future of society and civilisation. To laugh at political institutions; to fume with ire at the disappearing act which is taxation; to dismiss politicians as self-servers, or even deviants of the human race, does not bring understanding.

Perhaps the best we can do to begin with is to see politics as it is. This book is for anyone who is curious about how things get decided and done in modern Britain and who is willing to suspend judgement for a couple of hours. (You can go back to fuming after you've read it – perhaps with more reason.) It assumes no prior knowledge whatsoever on the part of the reader; but it is not meant to be a text book or a technical guide to the metamorphic constitution. Instead, it is best thought of as a series of portraits of the key elements of politics with a few less transcendental topics thrown in for light relief.

It is organised as a series of 156 themes arranged in alphabetical order. Each of these themes is a self-contained item (usually, but not always, in list form) so that you can read the book in any order, front to back, back to front, at random – or use it as an encyclopedia to look up a specific topic.

There are too many words written and spoken each day about politics and I believe brevity and clarity should be the guiding principles for anyone who adds to the subject. If anything in this book stimulates a desire to know more there are various pointers to further reading, listening and viewing in the text, especially in the bibliography and 'webography' at the end.

Beyond offering what I hope is a good read, there is an ulterior motive to all this: to make the political system plain so that there can be no doubt about where and how it needs reforming. We're often told that people in Britain are disengaged from politics; and when a third of the electorate doesn't bother to vote in a general election, we'd be wise to ask what they prefer doing on polling day. There is evidence that most people are not so much uninterested in politics as disinterested: the system which they technically own and pay for is remote from them and difficult to understand. Those with a stake in the structures of power – politicians and civil servants – seem incapable of understanding how the political system is seen and experienced from outside, by the ordinary taxpayer and voter. If we're truly interested in slimming the state to its optimum size and making government transparent and responsive, we must start by making sure that the institutions and procedures of government adapt themselves to the needs of citizens, not the other way around.

Acronyms

30 appealingly articulateable abbreviations

Creep
Committee for the Re-election of the President. The president being Richard Nixon, this is possibly the most prescient acronym ever invented as it gives a sense of villainy afoot: it was this committee that channelled funds to the Watergate burglars.

Dora
Defence of the Realm Act 1914. A far-reaching measure to control the home front during the First World War through censorship, requisitioning and prohibition of suspicious activities – including kite-flying.

Gerbil
Great Education Reform Bill. Sadly (for acronym lovers) this became the more prosaic Education Reform Act 1988.

Grapo
Grupos de Resistencia Antifascista Primero de Octubre. Spanish terrorist organisation less well known than ETA (another acronym).

Grunk
Gouvernement Royal Unifiée Nationale Khmer. A Khmer Rouge-dominated government of Cambodia.

Mad
Mutually Assured Destruction. A system of defence devised by apparently sane people on the foolproof assumption that if at any time it did not work, no one would be around to notice.

Maff
(rhymes with "naff") *Ministry of Agriculture, Food and Fisheries.* Subsumed into Department for Environment, Food and Rural Affairs (Defra) in 2001.

Moab
Massive Ordnance Air Blast. A formidable piece of US weaponry. It is widely believed that the official name was dreamed up to fit the acronym which really comes from "Mother of All Bombs".

Natsopa
National Society of Operative Printers and Assistants. A union mouthful that was swallowed by Sogat (Society of Graphical and Allied Trades) which in turn became part of the blandly-named, unacronymic Amicus.

Neddy
National Economic Development Council. Created by Harold Macmillan in 1962 to give an overview of economic activity and dismantled by Norman Lamont in 1992 when planning had gone out of fashion. Little Neddies looked after certain sectors of the economy.

Nibmar
No Independence Before Majority African Rule. A principle urged upon Harold Wilson by African Commonwealth leaders in 1964-5 when Ian Smith's white Rhodesia was trying to win independence.

Olaf
Office Européen de Lutte Anti-Fraude (European Anti-Fraud Office), created in 1999. A name conjuring up the image of an incorruptible Scandinavian hunter who sets out on a simple-minded, malice-free quest to make those in power see that cheating citizens out of their life savings is wrong. It replaced the more guttural Uclaf, who you wouldn't want to meet on a dark night.

Pest
Pressure for Economic and Social Toryism. Now part of the Tory Reform Group.

Smig
Salaire Minimum Interprofessionnel Garanti. The French minimum wage.

Thigmoo
This Great Movement of Ours. Jocular 1970s shorthand for the trade union movement.

Acts of Parliament

16 lumps of legendary legislation

Parliament churns out a great deal of legislation each year, some trivial, some significant. Only with hindsight is it possible to say which laws have a lasting impact on politics and society and even then, to paraphrase Mao when he was asked whether the French Revolution had had any lasting effects, it's always "too early to tell."

Below are 16 of the most important statutes passed by Parliament.

Parliamentary and Municipal Elections Act 1872 (Ballot Act)
Introduced secret voting in place of a show of hands and other public systems which were open to intimidation and corruption.

Offical Secrets Act 1911
A measure which was rushed through parliament in a single sitting in response to a particular but short-lived crisis in Morocco. It has been used since then, with updates, as a blanket restriction on the freedom of speech for anyone working for the government. In the same year the Parliament Act curbed the power of the Lords.

Representation of the People Act 1928
Allowed women to vote under the same conditions as men (a full 35 years after New Zealand, which gave women the vote in 1893).

National Health Service Act 1946
Created the NHS.

Coal Industry Nationalisation Act 1946
The first symbolic step towards increasing state ownership by the Attlee government. It was followed by the Transport Act 1947 which nationalised the railways.

Indian Independence Act 1947
Accepted the loss of the British Empire's "jewel in the crown" and marked the beginning of the end of the empire itself.

Murder (Abolition of Death Penalty) Act 1965
Introduced a trial abolition of capital punishment for five years. This became permanent (although the death penalty is still legally possible in certain circumstances) in 1969. The issue has since been debated several times but the death penalty was definitively killed off by the Human Rights Act of 1998 (see overleaf).

Race Relations Act 1965
A milestone in Britain's acceptance of its multicultural self.

Abortion Act 1967
Marked the end of the lottery of back-street abortions.

Sexual Offences Act 1967
Decriminalised homosexual acts in private between men over 21 years old (reduced in 1994 to 18).

Divorce Reform Act 1969
Permitted the ending of a marriage on the grounds of irretrievable breakdown rather than requiring the 'guilt' of one party or other. It marked the end of defended divorce cases and the introduction of what critics called 'quickie' divorces.

European Communities Act 1972
Confirmed Britain's accession to EU membership (the EEC as it then was). The act was the culmination of more than a decade of negotiations and frustrations. It was endorsed by a referendum in 1975 but a section of the British political class (the 'eurosceptics') continues to oppose membership as vehemently as ever.

Sex Discrimination Act 1975
Protects women, men and transgender people from discrimination, particularly in the workplace.

Telecommunications Act 1984
The first and most symbolic step in the Thatcher privatisation programme created the phone company BT by selling over half the shares to the public. Many other state-owned industries were similarly sold off in the following years.

Human Rights Act 1998
Came into force in October 2000 bringing Britain in line with the European Convention on Human Rights.

Scotland Act 1998
Set up the Scottish Parliament and established the principle of (limited) devolved powers within the United Kingdom.

Freedom of Information Act 2000
A significant, if some say unsatisfactory, step towards open government.

Alternative Politics

10 new ways to use or think about power

> *"Government itself is an awesome strategy for avoiding pain and conflict. For a considerable price, it relieves us of responsibilities, performing acts that would be as unsavoury for most of us as butchering our own beef. As our agent, the government can bomb and tax. As our agent, it can relieve us of responsibilities once borne face to face by the community... It takes our power...our consciousness. Many social tasks have reverted to government by default, and the end result has been creeping paralysis - unreality.... Above the citizens stands an immense, mild, paternal power that keeps them in perpetual childhood."*
>
> Marilyn Ferguson, 'The Aquarian Conspiracy'

Can politics be conducted in any other way than that traditionally practised by the politicians of the world? Does it always have to involve polarisation, argument, conflict, duplicity, mendacity, compromising, deal-cutting, lying, cheating, distorting the truth, manipulation, coercion, repression, corruption and all the other undesirable qualities we associate with political systems? Is it possible to organise societies without power structures?

Outside the conventional field of politics, a lot of political thinking and experimentation goes on which doesn't always get the consideration it deserves – or even get taken seriously. If we can break from our habitual ways of analysing politics – left versus right, governors versus governed etc. – maybe we can find better ways of doing things. In her 1980 book *The Aquarian Conspiracy*, Marilyn Ferguson discusses some different ways to think about political power. The list that follows is based on her work, with adaptations and additions.

Power of each person
Individuals can make a difference if they use their resources effectively. Anyone can start a national or international campaign for some cause or other. "Cast your whole vote, not a strip of paper merely, but your whole influence," wrote Thoreau. "Let your life be a counter friction to stop the machine."

Ego-free leadership

Leadership does not necessarily imply an authority figure convincing and coercing subservient followers to act against their will. A good leader acts from selfless motivation; he rises above popularity and adulation; he sees him or herself as empowering others; sharing rather than delegating; and he knows when to give up power for the greater good.

Network power

"The network is the institution of our time," says Marilyn Ferguson: "an open system, a dissipative structure." In a network, power is spread equally; it is everywhere and it is nowhere; it is a collective will. Modern communications – especially the internet – have freed us to form networks without central nodes, censors and someone always in charge.

Power of paying attention

If we stay alert when everyone around is half-asleep, distracted, cynical or in denial of reality, there is much we are able to learn and there are many new opportunities to put to good advantage. Just listening to people – listening especially to the fears, hopes and passions behind the words they use – can give us the means to transcend the normal divisions in society.

Power of self-knowledge

It sounds obvious, but you have to change yourself before you change the world. If you know your own strengths and weaknesses, your selfish impulses, which emotions drive you, you can better understand others and remove yourself from power games. Go into psychotherapy before you go into politics.

Political aikido (or the 'power of flexibility')

Rigid organisations, such as political parties, pride themselves on holding fast to assumptions (dogma) made in the past and sticking to methods that are familiar if not always effective in times of rapid change. Flexibility is a more apt response to the modern world. This does not mean being opportunistic, or amoral: rather it means moving towards a fixed goal but acting in the best way to fit the circumstances while always being aware of the needs and feelings of other people.

Power of creativity

The future is always unwritten and we have more choices than we think we have. Experimentation and innovation can throw up unexpected new ways of acting. "There is no riskless route into the future," says Robert Theobald, economist and futurologist. "We must choose which set of risks we wish to run."

Power of a new paradigm

Rather than seeing traditional political structures and concepts as essential for continuity and security we can question them in part or as wholes. We can spend so much time thinking about how to preserve something sacred that we don't allow ourselves to realise that we would be better off without it.

Power of withdrawal

We give authority power to use on our behalf, unconsciously, by default. We can always take back the power we have temporarily given up through boycotts and abstentions, but we can do it in a positive way rather than as a reaction. "... in the great game being played, we are the players as well as the cards and the stakes," observed Teilhard de Chardin. "Nothing can go on if we leave the table. Neither can any power force us to remain."

Satyagraha

The political philosophy of Gandhi has often been translated as "passive resistance" to authority and he himself used the terms synonymously to begin with. But later he sought to make it clear that satyagraha is not resistance in any violent sense and it can never be from a position of passivity or weakness. The doctrine is best summarized as the unbending pursuit of what is right or truthful while paying as much attention to one's inner, spiritual source of strength as to outside events. It may involve non-cooperation and civil disobedience but it is not antagonistic towards an opponent: it seeks not to beat authority but to transform it.

Anarchists

7 schemes for the subversion of the state

"I sit on a man's back, choking him and making him carry me, and yet assure myself and others that I am very sorry for him and wish to lighten his load by all possible means – except by getting off his back." Tolstoy

Far from signifying lawlessness or chaos, anarchy is a respectable political philosophy which holds that society can be run in an orderly way without the need for an authoritarian state and a ruler. It assumes the best in people and the worst in governments. Anarchist thinkers and doers have attempted several times in the last 150 years to demonstrate how life could be if we all took responsibility for ourselves. Sometimes their experiments have begun and ended in violence – which tends to get the headlines – but mostly they have been peaceful, collaborative ventures. Always, anarchist thought and deed provides a powerful commentary on conventional politics. Britain, unlike some other European countries, has never had a strong leaning towards anarchy but it has always had an anarchist presence and could claim to have the longest anarchist tradition of all.

- **William Godwin (1756-1836)** The author of *Enquiry Concerning Political Justice* never called himself an anarchist – he was technically a minarchist (a believer in small government) – but his thinking in response to the French Revolution was enormously influential on anarchists to come. He asserted that all men and women were endowed with reason and all individuals had the capacity to learn. His first disciple was his son-in-law, the poet Shelley.

- **Rudolf Rocker (1873-1958)** Although Rocker wasn't himself Jewish he is remembered as 'the anarchist rabbi' because of his work among immigrant Jews in Whitechapel in the early 20th century. While in London, he met Kropotkin, the influential Russian theorist of anarchism. Rocker's activities in Britain came to an end in 1914 when he was interned because of his German nationality (although he opposed both sides in the war) and in 1918 he was deported. He was opposed to both the Bolshevik revolution and a critic of the Nazis. "I am an anarchist not because I believe anarchism is the final goal," he wrote while in London, "but because there is no such thing as a final goal."

- **Sidney Street Siege or the Battle of Stepney, 3 January 1911** A gun battle between two or three Latvian anarchists, led by a man called Peter the Painter, and police in the East End of London. The Home Secretary, Winston Churchill, watched the siege first hand and ordered in troops to help the police. The siege ended with a fire and the defenders apparently being burned to death.

- **Great Unrest 1911-14** Until the Bolsheviks proved that they could complete a successful revolution in the name of communism, anarchism was the most tempting option among the working class and early trade unionists. There was a strong anarchist impulse behind the four years of strikes which preceded World War I and which principally affected the coal and steel industries, the docks and the railways. One member of the government described the country as, for a time, close to civil war.

- **The General Strike 1926 (anarcho-syndicalism)** The success of the socialist cause in the Russian Revolution, the rise of trade unionism and the involvement of the Labour Party in parliamentary politics diminished the attraction of anarchism after World War I but anarchists were still active in the syndicalist movement which sought to disrupt industries, topple bosses and put workers in charge of their own factories. The failure of the General Strike finally relegated anarchism to no more than an undercurrent of British politics.

- **Angry Brigade 1970-72** A radical 'urban guerilla' group influenced by libertarian communism and anarchism carried out bombings of embassies, police stations, banks and the homes of important Conservative MPs. The attacks were aimed at property and only one person was injured. Four members of the group were sentenced to 10 years in prison.

- **Direct Action** Anarchy lives on today as an influence behind a disparate array of political and social causes from the squatter movement (an application of Proudhon's dictum that "property is theft") to contemporary environmentalism and anti-globalisation protests. (see 'Direct Action' p96)

Animalism

7 Commandments from George Orwell's Animal Farm

1. Whatever goes upon two legs is an enemy.
2. Whatever goes upon four legs, or has wings, is a friend.
3. No animal shall wear clothes.
4. No animal shall sleep in a bed.
5. No animal shall drink alcohol.
6. No animal shall kill any other animal.
7. All animals are equal.

In chapter 10, when the farm is being run by pigs walking on their hind legs, the seven commandments are replaced on the wall by a single commandment:

> **ALL ANIMALS ARE EQUAL**
>
> **BUT SOME ANIMALS ARE**
>
> **MORE EQUAL THAN OTHERS**

Backbench Rebellions and Government Defeats

10 troubled times of in-house insurrection

> *"When in the House MPs divide,*
> *If they've a brain and a cerebellum too,*
> *They have to leave their brains outside*
> *And vote just as their leaders tell 'em to."*

Gilbert and Sullivan, 'Iolanthe'

Party discipline – exercised by the whips who can resort to virtual blackmail in order to bend the will of their MPs – is meant to ensure that the government's legislation gets on to the statute book with the reliability of a production line; but some MPs in every parliament vote against the more controversial measures sponsored by their own party, out of conscience or obstinacy.

MPs know that they risk condemning themselves to a life on the backbenches – or might even be forced to look for another job – if they step out of line. Some rebel only once and their careers do not suffer for it. Others are repeat offenders and accept that their independent-mindedness will bar them from ever holding government office.

When everyone knows that a vote is going to be close, the House of Commons wakes up. Behind the scenes much wheedling and coercing goes on before the divisive division. The government's last weapon – to be used sparingly, but better than outright defeat – is to negotiate or even back down over a contentious issue but then it risks denting its own self-esteem.

In normal circumstances, when a government has a large majority and can count on the *de facto* support of smaller parties and independents, backbench rebellions do no more than register a protest vote that is at worst an embarrassment. But just occasionally, a government faces more than a backbench tantrum; it can actually be defeated. Minority governments are naturally most vulnerable. If the vote is over one amendment or even a pet bill it is bad enough, but things are dire if it is a vote of no-confidence in its ability to govern.

✗ 1924

Only three no-confidence motions have brought down a government since 1900, two of them happening in the same year. On 21 January Baldwin's government ceded to the first, short-lived Labour government which was itself unseated on 8 October 1924, triggering dissolution of parliament and an election.

✗ 8 May 1940

Days after Hitler's Germany invaded Norway, and the day before it overran the Low Countries, Chamberlain survived a censure motion in the House of Commons but 40 of his own MPs had voted against him and several more had abstained. He was forced to question his position as war leader. On 10 May, Chamberlain resigned and Churchill took over.

✗ March to July 1974

The Labour minority government was defeated 17 times between the two elections that were held in this year. The Wilson-Callaghan governments of 1974-79, with only a dwindling majority in the Commons, had to endure 42 backbench rebellions in four and a half years.

✗ 25 January 1978

A Labour backbench rebellion led to a wrecking amendment being inserted into the bill allowing Scotland a referendum on devolution. The amendment stipulated that 40% of the electorate, irrespective of turnout and without regard to discrepancies in the electoral register (for instance, not discounting voters who had died since the register was drawn up), must vote in favour for the result of the referendum to be accepted. The referendum on 1 March 1979 produced a narrow majority in favour of devolution but only 32.9% of the electorate were in favour. The Scotland Act had to be repealed – the Blair government would later pick up this piece of unfinished business – and this contributed to the historic government defeat four weeks later.

✗ 28 March 1979

The Labour government under Jim Callaghan was defeated on a vote of no confidence moved by the Conservatives under Margaret Thatcher. An election had to be called and the rest is history.

✗ **14 April 1986**

The second reading of a bill (the occasion on which it is first discussed by the House of Commons) is normally a formality and governments have only faced defeat at this stage on three occasions in the past. The most recent and well known was the second reading of the Shops Bill when 72 Conservative MPs voted against it and 20 abstained. It was one of only four rebellions that Margaret Thatcher experienced during her eleven years in office.

✗ **6 December 1994**

When the Chancellor of the Exchequer Kenneth Clarke proposed to increase VAT on domestic fuel, the move prompted seven Conservative MPs to vote against it and a further eight to abstain. He adjusted his plans in a 'mini-budget'.

✗ **11 December 1997**

With a huge majority in parliament and fresh from historic electoral success, Tony Blair suffered his first major rebellion after only seven months in office when 47 backbenchers opposed plans to cut benefits to single parents. In the years that followed, the Labour government had to deal with a succession of rebellions against student grants and university tuition fees, changes to incapacity benefit (won by a majority of only 40), measures in the Freedom of Information Bill (which incurred five backbench revolts), the privatization of air traffic control, anti-terrorism measures, the promotion of faith schools and the creation of foundation hospitals.

✗ **26 February 2003**

122 backbenchers voted against the government's policy of war against Iraq.

✗ **14 March 2007**

The government's intention to replace the Trident nuclear missile system was approved by 248 votes in the House of Commons but the victory was only won because of Conservative support. All but two Tories supported the government while 95 Labour MPs, including four ex-Cabinet ministers, rebelled.

Afterthought One

> *"But then the prospect of a lot*
> *Of dull MPs in close proximity,*
> *All thinking for themselves, is what*
> *No man can face with equanimity."*

Gilbert and Sullivan, *'Iolanthe'*

Afterthought Two

"Only those who are prepared to make a mockery of representative democracy can prosper under the parliamentary whip... It should be illegal to interfere in an MP's decisions. If parties wish to persuade their members to vote in a particular way, they should do so by means of argument, not threats. Any suggestion that someone's voting record will affect the course of her career would be referred to a parliamentary ombudsman."

George Monbiot, *The Guardian*, 12 June 2001

BBC Objectivity

10 iffy instances of impartiality

> *"It is much more dangerous to trivialise than ever it is to criticise politicians."*

William Rees-Mogg
Times editorial about the BBC 1971

Licensed by Royal Charter and dependent on government for its funding, the BBC has a duty to be politically impartial. Its sense of balance has been called into question a number of times and the arguments continue about whether or not it is intrinsically biased and/or susceptible to covert pressure from the government of the day – and therefore abusing the public funds it obtains from viewers' licence fees. The BBC claims to always act in good faith, behave as transparently as possible and to be in a constant state of soul-searching. Perhaps the only way we can know that it is doing its job properly is when no one in politics loves it.

General Strike 1926

Many newspapers weren't printed during the General Strike and the Chancellor, Winston Churchill, wanted to commandeer the then British Broadcasting Company as a means for the government to communicate with the public. The founder and Director-General Lord Reith argued that the company's independence was at stake and this was accepted by Prime Minister Stanley Baldwin. Churchill was furious. The Labour Party and the TUC were angry with the BBC for refusing airtime to their representatives – including the leader of the Opposition, Ramsay MacDonald, former and future prime minister.

The Vernon Bartlett Affair 1933

In October 1933, BBC journalist Vernon Bartlett added a personal comment to a straight news report about Hitler pulling out of the League of Nations Disarmament Conference: "I believe the British would have acted in much the same way as Germany if they had been in the same position." The *Daily Telegraph* and *Evening Standard* launched into him saying that it was for the government to make such remarks, not a BBC correspondent. Bartlett was forced to resign.

Suez 1956

Prime Minister Anthony Eden expected the BBC to give its patriotic support to the government of the day during wartime, just as it had done (uncontroversially) during World War II. The nation was split over the three-day Suez conflict and the BBC's decision to grant airtime to the anti-war Labour Party leader Hugh Gaitskell enraged Eden. The government considered action to "discipline" the BBC and it was rumoured that this might include taking over the editorial control of the corporation. For Eden, of course, Suez spelled his downfall.

The Satire Boom 1963-4

The BBC didn't instigate the sudden explosion of anti-Establishment comedy in the early 60s but Conservatives were surprised that it joined in so enthusiastically – wasn't it part of the Establishment itself? The BBC's *That Was the Week that Was*, better known as *TW3*, found an easy target in the dying Macmillan-Home government which seemed to represent an anachronistic Britain in which deference was expected towards the aristocrats and old Etonians in office. The staid BBC appeared suddenly to have grown rude and cynical and the Prime Minister Alec Douglas-Home complained that it wasn't so much satire that *TW3* was producing, as personal insult.

Yesterday's Men 1971

The BBC broadcast a documentary that ridiculed the outgoing Labour government a year after losing the election. It took its title slyly from an insult Wilson had used against the Tories during the election campaign but neither the title nor the scathing journalistic approach was revealed to the Labour MPs who were asked to take part. In the BBC's own words, the tone of the film was "waspish". Wilson's press secretary called the finished production "calculated, deliberate, continuous deceit". For a long time afterwards the Labour Party distrusted the BBC.

Real Lives 1985

Mrs Thatcher had recently stated her wish that terrorists be starved of "the oxygen of publicity" when she found out the BBC had interviewed a Republican paramilitary for one of its *Real Lives* documentaries. The Home Secretary Leon Brittan declared that the programme was against the national interest and wrote to the

Chairman of the BBC asking him to cancel the broadcast. The governors complied but staff were furious at what they saw as government censorship and went on strike. The programme was eventually shown, with modifications.

Falklands War 1982

The BBC was put under pressure to take a patriotic stance on the Falklands war, just as it had been encouraged to knuckle under for Suez. John Snow on *Newsnight*, began one sentence: "If we believe the British..." which one MP described as "almost treasonable". *Panorama* meanwhile produced a programme called 'Can We Avoid War?' Success in the military campaign eventually defused tensions between the Government and the BBC but the corporation was adamant: "it is not the BBC's role to boost British troops' morale" and "the widow in Portsmouth is no different from the widow in Buenos Aires".

Libyan bombing 1986

Norman Tebbit accused the BBC of unbalanced reporting of the US bombings of 14 April 1986. He produced a point-by-point analysis of the BBC's reporting compared with ITN's and concluded that the BBC's coverage was "riddled with inaccuracy, innuendo and imbalance". The BBC responded by rebutting Tebbit's charges and the affair ended in stalemate.

Rod Liddle 2002

The editor of the flagship *Today* programme on Radio 4 was forced to resign after an article he had written in the *Guardian* criticising the Countryside Alliance brought into question his impartiality.

The Kelly Affair 2003-4

When BBC reporter Andrew Gilligan suggested that the government had deliberately misled Parliament with the claim that Iraq could deploy weapons of mass destruction within 45 minutes, the government demanded an apology. Gilligan's source for the story, weapons specialist Dr David Kelly, committed suicide because of the pressure of public exposure. The BBC was found to have made unfounded allegations by the ensuing enquiry and its chairman and director-general resigned.

Bill Boaks

10 facts about Britain's most eccentric campaigner

After a distinguished military career which included being at Dunkirk and taking part in the action which sank the Bismarck, Lieutenant-Commander William Boaks (1921-1986) devoted the latter part of his life to an heroic (or futile, depending on how you choose to see it) political career.

Like the greatest well-intentioned eccentrics, there was some sense and wisdom hidden behind what most of the world mistook for buffoonery. "Always steer towards the gunfire," he remarked, not of his military experiences but of his civil campaigns.

1. Bill Boaks started his campaigning career by trying to stand against Clement Attlee in 1951 but registered in the wrong constituency (Walthamstow East rather than Walthamstow West) by mistake.

2. He stood in 40 general elections and by-elections between 1951 and his final appearance in 1982. At one election he stood for three constituencies simultaneously.

3. His worst result was 5 votes (less than the number of nominees he needed in order to stand in the first place) and his best 240 votes. He was an important influence on Britain's other eccentric campaigner, Screaming Lord Sutch.

4. His perennial campaign theme was road safety. "More people have been killed on the roads this century than in war," he claimed in 1974.

5. One of his policies, if elected, would have been to invert the Highway Code as it applied to zebra crossings so that the roads between crossings would become places for pedestrians to walk in safety and the black and white stripes themselves would be considered ordinary road.

6. He also had a more serious awareness of the problems of Westminster politics. He proposed scrapping the division lobbies in favour of secret ballots so that MPs could vote according to their consciences not according to instructions given by the whips.

7. Boaks gave his 'movement' a different name for each election but a typical one was 'Land Sea and Air Democratic Monarchist Public Safety White Resident and Women's Party'. Some elements of the name were added just to provoke people.

8. Apart from standing for elections, Boaks's other tactic in his campaign for road safety was to launch private prosecutions against public figures who had been involved in road accidents.

9. In October 2000, Lord Hodgson of Astley Abbott referred to Boaks during a debate in the House of Lords: "His campaigning methods mostly consisted of climbing inside a large cardboard box, on the outside of which were painted his slogans, renting a bicycle and slowly cycling around the constituency. It cannot be said that he obtained great public support. I think that 30 votes were cast in his favour. Perhaps Mr Boaks was what one might call a one-club golfer. But he was not sexist; he was not racist; he was not ageist; he was not any other 'ist'. He was in effect a slightly eccentric elderly gentleman."

10. Ironically, after half a lifetime campaigning for road safety, Boaks died in 1986 as the result of being hit by a motorbike.

British Empire in the 21st Century
14 spots on the globe where the sun hasn't yet set

Britain's Overseas Territories, most of them called 'colonies' until 1981, are not part of the United Kingdom, but belong to it. They have little in common with each other apart from being British: the island of Pitcairn, lost in the Pacific Ocean, has only 47 inhabitants, whereas Bermuda has a population of over 62,000 and is an important centre for international finance.

Anguilla

British Antarctic Territory

Bermuda – Britain's oldest colony

British Indian Ocean Territory

British Virgin Islands

Cayman Islands

Falkland Islands (called Las Malvinas by Argentina which disputes sovereignty)

Gibraltar

Montserrat

St Helena and Dependencies (Ascension Island and Tristan da Cunha), Turk and Caicos Islands

Pitcairn Island

South Georgia and South Sandwich Islands

Sovereign Base Areas on Cyprus

Broadcasting

A history of politics on radio and television

> *"If any sentence in a television broadcast has more than twenty words, when it gets to the end most people have forgotten how it began. Including the person speaking it."*
>
> Antony Jay and Jonathan Lynn 'Yes Minister'

Ask any totalitarian dictator: whoever controls the mass media, controls the terms of debate. Democracy depends on information and most people's primary source of information today is television – although increasingly challenged by the internet.

There are strict rules on political access to television in Britain, frequently argued over and maintained by a consensus of the main parties in agreement with the TV companies. TV news teams are charged with reporting politics as impartially as they can but politicians are also given direct access to the airwaves themselves.

Each political party in Britain that can muster a certain number of candidates for an election has the right to one or more party political broadcasts (sometimes called slots to make them sound less boring). It has never been established how effective these broadcasts are – even the most skillfully made probably only reassure supporters rather than win converts – but the parties make as much use of them as they can.

1923
From the start of the BBC (1922), there was an issue over political access to the airwaves. John (later Lord) Reith, the BBC's general manager, felt that the fairest way to cover politics was to let each party have a certain amount of airtime. Neville Chamberlain, Postmaster General, considered this idea subversive.

1924
The go-ahead for the first party political broadcasts – the radio equivalent of delivering manifestos by post. For the election of that year the three party leaders were given 20 minutes each on air. Ramsay MacDonald was the first to broadcast.

1929

The first attempt at a formalized system of political broadcasting. Reith proposed giving minor parties access dependent on the number of candidates they were putting up at the general election. The Communist Party made one broadcast. The favoured format was still to have a party official read the manifesto on air.

1938

The first prime ministerial speech on television, given by Neville Chamberlain after returning from negotiations with Hitler. Only 10,000 people were able to watch it.

1939

The television signal was switched off during the war by orders of the Home Office because it believed German bombers would attempt to lock their navigation systems on to it. It was switched on again on 7 June 1946, after the election the previous year. In the meantime, BBC radio served as a propaganda arm of the government, its only competition being Lord Haw-Haw's broadcasts of Nazi propaganda. Goebbels is said to have commented that the BBC had won "the intellectual invasion" of Europe.

1950

The first televised election night, complete with rudimentary graphs and results. The presenters weren't allowed to speculate on the outcome because they were legally curtailed by the Representation of the People Act 1948. Neither of the two party leaders of the time thought much of television. Attlee considered the medium too invasive and Churchill suspected the BBC to be full of communists.

1953

The first party political broadcast proper was delivered, outside election time, by Macmillan for the Conservatives. The coronation, live on television a month later, is thought to have inspired many people to buy their first TV set. By the time of the 1955 election a third of homes had one.

1955

Commercial broadcasting began (ITV), creating competition for the BBC, including in its news programming and other political coverage. Politicians suddenly became visual beings rather than just talking heads.

1956
The Suez Conflict became, in a sense, Britain's first televised war – that is, the first war to be discussed on television. Labour leader Hugh Gaitskell contributed to the downfall of Prime Minister Anthony Eden by making a broadcast criticizing the government's foreign policy.

1967
First TV broadcasts in colour. Politicians still looked grey and it will be a long time before they come to terms with the image-making potential of television.

1970s and 1980s
The widespread availability of video recorders and remote controls (and later the introduction of satellite TV) made it easy for people from now on to avoid watching party political broadcasts or even any discussion of politics at all.

1978
The start of regular radio broadcasts from Parliament on 3 April. The nation was unimpressed by MPs' behaviour.

1979
With the help of advertising agency Saatchi and Saatchi, the Conservatives under Margaret Thatcher used television to its fullest potential, producing the most compelling party political broadcasts to date on the theme of 'Labour isn't working'.

1990
Rules on party political broadcasting established by statute. Regular televising of the proceedings in the House of Commons began on 19 July after a five-year experimental period.

2000s
In the era of rolling news, spin-doctors, image-makeovers and soundbites, does television serve politics or does politics serve television? Most politicians seem to believe that they will never get elected unless they adapt their images to the requirements of television and there is a widespread public perception that style has been championed over substance. But is this the fault of the broadcasters or the politicians?

Budget on the Back of an Envelope

A lesson in bar-top numerology

Public finances are enormously complicated, and endless footnotes, parentheses and lengthy explanations must be added to any set of facts and figures to make them accurate. Or must they? Surely any idea can be expressed on a variety of levels, including as a set of simple statements. If the Chancellor of the Exchequer had to explain to the proverbial man in the pub what his job boiled down to, in language that even a taxpayer can understand, this is what he might say*. A beermat may be used if there isn't an envelope available.

What we earn

1. The United Kingdom creates £1200 billion (that's 1,200,000,000,000 pound coins) worth of wealth a year (technically known as GDP). If you laid this money out in £10 notes it would cover over 50,000 square miles, approximately the whole of England.

2. Of this amount, the government collects £500 billion in taxes. £135 billion of this comes from income tax.

3. Relatively few people pay tax. Of 60 million people in Britain, 29 million do not earn anything, or very little:

    - 3 million are still in nappies
    - 8 million are at school
    - 200,000 are at university
    - 1.7 million are looking for a job
    - 74,000 are in prison
    - 9 million are retired
    - an indeterminable number live off the proceeds of crime or (a slightly different thing) the black economy

---

*Note: the figures used in this section have been compiled from a variety of sources. They are rounded approximations and do not refer to any particular year. For the most up-to-date figures see www.hm-treasury.gov.uk and www.statistics.gov.uk.

- a few lucky people live off rents and inherited wealth
- the remainder are fulltime carers, disabled, housewives/ husbands/mothers and others who are not employed

4. Of the 31 million in employment, 5 million work in the public sector which means that although they pay their taxes it is the equivalent of the government paying itself. So 26 million people in the private sector have to produce the wealth to support everyone else.

5. It has been calculated by The Taxpayers' Alliance that the average household will contribute £600,000 in taxes over a working lifetime of 40 years followed by 15 years' retirement.

What we spend

6. All the money that comes into the Treasury, goes out again. Relatively minor amounts go to:

- interest payments for government borrowings: 5% of the tax take, or £25 billion pounds
- The EU. Estimates of Britain's contribution vary but one official figure puts it at £3,091,000,000 per annum, equivalent to £50 per person per year, or £1 per person per week (double if you assume the burden falls only on people earning an income)

7. Major chunks of tax money go on three items on the national shopping list:

- 'social protection' i.e. safety nets for those on low incomes 27%
- the NHS 16%
- education 13%

We all want to work less hours and less years, and we all expect to live longer. Only a handful of people in Britain pay for their own education, healthcare and pensions without troubling the state; or prefer to educate their kids at home; prescribe their own alternative medicine; or fend for themselves in their old age. The vast majority expects the government to provide as much education as they want for their kids, to lay on every form of medical treatment through the NHS (including ones deriving from 'lifestyle choices'), and to pay a humane pension and provide adequate care when they grow old.

Paradoxically, the better the NHS does its job, the longer people live, and the more the state has to keep shelling out on pensions.

8. Defence accounts for 6% of the total spend.

9. The government spends £137 billion or 27% of the tax take on wages for the public sector (including doctors, nurses and teachers, it should be noted, not just bureaucrats).

10. And finally, it costs over £4 billion just to collect the tax, account for it and decide who gets to spend it.

Burke's Brief

In 1774 Edmund Burke gave a famous address to the electors of Bristol, his constituency, in which he summed up his own rationale for serving as an MP. Some politicians would say that no one has put their calling in nobler terms since.

"It ought to be the happiness and glory of a representative to live in the strictest union, the closest correspondence, and the most unreserved communication with his constituents. Their wishes ought to have great weight with him; their opinion high respect; their business unremitted attention. It is his duty to sacrifice his repose, his pleasures, his satisfactions, to theirs; and, above all, ever, and in all cases, to prefer their interest to his own. But his unbiassed opinion, his mature judgment, his enlightened conscience, he ought not to sacrifice to you, to any man, or to any set of men living. These he does not derive from your pleasure; no, nor from the law and the constitution. They are a trust from Providence, for the abuse of which he is deeply answerable. Your representative owes you, not his industry only, but his judgment; and he betrays, instead of serving you, if he sacrifices it to your opinion.

My worthy colleague says his will ought to be subservient to yours. If that be all, the thing is innocent. If government were a matter of will upon any side, yours, without question, ought to be superior. But government and legislation are matters of reason and judgment, and not of inclination; and what sort of reason is that, in which the determination precedes the discussion; in which one set of men deliberate, and another decide; and where those who form the conclusion are perhaps three hundred miles distant from those who hear the arguments?

To deliver an opinion is the right of all men; that of constituents is a weighty and respectable opinion, which a representative ought always to rejoice to hear, and which he ought always most seriously to consider. But authoritative instructions, mandates issued, which the member is bound blindly and implicitly to obey, to vote, and to argue for, though contrary to the clearest conviction of his judgment and conscience; these are things utterly unknown to the laws of this land, and which arise from a fundamental mistake of the whole order and tenor of our constitution.

Parliament is not a congress of ambassadors from different and hostile interests, which interests each must maintain, as an agent and advocate, against other agents and advocates; but parliament is a deliberative assembly of one nation, with one interest, that of the whole; where, not local purposes, not local prejudices ought to guide, but the general good, resulting from the general reason of the whole. You choose a member indeed; but when you have chosen him, he is not a member of Bristol, but he is a member of parliament. If the local constituent should have an interest, or should form an hasty opinion, evidently opposite to the real good of the rest of the community, the member for that place ought to be as far as any other from any endeavour to give it effect....Your faithful friend, your devoted servant, I shall be to the end of my life: a flatterer you do not wish for. On this point of instructions, how ever, I think it scarcely possible we ever can have any sort of difference. Perhaps I may give you too much rather than too little trouble. From the first hour I was encouraged to court your favour to this happy day of obtaining it, I have never promised you anything but humble and persevering endeavours to do my duty. The weight of that duty, I confess, makes me tremble; and whoever well considers what it is, of all things in the world will fly from what has the least likeness to a positive and precipitate engagement. To be a good member of parliament, is, let me tell you, no easy task; especially at this time, when there is so strong a disposition to run into the perilous extremes of servile compliance or wild popularity. To unite circumspection with vigour is absolutely necessary; but it is extremely difficult...this city...is but a part of a rich commercial nation, the interests of which are various, multiform, and intricate...All these widespread interests must be considered; must be compared; must be reconciled if possible. We are members for a free country, and surely we all know that the machine of a free constitution is no simple thing, but as intricate and as delicate as it is valuable...A constitution made up of balanced powers must ever be a critical thing. As such I mean to touch that part of it which comes within my reach. I know my inability, and I wish for support from every quarter."

Business Scandals

6 cases of commercial questionability

> *"When I want a peerage, I shall buy it like an honest man."*
> Remark attributed to Lord Northcliffe by Tom Driberg

Power, business and money go hand in hand and politicians can get caught in the middle. A few give into the temptations created by their positions and some do stupid things, although usually they are guilty of poor judgement rather than wrongdoing or criminality. Often the worst sin is to associate with shady characters who can't tell the difference between a gift and a bribe and don't much care what it is.

Marconi 1912

When Marconi was contracted to build radio stations around the British empire, three Liberal ministers including Lloyd George (before he was PM) were accused of taking advantage of confidential information to profit from share dealing. The Conservatives attacked the three but the government escaped censure thanks to support from the fledgling Labour Party and Irish MPs. Rudyard Kipling wrote a poem, *Gehazi* (see p246) about one of the share dealers, Rufus Isaacs, the attorney general who later became the lord chief justice.

Cash for Honours (Round 1) 1921-22

This was the second drubbing for Lloyd George's reputation and proved more costly than the first. The discreet sale of peerages in return for party funds was nothing new but what was unusual was, as Beaverbrook put it, "a prime minister without a party" – Lloyd George had split from the official Liberal Party during the war – who needed to raise political funds for himself as quickly as he could. The flagrant abuse of the honours system became a scandal precipitating Lloyd George's fall from grace and leading to the Honours (Prevention of Abuses) Act passed in 1923.

The Poulson Scandal

In 1972 Heath's Home Secretary Reginald Maudling resigned as a result of investigations into the business practices of the Yorkshire architect John Poulson. Having filed for bankruptcy, Poulson was found guilty of the widespread bribery of local government councillors in order to win lucrative development contracts for his firm. Maudling was never accused of any illegality, only poor choice of business associates. His resignation probably spared the police the embarrassment of interrogating their own political master. The most important consequence of the scandal was the creation of the Register of Members' Interests which requires MPs to disclose the sources of any outside income or gifts which they receive.

The Westland Affair 1986

There was no suggestion of anyone in politics profiting personally from the deals to help Britain's last ailing helicopter manufacturer, Westland, but the government's interference in the company's affairs almost led to Margaret Thatcher's downfall. The defence secretary Michael Heseltine acrimoniously resigned by walking out of a Cabinet meeting on 9th January and made a public statement to the effect that the Prime Minister had not allowed him to make his case for Westland to become part of a European consortium. The Trade and Industry Secretary Leon Brittan (a supporter of a rival deal with an American company) resigned soon after over allegations that he had been concealing information. It is widely thought that Neil Kinnock had an opportunity in the Commons debate on 27 January to present the Cabinet split as being mortally damaging to Margaret Thatcher but his performance on the occasion was lacklustre.

The Matrix-Churchill Affair 1992

The Major government took a serious knock when it was revealed, after the first Gulf War, that four Midlands businessmen had been illegally selling armaments to Iraq with the connivance of civil servants and possibly with the knowledge of ministers.

Cash for Honours (Round 2) 2006-07

Every government elevates people who have donated to its party's funds to the peerage but for there to be foul play the one has to be linked *quid pro quo* to the other. It is alleged that the Labour government of Tony Blair boosted its coffers in this way. The near-scandal of a serving prime minister being questioned by the police during a criminal investigation has highlighted the role big money from not altogether wholesome sources plays in keeping parties functioning.

Cabinet Composition

The current line-up with job titles explained*

> *"An extraordinary affair. I gave them their orders and they wanted to stay and discuss them."*
> Duke of Wellington on his first Cabinet meeting in 1828

> *"I want them to have the courage of my convictions."*
> Margaret Thatcher on dissenting members of her Cabinet (attrib.)

Like any team the cabinet's personnel varies with the times and according to the whims of the team captain. This is a list of the most recent squad and their playing positions. The job description of most members of the Cabinet is clear from their job titles but a few need further explanation.

1. Prime Minister, First Lord of the Treasury and Minister for the Civil Service.

2. Deputy Prime Minister and First Secretary of State.

3. Chancellor of the Exchequer.

4. Leader of the House of Commons (who manages government business in the House of Commons) and Lord Privy Seal (a meaningless honorific dating from the 14th century. It is fifth in order of the Great Officers of State).

5. Secretary of State for Foreign and Commonwealth Affairs.

6. Secretary of State for Trade and Industry.

7. Secretary of State for the Home Department.

8. Secretary of State for Health.

9. Secretary of State for Culture, Media and Sport.

10. Minister for the Cabinet Office and for Social Exclusion (and Chancellor of the Duchy of Lancaster). The Duchy of Lancaster

---

*The composition of the Cabinet and the distribution of job titles changes. This is the Cabinet formation as Politipedia goes to press.

is the monarch's personal inherited property i.e. it doesn't belong to the Crown and from it he or she takes the Privy Purse which is not part of the Civil List. The Chancellor spends only a small amount of time on Duchy business.

11. Secretary of State for Northern Ireland, and Secretary of State for Wales.

12. Leader of the House of Lords and Lord President of the Council (presides over the Privy Council of which, constitutionally-speaking, the Cabinet is a sub-committee).

13. Lord Chancellor and Secretary of State for Justice.

14. Secretary of State for International Development.

15. Secretary of State for Education and Skills.

16. Secretary of State for Communities and Local Government, and Minister for Women.

17. Secretary of State for Work and Pensions.

18. Secretary of State for Environment, Food and Rural Affairs.

19. Secretary of State for Defence.

20. Secretary of State for Transport and Secretary of State for Scotland.

21. Minister without Portfolio – one of the few job titles in the world which actually specifies that there is no job attached to it. It is used as a way of getting someone useful, generally the chair of either the Labour Party or the Conservative Party, into Cabinet.

22. Chief Whip (Parliamentary Secretary to the Treasury).

23. Chief Secretary to the Treasury.

24. Lords Chief Whip and Captain of the Gentlemen at Arms Head of Her Majesty's Bodyguard of the Honourable Corps of Gentlemen at Arms. The duties of the Gentlemen are now purely ceremonial such as attending royal garden parties and mess dinners. The Chief Government Whip in the House of Lords is always appointed captain but he is not expected to bring his ceremonial battle axe to Cabinet meetings.

Cabinet Secretaries

The machinery of British government is famously secretive and until the middle of the First World War there was no record of decisions reached by Cabinet unless the Prime Minister put them down in a letter to the monarch. In 1916, Lloyd George charged a senior civil servant with the job of preparing the agenda for Cabinet meetings and taking the minutes. Ever since the Cabinet Secretary has been the most powerful, or at least most influential unelected member of the government. He is also the head of the home civil service. There have only been ten Cabinet Secretaries since the post was created and Tony Blair got through four of them.

Cabinet Secretary	In post	Served under	Distinguishing features
Sir Maurice Hankey	1916-1938	Lloyd George Bonar Law Baldwin MacDonald Chamberlain	Appointed first Cabinet Secretary during the First World War and served as a minister in Churchill's Cabinet in the Second World War.
Sir Edward Bridges	1938–1946	Churchill Attlee	Son of the poet laureate Robert Bridges.
Sir Norman Brook	1947–1962	Attlee Churchill Eden Macmillan	Described as "the supremely effective engine-driver of government – the greyest of grey eminences and the most powerful civil servant of his age" by Kevin Theakston, Professor of British Government at the University of Leeds.
Sir Burke Trend	1963–73	Home Wilson Heath	Cabinet secretary for the whole of Wilson's 1964-1970 government.

Cabinet Secretary	In post	Served under	Distinguishing features
Sir John Hunt	1973-1979	Wilson Callaghan	Not to be confused with the mountaineer, John Hunt, who led the first expedition to climb Everest and who photographed yeti footprints.
Sir Robert Armstrong	1979-1987	Thatcher	Famous for his "economical with the truth" remark in Australia in the Spycatcher case in 1987.
Sir Robin Butler	1988-1997	Thatcher Major Blair	Oversaw the transition from a long period of Conservative rule to the rule of New Labour.
Sir Richard Wilson	1998-2002	Blair	First of a new reforming breed of heads of the civil service, he sought to recruit more women and people from ethnic minorities.
Sir Andrew Turnbull	2002-2005	Blair	In March 2007 he controversially described the chancellor, Gordon Brown, as acting with "Stalinist ruthlessness".
Sir Gus O'Donnell	2005-Present	Blair/ Brown	The present incumbent just happens to have the initials, GOD.

Cartoons

The 7 stages of the satirical sketch

"A few years ago I recognised what the nature of my craft is, which is voodoo. It's doing damage to someone at a distance with a sharp instrument, in this case a pen. And it's about sympathetic magic; ancient, dark magic; it's about changing the way people appear by transforming them through the magician's, or cartoonist's brain."

Martin Rowson, political cartoonist and caricaturist,
'Midweek', BBC Radio 4

Cartoonists are the democratic equivalent of the medieval court fool: they scratch at the personality sores of the great and good so that they don't get too full of themselves and that we may be reminded of how gullible we are when it comes to placing our trust in them. A good cartoon – particularly a good caricature – makes us aware of 'defects' in our leaders that we may have been aware of subliminally but couldn't articulate ourselves. Curiously, an art form which relies on topicality and inaccuracy (i.e. distortion of the truth) for its impact also makes a valuable record of British political history. For just short of 300 years, cartoons have been essential toilet reading.

Age of the pisspot

Political cartooning began in the early 18th century, during the reign of the first prime minister, Walpole. It reached its apogee between 1780 and 1830, the era of James Gillray and Thomas Rowlandson, when caricatures were issued as loose prints and sold in coffee shops. They were often rude to the nth degree. One, for instance, shows coalition partners Fox and North defecating into the same chamberpot.

Retreat to the Victorian water closet

Around 1820 cartoons began to appear in newspapers and magazines. This meant that cartoonists could reach much wider audiences but they also had to be less outrageous so as not to offend sensitive and impressionable readers. *Punch*, founded in 1841, became the vehicle of delivery par excellence for the humorous drawing and the home of great artists such as John Leech and Sir John Tenniel. It would publish over 500,000 cartoons (only a few of them on political subjects) before its demise in 1992. In the late 19th century photography began to displace illustration as the visual component of newspapers and magazines but the cartoon survived because of its ability to give another dimension to reality.

Out to the backyard privy

The age of deference and decorum was already coming to an end before Queen Victoria died. The next few decades saw radical changes in politics with the decline in influence of the aristocracy, the entrance of the working class into parliament and the social and economic reforms of Lloyd George. Cartooning, too, became more egalitarian. Great exponents of the age were the caricaturist Max Beerbohm and the pro-working class Australian Will Dyson of the *Daily Herald*.

The indoor flush toilet

The "first press baron of Fleet Street", Lord Beaverbrook, promoted cartoons in his papers the *Daily Express* and the *Evening Standard* as part of a populist attitude to design. He was responsible for the careers of David Low and later Vicky (Victor Weisz), amongst others, even though both of them were broadly left wing. Vicky famously cast Harold Macmillan as the superhero Supermac in the late 1950s. His intention was to ridicule the prime minister's exaggerated sense of his own abilities but he only succeeded in boosting Macmillan's image.

Installation of the low-level cistern

The scandals of the late Macmillan government, the appointment of the aristocratic Alec Douglas-Home as Prime Minister and the emergence of youth culture in the early 1960s fostered the satire boom which sought to attack 'the Establishment'. *Punch* had by now grown staid and *Private Eye* (launched in 1961) became a refuge for cartoonists who felt the politics of the 1960s required a response of overt savagery. Gerald Scarfe and Ralph Steadman typify the era.

Era of the en suite bathroom

Margaret Thatcher created a nation of owner-occupiers and gave fresh impetus to satire with her strident black-and-white world-view. She and her ministers (Michael Heseltine, Norman Tebbit, Norman Fowler, Sir Keith Joseph) were easily caricatured and left-wing cartooning thrived in opposition. The distinctive product of this age was Peter Fluck and Roger Law's *Spitting Image*, the political cartoon transposed to television, which was avidly watched by ministers and voters alike. It was direct and often cruel but by now we had come to believe that politicians deserved whatever they got. Margaret Thatcher was portrayed as a macho bully who used urinals; the puppet of Roy Hattersley sprayed copious amounts of spit whenever he spoke; and Dr David Owen, leader of the SDP, was cast as a miniature in relation to all other politicians.

DIY plumbing and the composting toilet

Everything after Margaret Thatcher was bound to be a come-down for satirists. The great ideological battles had been fought and the Cold War won. Steve Bell in the *Guardian* struggled to pin a personality on John Major and came up at last with the figure of a mediocre superhero (in contrast to Supermac) wearing high-street-bought Y-front underpants on the outside of his costume.

We now seem to see cartoons in a knowing, postmodern way because of three processes which have been going on simultaneously since the early 1990s. Cynicism with politics has become the norm; cartoons have less bite in an age in which everyone assumes all politicians to be venal, corrupt and self-deluding. Politicians (with exceptions) have grown more bland, more careful in what they say and do, less spontaneous and more attentive to their public images – all of which makes the cartoonist's job harder.

Finally, canny politicians have realized that they can disarm satirists by claiming to admire their work (and even collecting it for their own downstairs loo walls). They are probably not always telling the truth, but there is not much point in wielding satire against someone who claims to share the joke.

Catchphrases

10 easy formulae for remembering people, parties and their times

Every politician likes to be remembered for a memorable phrase, even if he or she didn't write it, as long as it evokes positive sentiments. Some phrases, however, stick for the wrong reasons. Almost always, such phrases capture the mood of the times, at least with the benefit of hindsight.

"Smack of firm government" Antony Eden
A newspaper phrase (from the *Daily Telegraph* 3 January 1956) that stuck to an unfortunate prime minister. Every prime minister would like to be remembered for applying the 'smack of firm government' but the *Telegraph* was complaining about the lack of it. The image was inspired by Eden's habit of emphasising a point by smacking his fist into the palm of his other hand.

"You've never had it so good" Harold Macmillan
In a speech to a meeting in Bedford in 1957 Macmillan said: "Let's be frank about it; most of our people have never had it so good."

"The pound in your pocket" Harold Wilson
Used in a broadcast on 19 November 1967 to explain the effects of devaluing the pound: "It does not mean, of course, that the pound here in Britain in your pocket or in your purse or in your bank has been devalued." It now sounds reassuringly inoffensive but at the time it seemed to sum up Wilson's deviousness in trying to present devaluation as a painless affair.

"Unacceptable face of capitalism" Edward Heath
Tory leaders do not traditionally condemn what we now call the "fat cats" of big business but during the Lonrho scandal in 1973 Heath felt obliged to distance himself from greedy but legal manipulation of the tax system by high-earners.

"Crisis? What crisis?" James Callaghan
Callaghan never said this or anything like it but he may as well have.

It comes from the headline of *The Sun* newspaper for 11 January 1979. Callaghan on returning home the day before from a summit in Guadeloupe had said of the mounting strikes in the UK (that would soon bring down his government and pave the way for the Thatcher era), "I don't think that other people in the world share the view that there is mounting chaos." *The Sun's* glib way with words almost certainly hastened Callaghan's end.

"Short, sharp, shock" William Whitelaw
Whitelaw was Home Secretary under Margaret Thatcher from 1979 to 1983. The phrase refers to a tough regime for punishing young delinquents based on the belief that prison had become too cushy to act as a deterrent and that a brief, painful experience was the best way to prevent re-offending. The "short, sharp, shock" had little effect on the crime figures but it did for a time pacify the law and order lobby of the Conservative Party.

"There is no alternative" (or *TINA*) Margaret Thatcher
The first Thatcher phrase to stick – encapsulating her stubbornness or tenacity, according to your point of view – was delivered in a speech she gave to the Woman's Conservative Conference in 1980.

"Rejoice! Rejoice!" Margaret Thatcher
Rather than being verbatim, these two words are a reporter's condensation of Mrs Thatcher's remarks delivered outside No 10 Downing Street on 25 April 1982 after she had heard about the recapture of South Georgia island at the start of the Falklands War. Edward Heath is said to have uttered the phrase on hearing about Mrs Thatcher's failure to win the leadership contest in 1990. Mrs Thatcher has more catch phrases associated with her than any other prime minister.

"Victorian values" Margaret Thatcher
This simple or simplistic summary of the Thatcherite moral highground was probably suggested to her by TV interviewer Brian Walden in January 1983 but in a radio interview three months later she happily elaborated on the notion: "I was brought up by a Victorian grandmother. We were taught to work jolly hard. We were taught to prove ourselves; we were taught self-reliance; we were

taught to live within our income...You were taught that cleanliness is next to godliness. You were taught self-respect. You were taught always to give a hand to your neighbour. You were taught tremendous pride in your country. All of these things are Victorian values. They are also perennial values."

"Roll back the state" Margaret Thatcher
The battle cry of the freemarket wing of the Conservative Party which makes the reduction of state bureaucracy sound as straightforward as rolling up a carpet. It has a whiff of King Canute about it and, paradoxically, echoes Marx's prediction of the "withering away of the state". A paraphrase from her speech in Bruges which freemarketeers quote to each other as often as they quote Henry IV's rallying cry outside Agincourt.

"Back to basics" John Major
A phrase used at the Conservative conference in 1993 to mean a return to the traditional values of the country and hence of the party. It has since come to be ironically associated with a series of sexual and sleaze scandals which bedevilled the later Major government.

"Tough on crime, tough on the causes of crime" Tony Blair
In these days of "political cross-dressing" Conservative leaders have to prove themselves compassionate and Labour leaders show their virility. This phrase from Blair's speech to the 1992 Labour Party conference (while he was still Shadow Home Secretary) was a clever way of appealing to wavering Conservative voters concerned that law-breakers should be decently punished while hinting to members of his own party that he would deal with the poverty and deprivation that they believed to be feeding crime.

"Joined-up government" New Labour
A slogan in frequent use from around 1997 but echoing an age-old desire of all governments for civil service departments to co-ordinate their efforts so as to avoid duplication of services and wasting money. Blair and his ministers found it just as hard as their predecessors to streamline Whitehall and the phrase became a taunt used by their critics.

The Chiltern Hundreds and the Manor of Northstead

A sinecureal exit strategy for MPs

According to a resolution of the House of Commons passed on 2 March 1623, an MP can only lose his seat (apart from through the dissolution of parliament and failure to win re-election) by being disqualified for legal reasons, expelled from the House or by dying – he or she can't simply resign it.

There is only one further option. The MP can accept a paid office of the Crown which automatically disqualifies the holder from sitting in the Commons. Two such offices are kept expressly for this purpose:

1. Crown Steward and Bailiff of the Chiltern Hundreds of Stoke, Desborough and Burnham.

2. Crown Steward and Bailiff of the Manor of Northstead.

They are granted by the Chancellor of the Exchequer and a letter confirming the appointment is sent to the applying member. The two offices are granted alternately. The office is held until someone else needs it. It's a charming or rather barmy tradition, depending on how you look at it.

Applying for one of these offices either means you are on your way up or down, or are making a career move out of politics.

The only exception to this genteel pattern was the mass resignation of 15 Ulster Unionist MPs – including James Molyneaux, the Rev Ian Paisley and Enoch Powell – on 17 December 1985 in protest against the Anglo–Irish agreement which had been signed a month earlier between the governments of Britain and Ireland. All these MPs were appointed to the Chiltern Hundreds and the Manor of Northstead alternately on the same day, each holding the office for a few minutes only.

Date	Name & Appointment	Direction	Reason
1 Jun 1973	Antony Lambton (CH)	↓	Resigned after scandal
11 Feb 1976	Selwyn Lloyd (N)	↑	Raised to peerage
27 Aug 1976	John Stonehouse (CH)	↓	Sent to prison
12 Oct 1976	Edward Short (N)	↑	Raised to peerage
5 Jan 1977	Christopher Tugendhat (N)	↑	Made EU commissioner
5 Jan 1977	Roy Jenkins (CH)	↑	Made EU commissioner
16 Jun 1977	Brian Walden (CH)	⇨	Became broadcaster
19 Jan 1984	Eric Varley (N)	⇨	Became director of private coalmining company
17 Apr 1986	Matthew Parris (N)	⇨	Became a journalist
1 Oct 1986	Robert Kilroy-Silk (N)	↘	Claimed victimization by Militant Tendency
18 Oct 1988	Bruce Millan (CH)	↑	Made EU commissioner
31 Dec 1988	Leon Brittan (N)	↑	Made EU commissioner
16 May 1994	Bryan Gould (N)	⇨	Became an academic
20 Jan 1995	Neil Kinnock (CH)	↑	Made EU commissioner
27 Oct 1997	Piers Merchant (N)	↓	Resigned after scandal
23 Oct 2000	Betty Boothroyd (CH)	↑	Retirement/elevated to the peerage
21 Nov 2000	Dennis Canavan (N)	⇨	Became an MP in the Scottish parliament
8 Sep 2004	Peter Mandelson (N)	↑	Made EU commissioner

Civil Servants

Who they are and what they are supposed to be doing

> *"Britain has invented a new missile. It's called the civil servant - it doesn't work and it can't be fired."*
> General Sir Walter Walker, Observer 1981

> *The Civil Service [has]* *"a difficulty for every solution"*
> Lord Samuel, Home Secretary 1916 & 1931-2

> *"The finest plans are always ruined by the littleness of those who ought to carry them out, for the Emperors can actually do nothing."*
> Bertolt Brecht, 'Mother Courage' (1939)

Anyone who is constitutionally an employee of the Crown, which in English means anyone who works for a government department, is called a civil servant. Confusingly, the monarch's own employees are not civil servants.

Civil servants are not employed by a particular department which means they can be moved around from one office to another at short notice. Special advisers – political appointees – are technically civil servants.

Most public sector employees are not civil servants. So, excluded from the definition are people employed by Parliament, quangos, the NHS, the Armed Forces, public corporations and local authorities.

The Civil Service Code sets out four 'core values' that civil servants must adhere to:

1. *Integrity* is putting the obligations of public service above your own personal interests. You must make sure public money and other resources are used properly and efficiently;

2. *Honesty* is being truthful and open;

3. *Objectivity* is basing your advice and decisions on rigorous analysis of the evidence; and

4. *Impartiality* is acting solely according to the merits of the case and serving governments of different political persuasions equally.

Civil Service Cross-Examination

9 questions to ask all bureaucrats everywhere

> *"The ideal civil servant should always be colourless, odourless and tasteless."*
> Roger Peyrefitte

It is easy to snipe at the civil service for being too big, too inefficient, too self-satisfied and too well-rewarded for what it does, and for any number of other reasons. But if we really want well-behaved public servants we would do better to ask them specific questions about what they think they are doing and how they are doing it.

Rather than pose these questions in the third person impersonal to the 'they' of our imaginations, it is more interesting to frame our mental questions as applying to people we can interrogate in person, 'you'. After all, civil servants are human beings with names; they can speak for themselves; and if we're paying them, they owe us some answers.

The questions below are for all civil servants but specifically for those at the top who make the strategic decisions. But note: every accusation we make against the civil service raises questions that we must ask and answer ourselves. If we are not clear about the brief we are setting civil servants, how can we expect them to fulfill their terms of employment?

"Are you (too) political?"

The convention in British government is that politicians are the masters and civil servants are, um, the servants. The former are elected and discharged according to their policies whereas administrators are career professionals who merely do what is asked of them and offer neutral advice when it is requested. In practice, however, government is a dynamic dance between ministers (politicians) and their permanent secretaries, locked in marriage at the head of every department. Civil servants occasionally make pronouncements on politics but mostly do their best to look as if it is nothing to do with them. Politicans sometimes see political distortion where none exists. When New Labour came to office in

1997 after 18 years in opposition, it assumed the civil service had turned into a wing of the Conservative Party. Sir Robin Butler, transition head of the civil service, claims that his staff overcompensated in the attempt to prove this to be a misconception.

"Are you wasting our money?"

For the taxpayer, every civil servant's salary is a salary too much – perhaps every politician's salary too – and every paper clip is a drain on public resources. Almost every organisation could be accused of spending money unnecessarily – who can ever know whether the right people would still be recruited if the pay package was 5% less? – but the civil service should rightly be scrutinised more closely than most.

"Are there too many of you?"

Organising and staffing a civil service is a constant managerial nightmare and for all the talk of shrinking states and joined-up government, civil servants, like death and taxes, will always be with us. Margaret Thatcher famously divested herself of a number of them (her privatisation programme helped) and there are periodic attempts to reorganise departments to avoid duplication of tasks. The appointment of special advisers and the creation of quangos (see p266) complicate the organigram.

"Are you accountable...?"

In what Peter Hennessy calls 'the governing marriage' at the head of each government department there is no such thing as a no-fault divorce. By cruel tradition, the minister takes all the blame, even for the incompetence of quite lowly bureaucrats while the permanent secretary who is their day-to-day boss remains in post for the sake of continuity. A consequence of this system is 'trial by tabloid' in which pressure from newspapers can force the resignation of a minister, as the public face of the department, while his civil servant opposite number remains in the shadows. One solution to the accountability problem would be to have a written contract between minister and permanent secretary defining each other's areas of responsibility.

"...which means, can we fire you if we want to?"

Some politicians believe the lopsided arrangements for accountability to be unfair. They accuse the civil service of hiding behind ministerial scapegoats while safeguarding jobs for life for all their staff regardless of their performance. The current head of the civil service, Gus O'Donnell, however, claims that poorly performing staff are sacked.

"Don't you have any feelings?"

Do we want impersonal unflappable 'below stairs' flunkeys to wait on us or people who put some enthusiasm into their jobs? Can people do their job without a degree of commitment? Gus O'Donnell espouses what he calls 'the four Ps': *pride, pace, professionalism* and *passion* – as in 'passionate about making the world a better place'. Fostering esprit de corps and individual job satisfaction is not a superfluous luxury: politicians who want to take all the decisions themselves, to centralise power, without leaving any to the initiatives of civil servants can find their most ambitious policies derailed by officials who feel no sense of ownership of government.

"Aren't you too secretive?"

"The default setting of the civil service is still secrecy", Anne Perkins pronounced in a BBC radio investigation of the civil service. It could be argued that some measure of closed-door confidentiality is necessary if business is to be discussed with frankness and clarity, and decisions taken by those in positions of responsibility rather than by pundits in the media. But there again, transparency is always a virtue in public organizations and perhaps the ideal is operational secrecy day-to-day, but full disclosure of information at determined intervals.

"Are you delivering more than your own career structures, salaries and knighthoods?"

The job of the civil service is, in the end, to deliver government services to the public. Politicians often complain that the promises they make are not fulfilled by civil servants. Civil servants, on the other hand, complain that politicians make unrealistic promises thus putting them in an impossible situation. In recent years there have been institutional attempts to make the civil service work to targets but it is never easy to measure productivity in public administration, especially if politicians are setting unachievable goals.

"Are you reformable?"

If we aren't satisfied with the answers to the above questions, can we modify or overhaul the bureaucracy or is it going to be resistant to all change? By its very nature, the British civil service doesn't like too much change and it could be said that change only hinders the very continuity on which democracy relies. The answer must be to always search for a balance between structures that work and the overhauling of those that have become obsolete. Sometimes it is not the organisation that needs to be reformed but the 'mindsets' of those who inhabit it – and such things are, by definition, hard to alter.

Clichés

10 phrases that should be put out to grass at this point in time

'anecodotal evidence'

Non-existent evidence which is evidence of nothing – that is, gossip. Politicians cite 'anecdotal evidence' as a vindication of their policies in the same way that journalists quote 'unnamed sources', knowing that such 'evidence' can't be confirmed but can't be refuted either.

'clear blue water'

The invisible gap which separates you from an opponent who is trying to steal your meticulously thought out policies and pass them off as his own.

'core values'

There is something solid and unmoveable about a 'core' and something reassuring about 'values'. Any politician who dared spout about 'ethics', 'virtues' or 'morals' instead would be dismissed as a religious nutter.

'issues around'

This phrase from psychotherapy means 'problems with' ('challenging issues' means 'intractable problems') and the reason why it is used so often is obvious: who wouldn't rather have issues than problems? David Blunkett for one. In 2003 he told the *Today* programme:

> *"It is about addressing issues that you don't have to address now, but if you don't will come back to bite you . . . Clandestine entry and working in this country, the misuse of free public services, the issues around organised crime and terrorism – all these issues will be the ones for years to come."*

'legacy'

Something you try to 'secure' especially if you are a departing prime minister. Failure to do so is to be consigned to Trotsky's 'dustbin of history'.

'put in place'

Derived from management speak and used to make public administration sound like a homely trade, akin to carpentry or car mechanics. It means 'implement'.

'renewed'

A pleasing way to describe anything rehashed or recycled, especially anything your opponents have described as failing. That which is renewed combines the best of two policies – the old one and the one to come. It is a way of admitting that things were going badly without being accused of doing a u-turn.

'robust'

An all-purpose combination of *strong, no-nonsense, good, efficient, effective, admirable, appropriate* and whatever else you can cram into it.

'(smooth) transition'

A more reassuring process than change. A transition, by implication, is always heading in the right direction and is under control.

'u-turn'

What you must never do, or at least admit to doing. The term originated in the US in 1961, came to Britain during the Heath government, was famously eschewed by Margaret Thatcher and is still used as the insult of choice to identify hypocrisy or failure.

Coalitions

7 civil partnerships for the greater national good

It is often said that one of the advantages of the first-past-the-post electoral system is that it produces strong governments rather than reluctant coalitions. Yet there have been a surprising number of years when Britain was either ruled by coalitions or in which there were attempts to build them.

☙ Lib-Lab Pact, 1906

By a secret agreement hatched in 1903, the Liberals agreed not to oppose a selected number of candidates appointed by the Labour Representation Committee (the forerunner of the Labour Party) at the 1906 general election. In return, the Liberals were spared having Labour opponents for a far larger number of seats. The deal worked to the short-term benefit of the Liberals but could be said to have contributed to their later demise by allowing Labour to drive a wedge into the two-party parliamentary system.

☙ First World War, 1915–1918

Asquith entered the war at the head of a Liberal cabinet but was forced into a coalition by events on the western front and in the Dardanelles. In 1916, Lloyd George ousted him in an internal coup and assumed the leadership of the coalition.

☙ Lloyd George's Postwar Coalition, 1918–1922

Lloyd George's decision to fight the 1918 general election as a coalitionist split and weakened his party and damaged his reputation. Although he was prime minister, the majority shareholder in government was the Conservative Party. This uneasy arrangement continued until 1922.

☙ National Government Part 1, 1931–1935

When Ramsay MacDonald's second Labour government was brought down by the economic crisis he formed a national government but was disowned by his party for doing so. The coalition was confirmed in office by the 1931 general election (a massive win for the Conservatives, despite being led by an ex-Labour prime minister.) As with Lloyd George before him, the arrangement damaged both MacDonald and his former party.

❂ National Government Part 2, 1935–1945

Neville Chamberlain took over the National Government from MacDonald at the 1935 election and it transmogrified into a government of even greater national emergency under Churchill for the duration of the Second World War. By 1945, Britain had been a one-party state for 14 years in everything but name and this perhaps explains the compensating effect of the 1945 election which returned the Labour Party to power with a large majority.

❂ The Hung Parliament, 1974

The first of the two indecisive elections of this year (in February) could easily have resulted in a coalition between Heath's Conservatives and the Liberals, but Harold Wilson managed to form a Labour government eventually and earn it a mandate from the October election.

❂ Lib-Lab Pact, 1977–8

The Labour government that took power in the two close-fought elections in 1974 saw its majority dwindle to one shortly after Jim Callaghan had succeeded Harold Wilson. The Liberals agreed to act as buttress in return for a veto over measures to go before Cabinet and for serious consideration to be given to introducing proportional representation. It was always a lopsided arrangement and the Callaghan government was doomed. The Liberals withdrew in 1978 and avoided being tainted by association in the general election the following year.

Comedies

*The 30 Greatest Political TV Comedies according to MPs**

Comedy is just entertainment whereas satire has a more deliberate purpose but often the borderline between the two isn't clear and the decisive factor is how politically aware the writers are.

What *is* certain is that political comedy is only good for a laugh if you are not on the receiving end. A politician who becomes the target of primetime jokes – which can easily degenerate into personal attack – can only respond by revealing him or herself to have a thick skin and a good sense of humour. Bizarrely, some gullible politicians vainly chasing the youth vote will allow themselves to be set up for ridicule by the comedians and the only course then is to bow to the guile of one's tormentors.

Even the cruelest practical jokes don't usually have any impact outside the studio and the nation's sitting rooms, but political comedy does sometimes land a punch and lead to a question being asked in the House of Commons. Occasionally, comedy can be of service to politics. It can be a good guide to how a party or policy is being perceived by the public and an astute politician can read useful omens in the entrails of his friends and enemies spilled on television. Laughter isn't always just a release of emotions: it can be full of political insights.

---

* results of a survey carried out for Channel 4, broadcast in 2007

#	Programme	Channel	Year(s)
1.	Yes Minister	BBC2	1980-84
2.	Spitting Image	ITV	1984-1996
3.	Bremner, Bird and Fortune	Channel 4	1998-present
4.	Have I Got News for You	BBC1/2	1990-present
5.	Drop the Dead Donkey	Channel 4	1990-1998
6.	Little Britain	BBC	2003-present
7.	That Was the Week that Was	BBC1	1963-64
8.	The New Statesman	Yorkshire TV	1987–92
9.	Not the Nine O'Clock News	BBC2	1979-82
10.	Dead Ringers	BBC2	2002
11.	The Ali G Show	Channel 4	2002-03
12.	Comic Strip Presents: The Strike	Channel 4	1988
13.	Absolute Power	BBC2	2003-05
14.	The Mike Yarwood Show	Thames	1978
15.	The Thick of It	BBC4	2005-present
16.	Brass Eye	Channel 4	1997-2001
17.	Till Death Us do Part	BBC1	1965-1975
18.	Monty Python's Flying Circus	BBC1	1970
19.	Tory Boy	BBC	1994
20.	The Daily Show with John Stewart	More 4	2005-present
21.	Alexei Sayle's Stuff	BBC2	1988-91
22.	Double Take	BBC2	2002-04
23.	A Very Social Secretary	Channel 4	Oct-05
24.	Jeffrey Archer: The Truth	BBC1	2002
25.	Don't Watch That, Watch This	BBC4	2005-present
26.	Crossing the Floor	BBC2	1996
27.	Michael Moore's TV Nation	BBC2	1994-95
28.	Normal Ormal: A Very Political Turtle	BBC1	1998
29.	The Day Today	BBC2	1994
30.	The Mark Thomas Comedy Product	Channel 4	1996-1999

The Commons is...

"... better than a play." *Charles II*

"... the longest running farce in the West End." *Cyril Smith*

"... a parcel of button-makers, pin-makers, horse jockeys, gamesters, pensioners, pimps and whoremasters." *James Otis*

"... an elaborate conspiracy to prevent the real clash of opinion which exists outside from finding an appropriate echo within its walls." *Aneurin Bevan*

"... hours and hours of exquisite boredom." *Aneurin Bevan*

"... a place of illogicalities." *George Brown*

"... the Asylum for Incapables." *Robert Cunninghame-Grahame*

A Conservative is...

"... someone who admires radicals a century after they're dead." *Anon*

"... someone who demands a square deal for the rich." *David Frost*

"... a man who is too cowardly to fight and too fat to run." *Elbert Hubbard*

"... a man with two perfectly good legs who, however, has never learned to walk forward." *Franklin D. Roosevelt (attrib.)*

"... someone who believes in reform, but not now." *Mort Sahl*

"... a statesman who is enamored of existing evils, as distinguished from the Liberal who wishes to replace them with others." *Ambrose Pierce*

"... a man who just sits and thinks, mostly sits." *Woodrow Wilson*

"... a man who thinks nothing new ought to be adopted for the first time." *Frank Vanderlip*

"... a liberal who has been mugged." *Anon* (and "a liberal is a conservative who has been arrested" said the writer Thomas Wolfe)

The Constitution

8 facts about a missing document

> "*[The British constitution] presumes more boldly than any other the good sense and the good faith of those who work it.*"
> William Gladstone

While everyone agrees that there is always scope for reform, no one really knows how much of the ethereal British Constitution you could take away or radically alter without the whole thing collapsing in a meaningless heap. Which is why so many people advise not tinkering with it at all.

1. There isn't a British constitution

It is unwritten. It is 'the rules of the game' or 'how things are done', a collection of laws and conventions. Politicians and civil servants are expected to know how things have always been done, and conform. As Sidney Low put it in his *The Governance of Britain* (1904): "we live under a system of tacit understandings, but the understandings themselves are not always understood". The constitutional variation of 'if it ain't broke, don't fix it' is 'don't write it down unless you have to.'

2. Walter Bagehot

Bagehot famously published his *The English Constitution* in 1867. He divided political structures into the 'Dignified' (symbolic and ceremonial, necessary to sustain certain illusions that hold the thing together) and the 'Efficient' (how things actually get done, whether they are apparent or not). "We must not let daylight in upon the magic," he warned.

3. The constitution does change

Leo Amery called it "a living structure". James Callaghan described it as being developed "on the back of an envelope". Power shifts subtly according to personalities, the needs of the day (in order to fight wars), the size of the state and the multiplying of its functions, and the changing nature of the economy.

4. The main elements of the constitution (in order of power)

- The prime minister
- The cabinet
- The civil service
- Parliament
- The monarchy

5. The cabinet

The Cabinet has always been an uneasy, rather inconspicuous committee adrift in the constitution. It was only formally recognised by statute in 1937 but prime ministers of late have not treated it as the sacred repository of collective decision-making that it is sometimes made out to be.

One analysis is that members of the Cabinet are not expected to take collective responsibility for decisions which the prime minister has made in private with one colleague or another. "A willingness to consult your senior colleagues indicates a willingness not to proceed with the decision," said Australian Prime Minister Malcolm Fraser.

6. The drift of power

Either Lord Hailsham or Peter Hennessy coined the phrase 'elective dictatorship' to define the drift of the British constitution from parliamentary government to government by the prime minister in his cabinet, to presidential government by the prime minister who treats his cabinet as a committee to rubber-stamp initiatives. As long as the prime minister has a majority behind him there are very few effective checks and balances that can limit his power. In the 18th century Rousseau observed that "the English people are free for one day in every five years – on the day of a general election."

7. Charter 88

Charter 88 is a pressure group formed following a letter to the *New Statesman* in 1988 and echoing the Czech Charter 77 (and the 19th century Chartists). It called for a written constitution for Britain.

The Original Charter 88

We have had less freedom than we believed. That which we have enjoyed has been too dependent on the benevolence of our rulers. Our freedoms have remained their possession, rationed out to us as subjects rather than being our own inalienable possession as citizens. To make real the freedoms we once took for granted means for the first time to take them for ourselves.

The time has come to demand political, civil and human rights in the United Kingdom. We call, therefore, for a new constitutional settlement which will:-

1. Enshrine, by means of a Bill of Rights, such civil liberties as the right to peaceful assembly, to freedom of association, to freedom from discrimination, to freedom from detention without trial, to trial by jury, to privacy and to freedom of expression.

2. Subject Executive powers and prerogatives, by whomsoever exercised, to the rule of law.

3. Establish freedom of information and open government.

4. Create a fair electoral system of proportional representation.

5. Reform the Upper House to establish a democratic, non-hereditary Second Chamber.

6. Place the Executive under the power of a democratically renewed Parliament and all agencies of the state under the rule of law.

7. Ensure the independence of a reformed judiciary.

8. Provide legal remedies for all abuses of power by the state and by officials of central and local government.

9. Guarantee an equitable distribution of power between the nations of the United Kingdom and between local, regional and central government.

10. Draw up a written constitution anchored in the ideal of universal citizenship, that incorporates these reforms.

11. The inscription of laws does not guarantee their realisation. Only people themselves can ensure freedom, democracy and equality before the law. Nonetheless, such ends are far better demanded, and more effectively obtained and guarded, once they belong to everyone by inalienable right.

From the official Charter 88 website, www.unlockdemocracy.org.uk

The Constitution According to Bagehot

8 extracts from Wise Walter

Britain doesn't have a written constitution (see page 55).

Oh yes it does: Walter Bagehot's *The English Constitution* (1867) is considered to be as good a summary of the residue of statute and convention that Britain is governed by as you are likely to get.

Naturally, it's out of date, having been written in the days when the working class worked and the ruling class didn't. No one then ever thought that women would one day vote or cheesy candidates descend from battlebuses to harangue passers-by. In Victorian England, things were dignified on the surface and efficient beneath it. Society was governed by gentleman's agreement and Bagehot observed it all with a little mockery but mainly with respect.

The quotes on the opposite page are from *The English Constitution* unless otherwise stated.

C

The Constitution

"When you put before the mass of mankind the question, 'Will you be governed by a king, or will you be governed by a constitution?' the inquiry comes out thus – 'Will you be governed in a way you understand, or will you be governed in a way you do not understand?'"

The Monarch

"The Queen...must sign her own death-warrant if the two Houses unanimously send it up to her."

Parliament

"A Parliament is nothing less than a big meeting of more or less idle people."

The House of Lords

"A severe though not unfriendly critic of our institutions said that 'the cure for admiring the House of Lords was to go and look at it.'"

The Civil Service

"It is an inevitable defect that bureaucrats will care more for routine than for results."

The Government

"Dullness in matters of government is a good sign, and not a bad one – in particular, dullness in parliamentary government is a test of its excellence, an indication of its success." *Saturday Review,* 1856

The People

"The being without an opinion is so painful to human nature that most people will leap to a hasty opinion rather than undergo it." *The Economist,* 1875

Prognostic

"The whole history of civilization is strewn with creeds and institutions which were invaluable at first, and deadly afterwards." *(attributed to Bagehot)*

The Constitution in Evolution

20 steps from autocracy to democracy

> *"In England we have come to rely upon a comfortable time-lag of fifty years or a century intervening between the perception that something ought to be done and a serious attempt to do it."* HG Wells, 1931

Over the centuries, power in Britain has been gradually shifting from God, who had the right to annoint an absolutist sovereign, to (ostensibly) the will of the people, expressed through a general election and vested in a prime minister. It has been a long process and not a smooth one, proceeding as a series of brusque or violent constitutional jumps rarely made for altruistic reasons and usually contested by losing factions.

1. **Norman Conquest 1066–1072**
   Feudalism is established in Britain. Creation of the Great Council of Tenants-in-Chief which will later grow into Parliament.

2. **Magna Carta 1215**
   King John pacifies his barons at Runnymede by signing a charter accepting their right to be tried by their equals and not taxed unless they are represented. The first significant weakening of royal power.

3. **Act of Supremacy 1534**
   The formal moment of Reformation under Henry VIII. The monarch severs allegiance to Rome and assumes control over the Church of England, uniting religious and secular power.

4. **Civil War and Interregnum 1642–51**
   The political and military contest between parliament and the king is temporarily settled in favour of the former. Britain is, for a short time and the only time in its history, a republic.

5. **Restoration 1660**
   Britain becomes a monarchy again.

6. **Habeas Corpus Act 1679**
   Establishes that imprisonment is unlawful without fair trial.

7. **Glorious Revolution 1688 and Bill of Rights 1689**
    Make Britain a constitutional monarchy.

8. **Act of Settlement 1701**
    Establishes the rules and order of succession for monarchs.

9. **Act of Union 1707**
    Unites England (with Wales attached to it) and Scotland to form Great Britain (even if Scotland is effectively reduced to the status of a province from now on).

10. **Appointment of first Prime Minister 1721**
    Robert Walpole is appointed, although with less power than the prime minister today.

11. **Last use of royal veto 1708**
    By Queen Anne, on advice of her ministers. From now on it is accepted that the monarch doesn't impede the work of parliament.

12. **Union of Britain and Ireland 1800**
    To form United Kingdom of Great Britain and Ireland.

13. **Reform Acts 19th century**
    Voting is made fairer. Simultaneously, the franchise is extended to include all men (1918) and all women (1928).

14. **Establishment of the Labour Party 1900**
    As the representative of the working class and the trade unions in mainstream politics.

15. **Ireland (the southern part) becomes independent 1922**

16. **Reform of the House of Lords, 1911 and 1949**
    Severe weakening of the second chamber.

17. **Britain joins the EEC (later the EU) 1973.**

18. **Maastricht Treaty, signed 1992, came into force 1993**
    Ceded more sovereignty to what was now called the European Union.

19. **Human Rights Act 1998**
    Partial acceptance of a humanitarian bill of rights for Britain.

20. **Reform of the House of Lords 2007**
    Labour plans definitive changes for Britain's senate.

Days

7 days of significance

"A week is a long time in politics" Harold Wilson, 1964

Sunday

Election day in many countries, such as France, so that work doesn't provide an excuse for not going to the polls.

Other than that, it is a bloody day for some reason. There were at least ten 'Bloody Sundays' during the 20th century (in Britain and abroad). The most famous of them is Bloody Sunday, 30 January 1972, when 26 civil rights protesters were shot dead in Northern Ireland by British soldiers. The incident fostered a mistrust of the British government among the province's Catholic community which lingered for over two decades after.

Monday

'Black Monday', 19 October 1987 was the largest drop on the stock market in living memory. One theory is that it was triggered by the Great Storm on the Friday before which prevented many traders from getting into the office to settle up their affairs before the end of the week: after a nervous weekend, as soon as they got back into the office they began panic selling.

Tuesday

The day on which the prime minister has his regular evening audience with the reigning monarch. The Queen has regularly entertained all ten of the prime ministers who have been in office during her reign.

Wednesday

The 'unofficial cabinet' of ministers' permanent secretaries (top civil servants) meets in Whitehall.

On Black Wednesday 16 September 1992 the Conservative government of John Major was forced to make a humiliating withdrawal from the European Exchange Rate Mechanism (ERM) because of pressure on the pound from currency speculators.

Thursday

The traditional day for general elections in Britain. The Cabinet meets at 10 Downing Street on Thursday mornings. Black Thursday, 24 October 1929, was the day of the Wall Street Crash which sent its shock waves across the Atlantic.

Friday

Parliament sits on some Fridays, known, as 'Sitting Fridays'.

On Red Friday, 31 July 1925, coal mine owners announced that they would be cutting miners' wages. When the TUC gave its support to the miners the Conservative government agreed to subsidise a return to original pay levels. The truce, however, was short-lived as 8 months later the employers' effectively reapplied the pay cut thus triggering the General Strike.

Saturday

Typically the day on which MPs hold their constituency surgeries.

The Saturday Night Massacre on 20 October 1973 was Nixon's last battle – a night which ended in two firings and one resignation – to avoid handing over the incriminating tapes he had made of conversations in the White House.

Debates

10 tactics for winning any political debate

"The best way I know to win an argument is to start by being in the right." Lord Hailsham

There is no finer moment in life than when the person sitting off-guard across the dinner table from you, or slouched at peace in the other sofa, disingenuously reveals himself (occasionally herself) to hold political views which are utterly uninformed and ill-thought out – that is, opposed to your own.

Like a lazy predator who knows there is only one possible outcome, you lay a provocative remark as a trap and your interlocutor suddenly bristles with the need to defend what he has just said to the reputational death. But don't rush it. The pleasure of taking apart someone else's world-view is worth savouring.

All the weaponry you need is contained in the following three lists but it's best to supplement the advice given here with examples of your own drawn from a selective scanning of the press and television in support of your prejudices.

The first list explains, step-by-step, how to deal with anyone less experienced or tenacious than yourself: use the tactics in the order they are given and stop just before you start to bore the rest of the company. If you can be gracious in victory (and not raise your eyebrows too high in condescension) you will inevitably rise a greasy notch in the social pecking order.

If you are up against someone who has an entrenched ideological position you need to follow the instructions in either the second or third list as appropriate – depending whether you dress to the political left or the political right.

Tactic 1 **Indisputable Evidence**

Used with a self-confidence that brooks no challenge, this can often be enough to win an argument before it has begun. As soon as your antagonist has delivered any sort of statement, refer to an obscure survey or statistic that disproves it – there's one to support every argument ever made. It's better if it comes from a reputable source but failing that anything that sounds like a reputable source will do: think tanks (see p316) called the Something Something Institute are perfect non-authoritative authorities for this purpose. If you are really bold and amoral, and winning an argument is all important to you, you can make your obscure survey and its source up.

Less satisfying is to cite a book your opponent hasn't read or a film he hasn't seen which contains essential evidence. Taking care not to sound too patronizing, you can conclude the argument with, "It's all in there. You should see it/read it/listen to it and then we'll come back to this discussion."

> *Disadvantage:* at best you will only win a pyrrhic victory or breathing space and if your evidence is shaky you may get found out. Be careful not to use two or more surveys which contradict each other in the same argument.

Tactic 2 **The Damning Definition**

Only a smug pedant who knows his stuff insists on looking up a disputed word in the dictionary, so providing a damning definition can be a good tactic if your opponent is not as smugly pedantic as you – he is bound to concede the point rather than risk the indignity of you reading the evidence aloud.

> *Disadvantages:* make sure there isn't a dictionary within easy reach as it probably won't back you up. If there *is* and if it doesn't, insist on a 'proper' dictionary e.g. Collins' Shorter Blackbacked Entymological Compendium of Political Terminology (3rd edition).

Tactic 3 **Complex Issue**

After you have patiently explained your case at least twice you can self-righteously throw up your hands in exasperation and exclaim, "You obviously don't understand the issue!" implying that you have done your best to dispel the cloud of ignorance but enough is enough.

> *Disadvantage:* your opponent may be composed enough to challenge you with: "I understand it only too well, it's you who doesn't understand it".

Tactic 4 "Come back to the real world"

Make it clear that only one of you can live in the real world and your opponent is the one who is in the world of wishful thinking.

> *Disadvantage:* you won't be able to appeal to your own ideology after using this tactic.

Tactic 5 "Give me an example"

Use this before he uses it. It's easy to shoot down any example of "socialism in action" or "a successful free market" but not so easy to come up with an example which is beyond criticism.

> *Disadvantage:* when an astute debater is asked "give me an example" he can reply, "no, you give me one". Whatever you do, don't respond with "I said it first". Instead, wave the challenge away with, "Let's not get bogged down in the details".

Tactic 6 Sins of the Others

It is imperative that you stick a label on your opponent as soon as you can so that you can heap guilt by association on to him. For instance, you can urge him to defend anything and everything done by Stalin or Margaret Thatcher or blame him for the policies of the present government or the wooliness of the opposition.

> *Disadvantage:* This tactic is not much use if he claims to be an independent without baggage.

Tactic 7 "You said ..."

Quote something your opponent said earlier that contradicts what he is saying now, preferably a throwaway remark he wasn't even aware of. Present him with the two statements and demand "Which is it to be?" You need a good memory to pull this off and you'll need to listen to your opponent which, of course, is a waste of your time. If you are really cunning you can make up a phrase which sounds like something he might have said.

> *Disadvantage:* if no one else is listening, it's your word against his. And even if he owns his own words he might not admit there is a contradiction between the two statements, giving him the opportunity to plunge into a explanation of the nuances that make them compatible.

Tactic 8 "What you really think/are trying to say is …"

There is nothing more infuriating than having someone make your argument for you, expressing it in a far crisper summary than you are capable of yourself. So, give him the benefit of your debating skills. But you must appear to be doing it as a genuine favour, as if you think there is something of worth in what he is trying to say. Of course, your intention is to phrase his arguments in terms that you can more easily demolish.

> *Disadvantage:* he might not agree with your summary. Great cunning is required to get away with this tactic.

Tactic 9 Defender of Democracy

With a few deft moves you can steer almost anyone into a corner known as the Repository of Unspeakable and Indefensible Causes. This sometimes requires a most outrageous reversal of the truth on your part. The goal is to get him to say something – anything– which you can twist into an admission of undemocratic, racist or even fascist sympathies.

> *Disadvantage:* make sure you don't have any undemocratic thoughts in your closet before you use this one.

Tactic 10 Invoke Hitler

If all else fails, accuse your opponent of thinking or talking "just like Hitler". You can only use this name once and by tradition the argument ends immediately if you can make the charge stick.

> *Disadvantage:* the comparison has got to have some substance to it. This tactic is not much use against someone who admires Hitler.

Debates – How to Be Right Because You Are

A Conservative strategy for winning an argument

1. **Socialism is idealistic in the bad sense of the word.** It is an attempt to impose an artificial theory on the real world, in the face of all evidence.

2. **Socialism rests on a false assumption about human nature:** that people can and will work together selflessly for the common good in all circumstances. They may do so in small-scale, limited, charitable causes but not in a way that you can depend on to run an economy or a society. Everyone's a capitalist at heart. People are born selfish and competitive – look at any playground. They don't want to be equal. They want pecking orders, incentives and rewards. You can't impose solidarity on people through legislation.

3. **Socialism is wrong about economic behaviour.** Marx's predictions of historical inevitability did not come true. Among other things, he failed to foresee: a) the growth and permeability of the middle class which has opened itself to rising working class people who then have no interest in revolutionary change b) the impact that technology would have in freeing people from drudgery, and c) that capitalism would turn everyone into a consumer with a decent standard of living and unlimited choice as to what, where and how they live.

4. **Socialism doesn't work in practice.** Look at the Soviet Union or any other state where it has been tried. Under communism, people are miserably poor, oppressed and denied the opportunity to improve their lives. Those that can, flee. Such systems crack at the seams and even if they spout socialist rhetoric they never come close to attaining their ideals. Socialism, in short, has been tried and it failed. The verdict of history is in, and the left lost.

5. **Socialism creates big, cumbersome, inefficient, repressive states.** All such states squash incentive and are wasteful – and no one ever takes responsibility for anything that goes wrong. The elites at the top of socialist regimes are as corrupt as any bred by capitalism.

6. **Socialism suppresses freedom.** Ever tried protesting in a totalitarian communist state? Freedom of speech goes with economic freedom. Even trade unions – which claim to be acting on behalf of workers – create restrictive conditions for them such as closed shops. Everything is geared towards collective power at the expense of individual freedom. Even if there aren't legal restrictions on what you can say and do, left-wingers try to force people to conform to standards of 'political correctness'.

7. **Socialists patronise people and interfere in their lives.** Most socialists are middle class people who believe they have a right to talk down to people and tell them what is best for them. Socialism, therefore, has nothing to do with working class solidarity.

8. **Only capitalism creates prosperity.** Socialists take advantage of the efforts of free enterprise. They are good at taking and spending other people's money but not at making money themselves, which is why socialism is the preferred philosophy of those who live on state handouts: teachers, social workers etc. Everyone benefits when business generates wealth in a society. And economic progress drives technological progress which makes living ever easier. Capitalism, therefore, gives people the means to seek their own happiness.

9. **All socialists are hypocrites.** Whether he lives in a capitalist or communist society, the average socialist doesn't mind living in a nice house and owning possessions. You never see one giving everything away to the have-nots whose cause he or she supposedly champions. While Karl Marx sat theorising about the destruction of capitalism in the British Museum he was living off the proceeds of Engels' family firm – how much more hypocritical can you get?

10. **Social democracy, or the mixed economy, is the worst compromise imaginable** because it stifles competition and makes businesses pay for an overbearing state that has an insatiable appetite for money.

Debates – How to Be Right When You Are Left

A socialist strategy for winning an argument

1. **Capitalism is an amoral system which only benefits greedy people.** It says that human nature is selfish and competition the norm but there are plenty of examples which prove that people are naturally disposed to work with, not against each other: the co-operative and trade union movements, and the act of politics itself. Capitalists are just as happy to back a dictatorship as a democracy if it creates stable economic conditions.

2. **Capitalism doesn't work in practice.** There is no such thing as a completely free market. Business people are never interested in removing all restrictions to free trade – only the ones that it suits them to remove. Even Adam Smith said that capitalists can never get together without fixing the rules between themselves to increase their profits. Behind closed boardroom doors anything goes: price fixing cabals, even bribery and corruption (under euphemistic names), are merely "the way business is done".

3. **Capitalists apply one rule to themselves and another to the workers.** They know the only way to reduce costs significantly (and hence increase profits) is to depress wages. For wages to be kept down, labour must be prevented from organising collective bargaining and strikes for better pay and conditions. As Marx said, politics always comes down to the competition between economic classes, with the state serving the interests of capitalism.

4. **Competition does not automatically lead to efficiency.** Capitalism is tremendously wasteful: look at the tiers of unnecessary management in any large corporation: at the gross amounts of money spent on naming and branding companies; the amount of waste produced by industry, such as pollution and inessential packaging. Capitalism is profligate with resources that belong to everyone (clean air and water) and even threatens to kill the earth and wipe out civilisation in its need for perpetual economic growth. The market will not produce solutions for climate change.

5. **Rolling back the state is an unrealistic dream.** The state is the logical provider of social services and infrastructures such as education, healthcare, public transport and policing which cannot be organised in a competitive way. Planning and wealth redistribution are the only ways to avoid unchecked pollution and a return to unfathomable, abject, 19th-century poverty.

6. **Capitalism has no idea what to do with the disadvantaged.** Left to itself, the free market creates far more losers than winners and they are expected to take care of themselves. The only solution capitalism can come up with is a little voluntary charity. Only socialism provides for anyone in society who, through no fault of his or her own, cannot compete.

7. **Real communism/socialism has never been tried in practice.** Stalin's USSR wasn't a true communist model but an aberration of Marx's ideas in the hands of an egomaniac. The Chinese revolution was also distorted by a mad man and his cronies. Castro's Cuba is a brave experiment but has always been hindered by the hostile attitude of its nearest neighbour, the US. The capitalist world always does its best to sabotage socialism to prove that caring and sharing cannot work.

8. **Many people prefer/preferred life under communism to life in a cut-throat economy.** The right-wing press in western countries always portrays life under communism as universally miserable. Many people in the ex-Soviet Union and Eastern Bloc countries – the ordinary people – had their basic needs met and lived in stable societies. The lack of freedom was only of concern to would-be capitalists and criminals.

9. **Capitalism is deceitful.** Capitalism creates rather than supplies demands. People must be made to feel as if they are always lacking something in order for them to consume. A satisfied customer who values the free things in life is no longer a contributor to the system. Capitalism does not and cannot make people happy. There is no 'trickle down' effect of prosperity; instead, wealth accumulates in the hands of a few.

10. **Social democracy or the mixed economy is the worst compromise imaginable** as society is always made subservient to the needs of business putting profit-making before people.

Decades – A Book a Decade

5 books for 5 decades

Why read more books than you have to? One every ten years is enough.

1940s

Never Again: Britain 1945-1951 by Peter Hennessy (1992)

1950s

Having It So Good: Britain in the Fifties by Peter Hennessy (2006)

1960s

Pendulum Years: Britain in the Sixties by Bernard Levin (1970)

1970s

The Seventies: The Decade That Changed the Future by Christopher Booker (1980)

1980s

If your political views are to the right read *Reasons to Be Cheerful* by Mark Steel (2001), a story of his coming-of-political-age under Thatcherism. If you are a lefty, read *The Downing Street Years* by Margaret Thatcher (1995).

1990s

A decade split in two by the 1997 election. *Thatcher and Sons* by Simon Jenkins (2006) connects the two halves, the 'sons' being Major, Blair and Brown.

The Naughties

Who Runs This Place? The Anatomy of Britain in the 21st Century by Anthony Sampson 2005.

Issues of the 20th Century

The top 5 topics of political conversation and 5 most important events of each decade

"We should be wary of politicians who profess to follow history while only noticing those signposts of history that point in the direction which they themselves already favour." Douglas Hurd

Every decade has its momentous events and its major themes – topics of home affairs or foreign policy which are endlessly discussed in the media, in political circles, in workplaces and over dinner tables.

Some issues are of their time and are settled relatively quickly with what looks now like the begrudging acceptance of inevitability. Others – especially the management of the economy, education, health, the fluctuating size of the armed forces, the trade-off between civil liberties and public security, the extent to which government can and should make free with information – rumble on without resolution. This list is not a historical appraisal of what we think is important but of what seemed important to people at the time.

1900s

"English policy is to float lazily downstream, occasionally putting out a diplomatic boathook to avoid collisions."

Lord Salisbury

Themes
Entrance of the working class into politics: rise of the Labour Party
Votes for women (suffragette movement)
Social reform: the alleviation of poverty
Free trade
Maintenance of the British Empire

Events

1900	Formation of the Labour Representation Committee (to become the Labour Party)
1900-01	Boxer Rebellion in China
1902	Second Boer War ended
1909	Lloyd George's 'People's Budget' defeated by the Lords
1904	Signing of the 'Entente Cordiale' between Britain and France

---

1910s

"What is our task? To make Britain a fit country for heroes to live in."
Lloyd George, speech in Wolverhampton, 23 November 1918

Themes
Reform of the House of Lords
Causes, aims and conduct of the First World War
After-effects of the war on international relations and the British economy
Home rule for Ireland
Votes for women

Events

1911	Parliament Act
1914-18	First World War
1916	Easter Rising in Ireland
1917	Russian Revolution
1918	Votes for women (but not on the same conditions as men)

1920s

"I would rather be an opportunist and float than go to the bottom with my principles round my neck."

Stanley Baldwin

Themes
After-effects of the war
Home rule for Ireland
Aftermath of the Russian Revolution: whether the Soviet Union would succeed or fail
Economic depression
First Labour Party governments

Events

1922	Irish Free State formed
1924	First Labour government
1926	General Strike, 3-12 May
1928	Votes for women (on equal terms to men)
1929	Wall Street Crash, October

1930s

"Dictators have only become possible through the invention of the microphone." Sir Thomas Inskip 1936

Themes
Rise of fascism in Germany, Italy and Spain (representing the failure of League of Nations and the post-war order); whether to respond with rearmament or appeasement.
Great Depression: unemployment, poverty
National Government; "betrayal" of the Labour Party by Ramsay MacDonald
Instability in India: calls for independence

Events

1929-33	Great Depression
1931	Formation of National Government under Ramsay MacDonald
1936	Jarrow March, October
1936	Abdication crisis
1936–9	Spanish Civil War

1940s

"Often the experts make the worst possible ministers in their own fields. In this country we prefer rule by amateurs."

Clement Attlee

Themes
Second World War: conduct of campaigns; Blitz; whether US would be drawn in.
Aftermath of the war: rationing, Nuremberg Trials, fate of European Jews
Reforming post-war Labour government: creation of the welfare state; nationalisation of industries
Britain's diminished role in the world: rise of the two superpowers
Independence (and partition of) India

Events

1939–45	Second World War
1945	Labour general election victory, July
1945	Atomic bomb dropped on Hiroshima, August
1945–9	Nuremberg Trials
1947	Partition of India

1950s

"It's pretty dreary living in the American Age – unless you're an American of course."

John Osborne, 'Look Back in Anger'

Themes

Loss of empire and Britain's international prestige
Cold War: proliferation of nuclear weapons
Death penalty: retention or abolition
First immigration from colonies and Commonwealth countries
Prosperity and the early consumer society

Events

1950-53	Korean war
1951	Festival of Britain
1951	Burgess-Maclean spy scandal
1952-54	Mau Mau rebellion in Kenya
1956	Suez crisis

1960s

*"Sexual intercourse began
In nineteen sixty-three..."*

Philip Larkin

Themes

Cold War: Berlin wall, Cuban missile crisis
Rapid social change: youth culture and the generation gap; sex, drugs and rock 'n' roll; legalisation of divorce and abortion; mass immigration
Technological revolution
Industrial relations
Management of the economy

Events

1961	Birth control pill available on NHS
1963	Britain's first EEC application rejected
1963	Kennedy assassination
1965	Abolition of the death penalty
1968	Start of the 'Troubles' in Northern Ireland

1970s

"Can you imagine lying in bed on a Sunday morning with the love of your life, a cup of tea and a bacon sandwich, and all you had to read was The Socialist Worker?"

Derek Jameson, Editor, Daily Express 1979

Themes
Feminism
Northern Ireland 'Troubles'
Britain's relationship to the EEC
Strikes and union power
Disillusion and cynicism with politics

Events
1971 Britain joins EEC
1972 Idi Amin expels the Asians of Uganda
1976 Maiden flight of Concorde
1977 Sex Pistols release "God Save the Queen"
1979 Margaret Thatcher becomes first woman prime minister

1980s

"He didn't riot. He got on his bike and looked for work."

Norman Tebbit on his unemployed father,
speaking at the Conservative Party Conference,
Blackpool, 15 October 1981

Themes
Power of the unions
Privatisation of nationalised industries
Poll tax
Weakness of the Opposition (Labour Party at its nadir; brief life of the SDP)
Disintegration of Soviet bloc and collapse of the Berlin Wall

Events
1980 Sale of council houses
1981 Formation of the SDP (merged with Liberals 1988)
1982 Falklands War
1984 Flotation of British Telecom
1989 Disintegration of the Soviet bloc

1990s

"Spin is only a posh word for deceit and manipulation."

Anne Widdecombe

Themes
Britain's role in the EU: integration and the 'threat' of federalism
Sleaze in politics
Devolution
Organisation and funding of education and the NHS: the era of choice
The transformation of politics from ideology to appearance: the rise of the spin doctor

Events
1991   First Gulf War
1997   Labour's landslide election victory
1997   Bank of England given the independent power to set interest rates
1998   Good Friday Agreement
1999   Partial reform of the House of Lords

2000s

"The threshold for war should always be high."

Robin Cook in his resignation speech

Themes
'War against terror' (Britain's unconditional support for the US in invasions of Afghanistan and Iraq)
Climate change
The EU: political union (the constitution) and whether to join the euro
National security vs. civil liberties including the introduction of identity cards
Continuation of the debate about the NHS and education

Events
2000   First mayor of London elected
2000   Fuel tax protest
2001   Terrorist attacks against the US, leading to 2003 invasion of Afghanistan and Iraq
2002   Introduction of the euro in continental Europe
2006-7 Cash for Honours scandal

Decades – Themes of the Past and Future Century

If we had to nominate the 5 most important themes of the last 100 years what would they be?

To answer this question we have to imagine how people will in the 24th century sum up the 20th century, in the way that we sum up the 16th century with soundbites such as "a struggle between religious freedom and religious persecution" and "competition for power between king and parliament".

Themes of the 20th century

- **The competition for industrial power between labour and capital** – with the government trying to mediate between the two. Whether large sections of industry should be nationalised or left in/returned to private ownership.

- **The rivalry between capitalism and communism** as the model for world order.

- **The mixed economy and the welfare state** as Britain's/Europe's social democratic solution to the capitalism/communism dilemma. The first half of the century was a demonstration of the need for it, and the creation of it; the latter half was a protracted debate about what resources it needed and whether the country could afford them.

- **The establishment of the principle of equal rights** for women, minority ethnic groups, homosexuals, children and the disabled.

- **Britain's place in the world:** the change in its international power and status. Its loss of empire; its relationship to the USA; and finding its place within Europe. The reduction in military capability and the shift in emphasis of warfare from mainly self-interest to mainly peacekeeping.

And what of the next 100 years? What are the issues that are still to be resolved?

Themes of the 21st century

- The distribution of power between local, regional, national, supranational and global levels. Will nation-states become ever less powerful in a 'globalised' world? How far can any community be autonomous in the modern world? Can significant power be returned to local or even personal levels? Is Britain's reluctance to fully engage with Europe stubborn resistance to an inevitable trend of pooling national resources or a model of independent thinking which the world will come to copy?

- The balance between liberalising the economy (encouraging the growth of free markets) and allowing politicians to manage it. At present the trend is away from the latter towards the former. Will healthcare and education become increasingly driven by consumer choice?

- The role and therefore the size of the state. What it should or should not try to do for us. What percentage of GDP should it consume? What is the optimum balance between public and private sectors? How can everyone be given access to the education and healthcare they need, and the disadvantaged looked after, at a price that society can afford?

- The balance between the privacy of the individual and the security of the state. How far can civil liberties be protected? Can we be free and safe from terrorism at the same time?

- The environment. How and how far should the world respond to climate change? Is there any point in one country acting alone? Is the care of the environment incompatible with a consumer society?

Defectors

An explicit diagram for political swingers

Party loyalty is everything in British politics but some MPs have risked damage to their reputations by 'crossing the floor', whether out of conscience or pragmatism.

The most famous ideological migrant was Ramsay Macdonald who set himself adrift from the Labour Party to form a coalition with the Conservatives in 1931.

Over the page is a selective chart of recent cross crossers. It ignores most MPs who become 'independent' because this denomination often masks an infraction of party discipline – an honourable member has not acted on a point of principle and has had the whip withdrawn by his party for misconduct. Few independents, whether convicted of bad behaviour or voluntary castaways, get re-elected. Most floor-crossers say they are doing it because the party has changed course, not them, or some variant on this theme.

The dustbin sign overleaf is not supposed to be a value judgement but an indication of a move which turned out to be a political cul-de-sac.

Independence Party (UKIP)		Lib/Lib Dem		SDP 🏛 RIP 1988
← 3 peers 2007	↘ Emma Nicholson 1995 ↘ Peter Thurman 1996	↘ Christopher Brocklebank Fowler 1981 ↗	Christopher Mayhew 1974 ↗ Paul Marsden 2001 ↗	Merged, 1988 ⇨ 'Gang of Four' + 28 more 1981 ←
CONSERVATIVE		Reg Prentice 1977 ⇨ ⇩ Alan Amos 1992 ⇩ Alan Howarth 1995 ⇩ Peter Temple-Morris (via "Independent One Nation Conservative") 1998 ⇩ Shaun Woodward 1999 ⇩ Robert Jackson 2005		LABOUR
George Gardiner 1997 ↓			Clare Short 2006 ↘	John Stonehouse 1976 ↘ → George Galloway 2003 (via being an independent)
REFERENDUM PARTY 🏛 RIP 1997		INDEPENDENT	ENGLISH NATIONAL PARTY 🏛 RIP 1981	RESPECT

Democracy is...

"a pathetic belief in the collective wisdom of individual ignorance."
HL Mencken

"the worst form of government except all the other forms that have been tried from time to time."

Winston Churchill

"being allowed to vote for the candidate you dislike least."
Robert Byrne

"simply the bludgeoning of the people by the people for the people."
Oscar Wilde

"government by discussion but it is only effective if you can stop people talking."

Clement Attlee (attrib.)

"the theory that the common people know what they want and deserve to get it good and hard."

HL Mencken

"the recurrent suspicion that more than half the people are right more than half of the time."

EB White

"a process by which the people are free to choose the man who will get the blame."

Lawrence J Peter

"an institution in which the whole is equal to the scum of the parts."
Keith Preston

"a government in the hands of men of low birth, no property and unskilled labour."

Aristotle

Demonstrations

10 public displays of disgust

However many people organisers manage to get onto the street, demonstrations rarely have a direct effect on policy. But to participants it still feels better to make their views known in public than it does to write a letter to the local paper or wait for the next election.

While some demos pass off peacefully, there are often minor disturbances. Occasionally a demo degenerates into a riot – the classification is often a matter of which TV footage is broadcast and how journalists choose to report the event.

By tradition, there is always a huge discrepancy between the number of people organisers claim have attended the demo and the number estimated by the police.

Below are some of the more notable political demonstrations to have taken place in Britain over the last two hundred years.

◄ϡ The Peterloo Massacre Manchester, 16 August 1819

The cavalry of the 15th Hussars charged a large but peaceable crowd which had assembled to hear a speech about parliamentary reform. Eleven people were killed and about 400 injured.

◄ϡ The Jarrow Crusade, October 1936

A 'hunger' march from the North East to London to present a petition for the alleviation of suffering after the closure of a shipyard had left two-thirds of the town unemployed.

◄ϡ The Aldermaston Marches

The Campaign for Nuclear Disarmament was formed in 1958 and at Easter in the same year the first mass march from Trafalgar Square to the Atomic Weapons Research Establishment at Aldermaston in Berkshire took place. The marches were a major annual event for about five years, until Vietnam became a more pressing focus for anti-war protests.

◀💬 Vietnam War Demonstration, Grosvenor Square, 17 March 1968

Britain made a relatively low-key contribution to the 'revolutions' of *soixante-huit*. This protest outside the US embassy degenerated into violence which is supposed to have inspired Mick Jagger and Keith Richard to write *Street Fighting Man* (see p279).

◀💬 Greenham Common Peace Camp, 1981-91

The women who lived in a makeshift camp at the gates of the Berkshire American air force base for ten years defined passive resistance in the 1980s. They were there to draw attention to the deployment of cruise missiles in Britain which, they said, formed part of the new Cold War strategy of preparing for a "limited" nuclear confrontation in place of MAD (mutually assured destruction).

◀💬 The Poll Tax Riot, 31 March 1990

Trafalgar Square, London. Margaret Thatcher's Community Charge, universally known as the poll tax, became the focus for a political generation which felt it had been disenfranchised for a decade. The series of protests against its imposition contributed to her fall before the end of the year. As the poll tax was withdrawn (and replaced with the council tax) it could be argued that this was one demonstration of people power which succeeded.

◀💬 Street Party Camden High Street, London, 1995

Everyone was invited but not everyone wanted to attend the forced closure of a principal artery of North London by Reclaim the Streets, a movement dedicated to reclaiming roads as public spaces by temporarily stopping the traffic.

◀💬 May Day

International Workers' Day is a traditional occasion for demonstrations by trade unionists. In recent years it has also become the focus for anti-capitalist rallies and in 2000 the occasion degenerated into violence.

◀» Liberty & Livelihood March, Westminster, London, 22 September 2002

Demonstrations are normally the preserve of the progressive left but the Blair government's measures to ban fox hunting led to the formation of a conservative campaign organisation, the Countryside Alliance, which staged a series of Barbour-jacketed marches to prove its strength. This was the largest of them, attracting an estimated 400,000 people.

◀» Anti-Iraq War Demonstration, 15 February 2003

The march through London on Sunday 15 February 2003 attracted at least 750,000 people according to police estimates and a million or more according to the organisers. Which means that 2-3% of the electorate (or, if you take into account low turnouts at elections, up to 6% of the politically active population) was on the streets of the capital objecting to a policy being implemented in its name.

Demos – Agnew's Ten Commandments of Protest

*"Freedom of speech is useless without freedom of thought.
And I fear that the politics of protest is shutting out the process
of thought, so necessary to rational discussion."*
Spiro Agnew, vice-president of the USA 1968-73

Thou Shalt Not Allow Thy Opponent to Speak.

Thou Shalt Not Set Forth a Program of Thine Own.

Thou Shalt Not Trust Anybody Over Thirty.

Thou Shalt Not Honor Thy Father or Thy Mother.

Thou Shalt Not Heed the Lessons of History.

Thou Shalt Not Write Anything Longer than a Slogan.

Thou Shalt Not Present a Negotiable Demand.

Thou Shalt Not Accept Any Establishment Idea.

Thou Shalt Not Revere Any but Totalitarian Heroes.

Thou Shalt Not Ask Forgiveness for Thy Transgressions,
Rather Thou Shalt Demand Amnesty for Them.

(from a speech given in 1969 when the protest movement –
particularly against the Vietnam war – was at its height.)

Desert Island Discs

10 washed up politicians

Every week since 1942 (with gaps between series) a famous person has been hypothetically marooned on a desert island by Radio 4. He or she is asked to choose eight favourite pieces of music (originally gramophone records), as well as one book and one other luxury with which to pass an indefinite isolation from the world. One wonders how any politician will get on with no one to talk to, let alone an audience for a speech.

Date	Name	Music	Luxury	Book
18.2.78	Margaret Thatcher	Beethoven's Piano Concerto No 5 in E Flat Major*	A photograph album of her children	*The Survival Handbook* by Michael Allaby
18.10.87	Jim Callaghan	Mozart's Jupiter Symphony	A big telescope and textbook on the stars	*War and Peace* by Tolstoy
3.3.96	Gordon Brown	Bach's Suite No 3 in D Major	A tennis ball machine and racket	*The Story of Art* by Ernst Hans Gombrich
24.11.96	Tony Blair	Recuerdos de la Alhambra by John Williams	A guitar	*Ivanhoe* by Sir Walter Scott
3.11.02	Robin Cook	No 3 The Siegfried Idyll by Wagner	A chess computer	National Hunt Form Book
17.10.04	Menzies Campbell	Ride of the Valkyries by Wagner	Set of golf clubs	*Treasure Island* and *Kidnapped* by Robert Louis Stevenson

30.10.05	Boris Johnson	Finale of Brahms Variations on a Theme by Haydn	A large pot of French mustard	*Homer* – an Indian paper edition (to translate)
4.7.05	Michael Howard	(Everything I do) I Do It For You by Bryan Adams	Hot shower and some soap	*The Years of Lyndon Johnson* by Robert A. Caro
29.1.06	Shirley Williams	How Beautiful are the Feet by Handel	PC linked to internet	Collected W.H. Auden
28.5.06	David Cameron	Tangled Up In Blue by Bob Dylan	Crate of Scotch whisky	*The River Cottage Cookbook* by Hugh Fearnley-Whittingstall

*according to much-repeated legend another of her choices was Rolf Harris's *Two Little Boys* but in fact this was not among her records.

Diaries

13 chronicles, confessions, and/or castigations of contemporaries and colleagues

"To write one's memoirs is to speak ill of everybody except oneself." Marshall Pétain, 1946

Too often these days politicians keep diaries with a view to publishing them as soon as they leave office: a means of taking revenge on their enemies and vindicating their own actions. You can almost hear the writer talking self-consciously to posterity as he selectively records events in which he sees himself as the fulcrum, putting the best gloss on his own thoughts and actions. The most illuminating diaries, however, are those kept as truly intimate, confessional journals (sometimes by political nonentities), which often give as much space to the mundane, the transient and the trivial as they do to historic affairs of state. The best diarists are controversial and outspoken figures who really were in the thick of things, who write well and who express themselves with shocking frankness.

❧ **Thomas Jones** (1870-1955) Deputy Cabinet Secretary – the second highest post in the civil service – from 1916 to 1930. His *Whitehall Diaries* are in three parts, the first two covering 1916-1925 and 1926-1930, and the third dedicated to events to do with Ireland over the same period.

❧ **Harold Nicolson** (1886-1968). A politician, diplomat and writer married to Vita Sackville-West whose complete diaries span 1907-1963.

❧ **Duff Cooper** (1890-1954) Diplomat, Tory cabinet minister and friend of Edward VIII who resigned over Chamberlain's policy of appeasing Hitler and heard of the outbreak of World War II while on the golf course. His diaries cover 1915-1951.

❧ **Harold Macmillan** (1894–1986) Conservative prime minister, although his diaries mainly cover the period before his premiership, 1950-1957.

❧ **Richard Crossman** (1907-74) Minister for Housing, Leader of the House and Secretary for Social Services under Wilson. It has been suggested that Crossman's diaries, covering the Wilson government 1964–70, provided the inspiration for *Yes Minister* (see p352).

❧ **Barbara Castle** (1910–2002) A Labour 'modernizer', she held various government posts. Her diaries cover 1964-76.

❧ **Tony Benn** (b 1925). The veteran, frank and often controversial Labour Party parliamentarian. His diaries cover his long political career and extend beyond his retirement (2001-2007) which he describes in his most recent title, *More Time for Politics*.

❧ **Alan Clark** (1928-99) A Conservative MP and junior minister who was described by Edward Pearce as a "walking controversy". His diaries were published in three parts: *In Power* (1994) covering the 1980s, *Into Politics* (2001) covering 1972-82 and *The Last Diaries: In and Out of the Wilderness* (2003) covering 1991-99 and filmed by the BBC in 2004. They are remarkable not only for their political insights, not least into the fall of his heroine Margaret Thatcher, but also for Clark's obsession with sex.

❧ **Paddy Ashdown** (b 1941) Although Liberal leader and therefore not officially at the heart of government, Ashdown worked closely with Tony Blair before and after the latter's watershed election victory which acts as the dividing line between the two volumes of *The Ashdown Diaries, 1988–1997* and *1997-1999*.

❧ **Robin Cook** (1946–2005) Former foreign secretary. A brief diary with a particular point to make, *The Point of Departure: Diaries from the Front Bench* (2004), looks at the build up to Blair's Iraq war between 2001 and 2003, a war to which Cook was opposed.

❧ **Edwina Currie** (b 1946) Opinionated Conservative MP and sometime junior health minister whose diaries on the years 1987-1992 became infamous for revealing that she had a four-year affair with John Major before he became prime minister.

❧ **David Blunkett** (b 1947) Some politicians think what they have to say is more interesting than it actually is but *The Blunkett Tapes: My Life in the Bear Pit*, spanning 1997–2006, still gives insights into the workings of the Blair government.

❧ **Alastair Campbell** (b 1957) Blair's Director of Communications ('spin doctor') from 1997 until his resignation in 2003 waited until after Blair's departure from office before publishing an edited version of his diaries, *The Blair Years*, consisting of 2 million words and covering the years 1994–2003.

Dictatorial Definitions

6 totalitarian terms transposed

Foreign political systems have generated so many colourful terms and expressions that politicians and journalists in Britain invariably reach for this exotic phrasebook when they wish to add a pinch of hyperbole to their speeches and writing,

Here are some of their most popular choices:

'Junta'

- *Original meaning:* In Spanish, a council or regional authority. As in the Junta de Andalucia, the local government for the Costa del Sol and the rest of southern Spain.

- *Modern usage:* a sinister-sounding, unelected, repressive, moustachioed South American military regime.

'Great Leap Forward'

- *Original meaning:* An economic initiative of Mao Tse Tung which involved the forcible placing of 700 million people in 26,578 communes and which was partly responsible for 20 million dying of starvation in 1959-1962.

- *Modern usage:* Any over-optimistic/unrealistic plan (called by its supporters "a bold objective") for sudden and rapid transformation of a party, department, society etc. Almost always used disparagingly in hindsight with the tone of "I told you so."

'Purge'

- *Original meaning:* The act of naming, shaming, expelling and usually eradicating ideologically suspect elements from the government, party, state television station etc.

- *Modern usage:* Ditto, but with an official enquiry replacing the show trial, removal from the media spotlight instead of internal exile, and "spending more time with one's family" as an alternative to gulag.

'Night of the Long Knives'

- *Original meaning:* The murder of Hitler's opponents by the Gestapo on 30th June 1934.

- *Modern usage:* To ruthlessly dispatch half one's Cabinet in one go. Most famous example: 12 July 1962 Harold MacMillan sacked seven members of his Cabinet including the Chancellor Selwyn Lloyd in an attempt to save his own skin. "Greater love hath no man than he who lays down his friends for his life," said Jeremy Thorpe at the time.

'Gang of Four'

- *Original meaning:* The leaders of the Chinese Cultural Revolution, Mao's widow among them. They were later discredited and the phrase has overtones of a criminal band.

- *Modern usage:* The founders of the SDP.

'Tsar'

- *Original meaning:* autocratic God-anointed despot of Russia.

- *Peculiarly modern British usage:* A man or woman who acts as a despot (or even minor god) for a section of the public sector. He is ostensibly appointed to make the public believe that someone is focusing 100% on a particular problem (e.g. drugs) even if they know that he can do nothing about it. Cynics say the real job of a modern tsar is to draw the flack from a failing department of the civil service and therefore obviate revolution from below.

Diplomatic definitions

A starter vocabulary to know who your friends are

"Diplomacy n. the art and business of lying for one's country."
Ambrose Bierce 'The Devil's Dictionary' 1911

Successful diplomacy is largely a matter of choosing your words carefully. Before you begin negotiations or make any public statement, you should ask the White House whether the country you are dealing with is in or out of favour: that is, whether it is one of us or one of them. Then you can describe it accurately using the vocabulary below.

Us	*Them*
admission	confession
alliance	axis
confidential, secret	hidden
political class	corrupt elite
defence capability, deterrent	(illegal) WMDs
defence policy	aggression towards neighbours
detained for interests of national security	imprisoned without trial
developing (poor) country	failing (failed) state
elections	rigged elections
federation, union	bloc
friendly government	puppet government
government	regime
incentive	bribe
independent country	diplomatically isolated rogue state
restoration of order	repression, suppression
influence	orchestrate

leader, president	dictator
liberation (of a country)	invasion
local business conditions	corruption
obvious, evident	flagrant
opposition forces	insurgents
plentiful, abundant	rife
policy	posture
principled	fundamentalist
politics	power struggle
public service broadcasting	state-owned television
regime change	invasion, coup d'etat
security forces	paramilitary police
security measures	repression
speech	proclamation, discourse
sphere of influence	sphere of control
supply economic and military advisers	infiltrate
support (a government)	prop up
(bring) stability to	destabilise
tough	brutal
resolute	intransigent, stubborn, inflexible
trading partner	satellite
free/unregulated market	black market
strategic interests	plans for expansion, conquest
transition	power vacuum
treaty	pact

Direct Action

10 cases when parliament and the government were sidelined

> *"First they ignore you. Then they laugh at you. Then they fight you. Then you win."* Gandhi

> *"Frighten the people of this country until they frighten the Government; that is the only way to get anything done."*
> Mark Kerr, British rear-admiral during First World War, 1923

A demonstration merely makes a point and it is easy for decision-makers to ignore it, play down its importance, or scoff at the ineffectualness of its organisers. But for a minority of motivated people, marching and talking are a waste of time; the only thing that people in power ever take notice of is a *passage à l'acte*.

Those who take direct political action know that they may have to break the law and accept the consequences. They will alienate some of their allies and give their enemies a justification to condemn them. Public opinion can swing for or against them or both ways at once. None of this really matters: they take the long view and believe that the righteousness of their cause will, with hindsight, be seen to justify whatever tactics they use.

The Tolpuddle Martyrs 1834

The labour movement regards as heroes the six Dorset farm workers who organised themselves into a trade union and who were transported to Tasmania for their troubles. In court, one of the six defended their actions by saying "We were meeting together to preserve ourselves, our wives, and our children from utter degradation and starvation."

The Suffragettes

Emily Davison made herself a martyr to the cause of political representation for women by throwing herself under the King's racehorse in the Derby at Epsom in 1913. Other suffragettes went on hunger strike in prison. Their militant tactics alienated some potential supporters but publicised their cause. Ultimately the movement was successful in getting votes for women in 1918.

Squatting

The occupation of vacant buildings seems like an unambiguous application of Proudhon's dictum that "property is theft", and hence a challenge to legal rights over private ownership. In fact, it is not quite as baldly subversive as it seems. It has a respectable pedigree going back at least to the Enclosures, and to 17th-century groups such as the Diggers and the Levellers, and is concerned with championing the effective, collective use of resources, not theft for theft's sake.

Squatting has enjoyed periodic revivals in the 20th century – whenever there is pressure for cheap housing and buildings are left empty or abandoned by their owners. A few squats have managed to establish themselves as community resources in deprived areas.

Hunt Saboteurs

The Hunt Saboteurs Association was founded in Devon in 1964 and for thirty years its members engaged in a battle over the use of the countryside.

Hunting was outlawed by Act of Parliament on 18 February 2005 but abolition has always been vehemently opposed by the Countryside Alliance (see p86) and in practice hunting has not been completely stopped.

Animal Rights

A broader effort to defend the rights of animals (for some a contentious notion) is carried out by the Animal Liberation Front, which grew out of the Band of Mercy in 1976. Most activists claim to be engaged in actions which are not violent to "human animals" but extreme elements of the movement have resorted episodically to violence, intimidation, and terrorism.

The movement is distinctive not only for its longevity and persistence but also for its ability to organise without leaders. Some animal rights campaigns attract support from moderates who have never protested in their lives but mostly their support takes the form of demonstrations rather than direct action – as in the protest against the transport of live animals in 1997-8.

Road and Airport Protesters

In the late 1990s most direct action was focused on the expansion of Britain's road network and the building of new runways for busy airports. Protesters in both cases argued that the easier it is to drive or fly, the more traffic there will be on the roads and in the sky, with ever increasing air pollution as a consequence.

The Newbury by-pass (which opened in 1998) was the scene of mostly pacifist resistance to bulldozers and bailiffs and in the 'battle' to prevent the building of a second runway for Manchester airport in 1997-1999, campaigners dug tunnels and chained themselves to the tops of trees to make it harder to evict them.

Fuel Tax Protest, September 2000

Blair's government was almost brought down by a blockade of oil refineries which was rapidly organised by disgruntled lorry drivers using a new tool of flying protest, the mobile phone. The 'revolt' against increased tax on fuel was a prime example of effective, single-issue political action carried out by a relatively unpoliticised group campaigning for a specific, self-interested goal.

Fathers 4 Justice

No suffragette of the 1900s or even a feminist of the 1970s could have imagined that by the end of the century men would be claiming to be the victims of a political consensus against them. Today's underdog in search of justice is the estranged father who has to pay maintenance but is denied access to his children. Fathers 4 Justice wants a Bill of Rights for the family to ensure that all parties of separation and divorce receive fair treatment and its tactic of preference is the 'cunning stunt' in fancy dress. When Batman climbed onto a balcony of Buckingham Palace to appeal for a fair deal for estranged fathers, he was probably testing public sympathy to its limit but for those who undertake direct action anything is justified if it gets attention in the media.

Environmentalism

Greenpeace is an international organisation founded in 1971 with the aim of pressurizing those responsible for environmental damage into changing their ways, and political decision makers into changing their policies. One of its most famous actions in Britain was to draw publicity to Shell's proposed dumping of the redundant Brent Spar oil platform at sea in 1996. Shell was forced by public opinion to dismantle and recycle the structure at a cost of £43m instead of dumping it which would have cost £4.5m (and untold environmental damage).

The Disruption of Parliament

The ultimate risk for activists is to take their cause into the House of Commons itself. On 15 September 2004 eight campaigners opposed to the government's bill to ban fox hunting tricked their way through the security systems of parliament by disguising themselves as builders and entered the chamber of the House of Commons.

Such a strategy, however, can easily backfire. In this case the TV and press publicity generated by the protest dwelt as much on the lamentable security in the Houses of Westminster as it did on the issue of fox-hunting, and public opinion in general was not sympathetic to the protestors' tactics – how can it be democratic to interrupt the workings of democracy?

Discipline in the House of Commons

An 8-step plan for auto-correction

As well as making the laws of Britain, the House of Commons also has a few laws of its own to deal with troublemakers in its midst. MPs are expected to behave with decorum in the Commons chamber and pay attention to debates. They are not allowed briefcases, newspapers and magazines, nor are they allowed food and drink lest they distract whoever is speaking by sucking oranges, cracking nuts or opening cans of fizzy drink. They are not permitted to interrupt someone who the Speaker has nominated to speak and it goes without saying that they must respect the venerable house in which they sit.

On 27 May 1976, Michael Heseltine famously committed the ultimate act of disrespect towards the House. Infuriated by the singing of the Red Flag by a group of Welsh Labour MPs he seized the mace – the silver club symbolising royal power vested in the Commons – and brandished it over his head. The sitting had to be suspended but he saved himself from discipline by apologising first thing the next day.

Serious breeches of the Parliamentary rules are referred to the Committee on Standards and Privileges for a ruling on what action to take. Parties also have their own methods of punishment, specifically withdrawal of the whip (even if it sounds like something desirable it's a form of ostracism), deselection or expulsion from the party (but not from Parliament – only losing an election or the procedure below can lead to that).

Sanctions for poor behaviour in the House

1. If a member persistently interrupts another the Speaker first asks him/her to resume his seat.

2. If he continues to interrupt or commits one of a number of infractions (using insulting, coarse, or abusive language, calling another member a liar or accusing him of being drunk), the Speaker will suggest that the culprit leave the Chamber for the remainder of the day's sitting although he can't oblige him to do so – the MP can still vote in divisions.

3. If the member refuses to go voluntarily, the Speaker can invoke Standing Order no. 43 and order him to leave Parliament altogether for the day, handing him over to the Serjeant at Arms for forcible eviction.

4. If the member resists, the next sanction is to 'name' him, parliamentary language for suspension. The member is disbarred for 5 sitting days without pay for an initial offence, 20 days for a second offence and for as long as the House wants if he proves an incorrigible recidivist.

5. Serious crimes, such as perjury, forgery, fraud and corruption, are punishable by expulsion. Three members have been expelled in recent times:

    • Horatio Bottomley, August 1922, convicted of fraud and sent to prison;

    • Garry Allighan, 30 October 1947, for lying to a committee and contempt of the House;

    • Peter Baker, 16 December 1954, convicted of forgery and sent to prison.

6. Certain behaviour in the world outside Parliament has an effect inside it. Anyone convicted and sentenced to prison, or declared bankrupt, is disqualified from voting and a by-election is held in his constituency. Treason is dealt with similarly but there has only been one case since 1900: in 1903 Arthur Lynch (Nationalist MP for Galway) was convicted of high treason for fighting against the Crown in the Boer War.

7. The House used to have the power to fine members but it lapsed in the 18th century. There have since been attempts to revive it.

8. Technically, the House can also imprison one of its number but it last did so at the end of the 19th century, and then only for one night.

Divisions

10 facts about how the House of Commons votes

The lynchpin of British democracy is an archaic, unautomated system of voting which dates from 1906. The division system is not so much manual as ambulatory: members must literally walk through the voting lobbies, give their names and record their votes as they exit. MPs don't want to modernize it because, amongst other things, it would take away the sociability of voting: the lobby is one place where you can be sure to run into your colleagues.

Voting procedure

1. When the House decides to put a matter to the vote, a strict procedure must be followed. The Speaker orders "Clear the lobbies" (to make sure no intruders vote by subterfuge) and the division bells are rung through the Palace of Westminster. Glasses are left on bars; plates of dinner half eaten as MPs hurry towards the lobbies. The lobby exit doors are locked.

2. Two minutes after the original motion for the vote, the Speaker puts the question to the House for a second time and the division only goes ahead if the question is challenged. Otherwise it is called off and everyone goes back to what they were doing, eating or drinking.

3. If the division is to go ahead, members file in to the lobbies as directed by the whips – those who have not been following the debate may have no idea what the division is about. Eight minutes after the question was put for the first time (measured by electronic clock) the lobby entrance doors are locked and counting begins.

4. An MP who is in the Palace of Westminster but too ill or infirm to make it to the lobby may be "nodded through" – that is, his vote is registered without him physically passing through the lobby.

5. The only way to abstain is to remain in your seat or go into the lobby and not register a vote. Occasionally, MPs will abstain to render a vote inquorate – quorum for a valid vote is 40.

6. Pairing is an unofficial arrangement whereby two members of opposing parties agree (with the Whips' consent) not to vote. The arrangement is temporarily cancelled for important votes.

7. When a government has a large majority it permits groups of its MPs to form 'bisques' (a term taken from croquet): groups of members who are unpaired but who are allowed to not turn up for a division because the government knows it will still get a sufficient majority for any piece of legislation.

8. If an MP votes in the wrong lobby by mistake he or she can vote again in the other lobby to counteract the effect – as long as there is time before the entrance doors are locked.

9. A division takes between 10 and 15 minutes, the average having been calculated as 11 and a half minutes.

10. If the result of the division is a tie, the Speaker has the casting vote, and uses it in conformity with certain rules set by precedent. The last time this happened was on 22 July 1993.

Downing Street

10 episodes in the history of an historic house

"More of a monastery than a power house." Marcia Williams

The world's most famous address belongs to the most intensively used and visited house of all time. It has been described as being like Doctor Who's Tardis – far bigger on the inside than it looks from the outside. Not only is it home to a family but it also provides office space for upwards of 250 people and reception rooms for summits of world leaders, press conferences and tricky negotiations.

1. The street is named after its 17th century developer George Downing, one of the earliest graduates of Harvard, who diarist Samuel Pepys described as "a perfidious rogue". No. 10 was No. 5 until 1779.

2. It is technically two houses combined: Downing's cheap terrace house and a grander house overlooking Horse Guard's Parade, also 17th century.

3. No. 10 has been associated with the prime minister since 1730 when the first prime minister, Sir Robert Walpole, refused to accept it as a personal gift, insisting that it be used by all 'First Lords of the Treasury'. In the same year the last private resident of Downing Street moved out, about whom nothing is known except that he was called Mr Chicken.

4. In 1908, under Asquith's premiership, suffragettes chained themselves to the railings outside No. 10 and policemen had to remove them with hacksaws.

5. Ramsay MacDonald was the first prime minister not to have a personal art collection. He set a precedent by borrowing art works from national collections.

6. Bombs caused damage to No. 10 during the Blitz of 1940 but there were no direct hits.

7. Harold Macmillan had the rectangular Cabinet Room table replaced with a curved, boat-shaped one so that he could see everyone sitting around it without anyone having to lean forward. The prime minister's chair, with its back to the

fireplace, is always left parked at an angle so that he can get into it at a trot at the start of a meeting.

8. In 1989 tall metal gates were erected at the end of Downing Street, putting protesters and other members of the public at a distance from the prime minister.

9. In 1991 the IRA fired a mortar bomb at No. 10 from a white Transit van parked in Whitehall. John Major was conducting a Cabinet meeting on the forthcoming Gulf War when the bomb exploded in the garden, blowing out windows and causing a crater but not killing anyone.

10. The Grand Staircase is lined with the portraits of all preceding prime ministers, ascending in chronological order. When a prime minister leaves office, the portraits are shuffled down to make space for him (or her) at the top.

Dystopias

10 places you wouldn't want to move to

If we know where we don't want to go, let's hope we can avoid going there whether by accident, apathy or some scheming leader's evil intent.

Erewhon by Samuel Butler (1872)

The giveaway title spells 'Nowhere' backwards – almost. Apparently a utopia but really a satire on Victorian society. Erewhonian law treats criminals as if they were ill and sick people as criminals.

We by Yevgeny Ivanovich Zamyatin (1921)

A major influence on Orwell and perhaps on Huxley as well. In it, the One State is governed by the Benefactor and a giant wall separates the inhabitants from nature.

Brave New World by Aldous Huxley (1932)

A more subtle dystopia than others because it could almost be a utopia. People live in a state of permanent drug and sex-fuelled happiness. Or do they?

1984 by George Orwell (1949)

Still the most chilling of dystopias, a depiction of the ultimate totalitarian state in which even language (see 'Newspeak and Doublethink' p207), and thereby thoughts, are controlled by the Party.

Fahrenheit 451 by Ray Bradbury (1953)

A science fiction novel set in a society dedicated to censorship and in which the only source of information for the citizens is television. Books are burnt to prevent critical thought, 451°F being the temperature at which paper ignites.

Consider Her Ways by John Wyndham (1961)

A short story about a future society in which men have been eradicated and only women exist. His post-apocalyptical novel, *The Chrysalids* (1955) also has dystopian overtones.

The Machine Stops by E. M. Forster (1909)
A short story in which human beings live underground and all their needs are met by an omnipotent machine.

Planet of the Apes by Pierre Boulle (1963)
The earth of the future has been taken over by super-evolved gorillas, orangutans and chimpanzees who rule over human beings with a mixture of intelligence and brutality, as we do the animal kingdom. Made famous by the film of 1968.

Blade Runner (a film made in 1982)
A loose adaptation of *Do Androids Dream of Electric Sheep?* by Philip K. Dick about a dysfunctional Los Angeles in 2019. It is not overtly political but is perhaps the best demonstration of the cinema's ability to show what life in a technologically advanced dystopia could be like.

Swastika Night by Katharine Burdekin (published under a pseudonym, 1937)
A dystopia which starts with the political reality of the 1930s and asks what would have happened if Hitler had succeeded in establishing his 'thousand-year reich'.

Economists

10 inflated gurus and their political messages

> "No real English gentleman, in his secret soul, was ever sorry for the death of a political economist." Walter Bagheot

> "There are two problems in my life. The political ones are insoluble and the economic ones are incomprehensible."
> Alec-Douglas Home

> "Every discipline has its academic disagreements, but in other subjects there is scope for future agreement... Economic theories don't die, they merely become unfashionable...the dispute between monetarism and Keynesianism could run for ever." Victor Keegan, The Guardian

Economics is more a superstition or religion than a social science. Its business is prophecy and the entrails it reads to make its predictions are history, technological progress and human behaviour.

While most economists agree on explanations of past events, when it comes to establishing laws which will be valid for the future they split into sects with violently differing world views. As an economist, you can believe what you want to believe but you can never prove it, and your opponent won't be able to prove its refutation either.

For an inexact science which hasn't come to any definite conclusions, economics has used up a lot of words, many of them invented. It is also very good at computer modelling (econometrics) which it clings to like a raft drifting ever further from the real world.

Nevertheless, economists have made many interesting observations about the world, observations which they generally expound in very large books. As any para-economist knows, everything anyone has to say which is worth saying can be said in a sentence. This list pares 200 years of self-important prestidigitation down to manageable size. And if you want economics itself summarised in a maxim to remember it is this (useful if you are betting on the horses or the next election):

'What goes up must come down.'

Adam Smith (1723-90)

Catchiest title: 'An Inquiry into the Nature and Causes of the Wealth of Nations' (1776)

Slogan: "We'll all be richer if we take away the red tape and let the market rip."

Note: it has been claimed that although Smith is regarded as a guru by the freemarketeering right, the left can find plenty in his writings to contradict this interpretation.

David Ricardo (1772–1823)

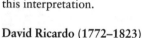

Catchiest title: 'Principles of Political Economy and Taxation' (1817)

Slogan: "The more you pay your workers, the less there is in it for you."

Karl Marx (1818-1883)

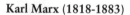

Catchiest title: 'Das Kapital' (Capital) 1867

Slogan: "Nice factory you've got – are you going to share it?"

Note: for more on Marx see p309.

Carl Menger (1840–1921)

Catchiest title: 'Principles of Economics' (1871)

Slogan: "Smith was wrong."

Note: Founded the Austrian school which refuted Smith and Ricardo.

R.H. Tawney (1880-1962)

Catchiest title: 'The Acquisitive Society' (1921)

Slogan: "Freedom for the pike is death to the minnows."

John Maynard Keynes (1883–1946)

Catchiest title: 'The General Theory of Employment, Interest, and Money' (1936)

Slogan: "To get people spending, and thus create demand which creates jobs, the governments should make people dig holes and fill them in again."

Friedrich Hayek (1899–1992)

Catchiest title: 'The Road to Serfdom' (1944)

Slogan: "The state will still need to put up road signs but the market will take care of everything else."

J.K. Galbraith (1908-2006)

Catchiest title: 'The Affluent Society' (1958)

Slogan: "Money doesn't make people happy by itself."

Milton Friedman (1912–2006)

Catchiest title: 'Capitalism and Freedom' (1962)

Slogan: "The only free lunch is one you cook for yourself."

E.F. Schumacher (1911-1977)

Catchiest title: 'Small is Beautiful: A Study of Economics As If People Mattered' (1973)

Slogan: "Let's not get things out of proportion."

Election Milestones

The 12 most important elections of the 20th century

Every election is unique because of the time and circumstances in which it is held, and the personalities who take part; but where some elections are routine affairs with predictable outcomes others are remarkable either for delivering shock results or for marking the start of a new political era.

1900 Khaki Election

Thus named because it took place at the height of the Boer War. It was the first outing for the Labour Representation Committee which would become the Labour Party.

1918 Coupon Election

The Liberal Party split during the First World War and Lloyd George fought this post-war election in coalition with the Conservatives. 'Coupons' or letters of approval were distributed to distinguish coalition candidates from Liberals who had stuck with Asquith during the rift. It was the first election in which women could vote, although not from the same minimum age as men. And it was the first election to be held on one day instead of two.

1924 Deliberalising Election

The 'two-party system' referred to the Conservative and Liberal parties until this election when support for the latter evaporated. From now on the Labour Party would be the other big player in British politics.

1929 Flapper Election

The first election in which women could vote on the same terms as men. Young women of the time were known as "flappers".

1931 Doctor's Mandate Election

The National Government's manifesto used this phrase to appeal for the power to do whatever it had to do to heal the sick patient – the

British economy. It could just as accurately be called the Depressed Election because it took place in the middle of the Great Depression. It was the last election not to be held on a Thursday.

1945 Nationalisation Election

Churchill, having won the war, might have expected an election victory in gratitude but voters turned en masse to the Labour Party which offered a radical programme of nationalisation and legislation to create the welfare state. The election was called before the war had been finally won – after Germany had capitulated but before the detonation of the two atomic bombs over Japan.

1964 Establishment Election

A surprise, skin-of-the-teeth win for Harold Wilson, mainly because of a series of setbacks and scandals that had plagued the Conservatives who were seen as synonymous with 'the Establishment'. The mood of the 1960s was to break with the past and to shatter the conventions of class deference. The in-coming Labour government seemed more in tune with the aspirations of the country as a whole.

1970 Yesterday's Men Election

Another election which did not go the way it was expected to. During the campaign, Labour had tried to portray the Conservatives as 'yesterday's men' and they were as surprised as anyone when Heath won. The BBC made a controversial documentary labelling the outgoing Labour government as the real "yesterday's men" which, technically, they were. (see 'BBC objectivity' p15)

1974 (February) Governing Government Election

Heath appealed to the electorate to decide who was running the country: his government or the striking mineworkers. Voters decided it wasn't him, but they weren't sure who it should be, and returned a hung parliament. Labour struggled to form a government and Harold Wilson was forced to call another election in October, which gave him a slight, but sufficient majority.

1979 Discontented Election

The Sun baptised the winter of 1978–9 'The Winter of Discontent' after Shakespeare's Richard III and the phase caught the mood of the times. Margaret Thatcher rode to power not because of a wave of support for her but because of intense and widespread dissatisfaction with the Callaghan government. Labour would remain out of office for the next 18 years.

1983 Falklands Election

A year after victory in the Falklands, with Margaret Thatcher's popularity peaking, there was nothing Labour could do to save themselves from spectacular defeat. It was probably unkind, but true, therefore for Gerald Kaufmann to call the party manifesto "the longest suicide note in history."

1997 New Labour Election

Tony Blair won landslide approval with the biggest postwar majority of any party. To achieve it, he had rebaptised Labour as New Labour and surrounded himself with spin doctors who knew that it wasn't so much substance which would win over floating voters but style and presentation.

The Establishment

A ready reckoner to see if your face fits (blood test advisable)

> *"It is impossible that the whisper of a faction should prevail against the voice of a nation."* Lord Russell

> *"Class is the basis of British party politics; all else is embellishment and detail."* Pulzer

The term 'the Establishment' was first defined in the 1950s. Before then, no one bothered to identify the components of the ruling class – weren't they obvious? Britain has since, supposedly, evolved into a semi-classless quasi-meritocracy but there is of course still an elite at the top of the societal heap. Influential rather than vested with formal powers, the Establishment perpetuates itself by birth, wealth, education and connections, and identifies the good of the country with its own interests. But it is not a homogeneous, close-knit, or immutable entity and is no longer as coherent as it was when Conservative prime ministers magically 'emerged', anointed, unelected, from its midsts.

In the old days you were either part of it or you weren't; now you can belong to it to a greater or lesser degree and you can worm your way in. One of the great things about the Establishment (and the class system) is the trickle of upward permeability it allows which refreshes the talents at the top even if the blood stays much the same.

You can infiltrate the Establishment if you behave properly, lunch, network and wheedle; but you can't buy your way in and you can't join by merit alone. New membership is by invitation only. Note that only those born with a stake in the status quo can hold non-conformist, eccentric, outrageous or leftist views and still be clutched to the bosom of the Establishment.

Take the test opposite to work out how 'Establishment' you are. Add the % scores for all categories that apply to you, deduct any allowances and divide by the number of boxes you've ticked. e.g. if you are a monarch of the UK tick the first item for your main job and also 'Church of England clergyman' as you are head of the Anglican church, making a total of 195. Divided by 2, this makes you 97.5% Establishment. You should make an effort to improve your social contacts with the people who count.

Affiliation		%	Running total
Royal Family	☐	100	....
Employee of Royal Family (only if you can keep schtumm for a lifetime)	☐	100	....
Member of the Monday Club (give yourself a 25 bonus if you have been a member for more than 25 years and 50 for 50 years)	☐	100	....
Privy Councillor	☐	100	....
Aristocracy (top up by 5 if you are from one of *the* families of Britain)	☐	95	....
Editor of the *Daily Telegraph*	☐	95	....
Church of England clergyman (upper echelons only; subtract 50 if you consider Jesus to have been the first Socialist; subtract 100 if you have evangelical views)	☐	95	....
Landed gentry (absentee landlords living in London)	☐	90	....
Senior judge	☐	90	....
Oxford or Cambridge don or employee	☐	90	....
Product of a top public school with orthodox career	☐	90	....
Member of a traditional London club	☐	90	....
Prime minister or ex-prime minister	☐	90	....
High-ranking officer in the armed forces	☐	80	....
Member of the Royal Academy	☐	80	....
Decision-maker in any other institution with 'Royal' in title	☐	80	....
Conservative cabinet minister	☐	80	....
Something in the City	☐	70	....
Labour cabinet minister (while in office; afterwards you're on your own)	☐	70	....
Spy (MI5 or MI6 but not double agent)	☐	70	....
Editor of the *Times*	☐	65	....
Senior civil service	☐	60	....
Conservative Party member	☐	50	....
On BBC board or BBC trust	☐	40	....
Quango appointee (if you sit on the board of more than one, add 5 for each)	☐	30	....

Middle-ranking civil servant	☐	20 ....
Editor of the Times Literary Supplement	☐	10 ....
If more than three-quarters of your close friends and shooting partners belong to the above categories and a word from you over the port is enough to "get things done"	☐	100 ....

Total number of affiliation points

Allowances

If your main residence is outside London and has less than 100 acres of land	☐	-60 ....
If you work because you have to rather than because you want to	☐	-80 ....
If you can't remember whether an earl outranks a marquess (you should know such things without even knowing how you know them)	☐	-90 ....
If you think things are better today than they were when you were a boy/girl	☐	-90 ....
If you have ever received any state benefit (except grant for repairing stately home)	☐	-95 ....
If you work in the arts, organic farming, journalism (except the Daily Telegraph) or social work	☐	-95 ....
If you ever wonder whether you are really a member of the Establishment	☐	-100 ....
If you had a state education (including grammar school)	☐	-100 ....

Total allowances

Net (affiliation points less allowancs)

Number of boxes ticked

Final score (Net divided by # boxes ticked)*

* Indicates eligibility to call yourself part of the Establishment

Note: if you even started reading this page, and especially if you did the exercise, you are definitely *not* part of the Establishment.

Eurolovableness

8 reasons why you might want to give the EU a cuddle

> *"The last time Britain went into Europe with any degree of success was on 6 June 1944."* Daily Express 1980

Europe-bashing, led by the tabloid press, has become a national pastime in Britain. Our involvement is much like an office love affair gone horribly wrong. For a decade we were wooed and rejected in turn and then when the relationship was finally consummated we didn't experience the long-awaited closeness and multi-level satisfaction we had expected. Instead we found ourselves entangled with a promiscuous polygamist who was following her own agenda and who didn't care as much about what we thought as we had assumed. No wonder the eurosceptic half of our national personality feels confused and hurt. We'd change continent if we could, but why should we and where would we go?

Let's get wise: the more we sulk and brood, the harder we're making it for ourselves. It's time we stopped crying and started realising that even the toughest emotional experiences in life can teach us valuable lessons. All relationships take work, don't they? To rebuild our shattered self-confidence we have to start by remembering why we allowed ourselves to be seduced in the first place. It wasn't just the fault of the cheap booze at the office party.

The pacific notion

It's a cliché but not a banal statement that there hasn't been a war in Western Europe since the Common Market was formed 50 years ago. Germany and France were at each other's throats three times in the 70 years between 1870 and 1940 and Britain was catastrophically roped in twice.

It could be argued that geopolitical developments (the end of empires and the global dominance of the US) have made war in Europe less likely and that the existence of NATO is more responsible for peacekeeping than the EU. But peace isn't just an absence of war or the flexing of joint military muscle; it's a more subtle and fragile commodity than that and we shouldn't underestimate the role of European institutions in providing activities for countries to engage in that make aggression a less attractive option. The EU locks the politics and economic interests of larger and smaller countries together and the disappearance of borders makes arguments over disputed territories less likely. Some of the former Soviet Bloc states now in the EU could easily have become the loose cannons of Europe without a new economic fortress to be part of.

Europe also, hesitantly, grants political involvement to extreme, nationalistic political groups which might otherwise set about rearming and looking for a fight. Whether the EU is the paramount agency of the Pax Europea or not, the more peace-keeping mechanisms there are in what was once a tinderbox the better, and if we think the price of too much bureaucracy is too high, perhaps we should remember what happened between 1939 and 1945.

Power hunger

Eurosceptics are always rabbiting on about loss of sovereignty to Brussels. *Guardian* journalist Polly Toynbee has suggested that this may be because British subjects feel they have so little sovereignty to begin with that they daren't lose any more. Power in the British political system has never been evenly shared and as it becomes increasingly more centralised so it becomes more remote from the people who supposedly legitimate it. The average Briton feels he has no more of a stake in Westminster – or even his local town hall – than he has in Brussels but whereas he is stifled by patriotism from addressing the failings of his own constitution the power-hungry European Union is an easy and safe target for his frustrations.

If the European Union starts to open people's eyes to the way in which they are being disempowered by *all* layers of government, then it will be doing them a favour. There seems to be a collective myth afoot in Britain that were the country to pull out of the EU, clouds of sovereignty would waft down every high street to be inhaled by every freeborn man or woman.

A lack of proportion

One of the failings of the Westminster political system is illuminated in fairground lights whenever elections are held for the European Parliament. Ironically, a small, anti-EU party such as UKIP is blocked from winning seats in the House of Commons by our anachronistic first-past-the-post voting system but has a fair chance of getting representatives into the European Parliament. Sooner or later a British government is going to have to explain to its electorate why proportional representation is appropriate for choosing MEPs but not for choosing MPs.

Common currency

There may be plenty of good, macro-economic reasons to shun the euro but if you are a consumer, especially if you live near a border (which includes anywhere south of the river Thames), there is no question about its advantages: no more walking around with pocket calculators; no more getting ripped off because you can't think fast enough.

The single European currency may yet fail but until then it will be a bold, visionary experiment – and don't we wish that more politicians would be more daring more of the time? Rather than take a risk, however, the British feel it is their duty to go on paying the banks lush commissions to change their money from one abstract unit to another.

There is a superstition that to lose the pound would be to give away a part of our national soul but millions of Europeans have survived similar spiritual cravings for the franc, the lira and the peseta.

Little Britain

We may not have forgotten Agincourt and Waterloo but everyone else has. Britain is shrinking in relative importance to an increasingly internationalised world. We can't and shouldn't go on suffering post-colonialist stress disorder for ever and should start getting used to the idea that the North American continent is drifting ever further away from us. We need to make new friends and play with the kids who have moved in next door. Then, perhaps, we can have a say in what the next game is.

The right to roam

Our homeland is, let's face it, a damp and drafty little North Atlantic island and many of us can't wait to get away from it. It's always been possible to emigrate but the EU has made it easy. There was no guaranteed freedom of settlement before the union did away with borders and paperwork. No one was fool enough to build a Channel Tunnel in the days when the continent was cut off by fog. But now it is the old fogeys in Britain who are cut off by fog. Young people are catching up with the benefits of moving around and the benefits are two-way. French entrepreneurs install themselves in Kent, and Spanish students staff London restaurants to the benefit of local economies, while Brits cash in on a booming housing market and emigrate to the Dordogne or Costa del Sol. Does anyone really want to re-erect border posts staffed by truculent paramilitary police officers?

The withering away of the nation state

As for the bogeyman of federalism: what is the United Kingdom of Great Britain and Northern Ireland if not a four-part federation already? Does it make that much difference if the fragments are subsumed into another federation? The United Kingdom isn't a permanent entity: it was only formed in the 18th century and immediately started falling apart until most of Ireland was hived off in 1922. Scotland now has itchy feet. So we're not really talking about an inviolate tribal area. The nation state is, in any case, an outdated invention which has served its purpose. It's time to move on from our petty nationalistic preoccupations by turning Europe into a continent composed of regions with political powers taken at the most appropriate level, from the supranational to the empowered comune (or parish).

Invisible exports

It may seem a mad idea for 27 countries to get together and try to make a common foreign policy but it is also a mad idea for 27 small countries which live so close to each other, and which have so many similiar geopolitical interests, to practise separate foreign policies. Europe has the possibility of doing some good in the world. Professor Timothy Garton Ash recommends that if we are worried about globalisation we should actively favour Europeanisation as an alternative. Europe has created a lot more than its fair share of the world's post-middle age problems but these days it's a chastened continent anxious to do good and it has some remarkable virtues to export. Especially a non-American understanding of democracy, a respect for the freedom of the individual, for free speech, for human rights, for the rule of law, for minorities and multiculturalism, for religions (plural) and for social solidarity in general. Britain could be a willing party in promoting these values to the rest of the world.

You don't have to look far for examples of countries that were dictatorships in living memory and which are now partners in the EU. Who knows, perhaps Europeanisation could lead the way to some sort of world government.

All of the above

You can dispute the value of any or all of these reasons for giving Europe a chance but it is the combination of them which is important.

As a cluster of institutions, Brussels-cum-Strasbourg are no more and no less imperfect than Westminster-cum-Whitehall. They both wolf down taxes; they both spawn too much bureaucracy; they are both stuffed with people who are unelected and unaccountable and they both work in an idiosyncratic way. There are lots of problems with both British and European government which need to be solved but leaving the European Union would be a retrograde step by definition. It would be costly and complicated and would not necessarily achieve the aims of eurosceptics.

Resting within the union in a disgruntled, half-hearted sort of way doesn't seem like a good option either.

It's time Britain snapped out of its adolescent grump and either jumped fully into the arms of her eurolover or adopted the life of a celibate old matron of a certain age.

Expert Advice

12 tips from top people

"When the facts change, I change my opinion. What do you do?"
John Maynard Keynes

"The acid test of any political decision is the question: 'What is the alternative?'"
Lord Trend

"No man ever became great or good except through many and great mistakes."
William Gladstone

"Power without principles is ruthless, sour, empty, vicious .... principle without power is idle sterility."
Neil Kinnock

"Never complain and never explain."
Benjamin Disraeli

"Son, in politics you've got to learn that overnight chicken shit can turn to chicken salad."
Lyndon B Johnson

"If you want to succeed in politics, you must keep your conscience well under control."
David Lloyd George

"One final tip to rebels: always have a second profession in reserve."
Nigel Nicolson (who was unseated as a Tory MP for opposing government policy on Suez)

"Pennies don't fall from heaven. They have to be earned on earth."
Margaret Thatcher

"When it is not necessary to make a decision, it is necessary not to make a decision."
Lord Falkland, 17th century English politician

"Being powerful is like being a lady. If you have to tell people you are, you aren't."
Margaret Thatcher

"The candidate who takes the credit for the rain also get the blame for the drought."
Dwight Morrow, American lawyer and politician

Falklands Politics

10 diplomatic steps

"This has been a pimple on the ass of progress festering for 200 years, and I guess someone decided to lance it".
Alexander Haig, US Secretary of State, quoted in the Sunday Times, 1982

The Falklands War is remembered in Britain as a military campaign which boosted the nation's self-esteem and won an election for Margaret Thatcher. As wars go, it was small, short and limited, and it might seem of importance only to the histories of the countries that fought it. But the conflict provides a textbook example of a perennial problem: how do two countries resolve a dispute over a piece of property that each claims to own? Is there always a peaceful, diplomatic solution? How should potential loss of life be measured against such abstracts as national pride, justice and the right of a remote population of islanders to choose their nationality?

All these questions are political not military. What makes a great war leader such as Thatcher (and Churchill before her) is not the ability to manage a battlefield but the ability to wage politics before the troops go into action and, to a lesser extent, while they are actually fighting.

Military might, however, is usually the politician's weapon of last resort. Not because most politicians are ideologically opposed to force – they believe that in some situations there is no alternative – but because sending in the troops makes a situation unpredictable. Apart from any amount of human error and bad weather, modern war is bedevilled by equipment failure. Had one of Britain's two aircraft carriers broken down – and one almost did an hour out of Plymouth – the Falklands war would have been instantly lost and with it Margaret Thatcher's room for political manoeuvre. Such near scrapes only emphasise the political nerve needed to fight any war but especially one 16,000 km away.

1. Signal failure

The first skill in diplomacy is to read the intentions of an opponent. In early 1982, Argentina believed, with good reason, that Britain was not much interested in retaining sovereignty of the Falklands (known as Las Malvinas in South America) forever. The islands were almost a nuisance: they were far away from London, a drain on the national budget, strategically unimportant and, above all, almost impossible to defend at a reasonable price to the taxpayer.

Britain had engaged in inconclusive talks about the future of the islands with Argentina and immediately before the war broke out it was in the process of scaling down its military presence in the region. Is it any wonder that Argentina thought it had a chance of successfully occupying these fairly useless islands, far closer to Buenos Aires than London? On hearing that there was an invasion force on the way, the governor of the Falklands, Rex Hunt, remarked to a British army officer, "We've called their bluff for 20 years; it looks as though the silly buggers are going to do it."

2. War aims

On the morning of 2nd April 1982, shortly after Argentina had occupied the Falklands capital Port Stanley, the British Cabinet's war aim was decided on without argument: to recover stolen property from a thief caught red-handed, preferably by diplomatic pressure, possibly by military might (but this was still an uncertain option).

Argentina's military regime under General Leopoldo Galtieri, meanwhile, believed it had merely done what any country in its position would have done by recovering its rightful property from an absentee thief. It needed a shot of nationalistic prestige to settle civilian opposition and take attention away from an ever-worsening economic crisis.

The two governments were now engaged in a political struggle to force the other to back down. To achieve this each needed to keep critics at home silent and to convince the other countries of the world that it was a) behaving legitimately and b) making the maximum diplomatic efforts to achieve a just settlement.

3. Level pegging

The occupation of the Falklands began well for Argentina which managed not to kill any of the 80 British marine commandos who were defending the islands against an invasion force of 2,500. The plan was to effect a symbolic occupation and withdraw most of the troops. Handled correctly, the operation would look to the world like a *fait accompli* to end an argument over sovereignty between states which had roughly equal claims to the territory. The generals who ruled Argentina assumed an effete western democracy would be incapable of taking resolute, risky military action from such a long distance away.

4. First impressions

When the British government first heard what had happened, it was outraged and embarrassed. The invasion represented a failure of the Foreign Office to read Argentina's intentions and it was seen as an act of impudence by a tinpot dictator. The Cabinet knew that it must be seen by its own public opinion to be doing something and the first orders to assemble a task force were given. But war was still a long way off – geographically and diplomatically. To pass from a muster of smartly-dressed sailors on the decks of warships to a massed landing of troops under fire, there would have to be sustained political resolve that the islands were worth all the fuss.

5. Incriminating photographs

Back in the Falklands the Argentinians had done something militarily understandable but politically stupid. After the commandos defending the islands had surrendered, they were made to lie face down on the ground. Photographs were taken of them in this humiliating position and these images were suddenly all around the world. In Britain they conjured up memories of 1930s dictators and that dirtiest of political words, appeasement. When it became known that the Argentinians had made Spanish the official language of the islands and moved traffic on to the right of the road (for safety reasons, they claimed), it became hard for any politician in Britain to object to the momentum of war.

6. Show of force

The British government almost certainly did not want to go to the expense, trouble and risk of actually fighting a war in order to take back its own territory, and it still hoped that the threat of overwhelming force would result in an Argentinian withdrawal. But by flexing its national muscle, Britain might well have achieved the opposite effect. The Argentinian regime realized that it no longer had the option of maintaining a minimal occupation of the islands until Britain was made to see reason at the conference table. Instead of retreating, it doubled its bets and poured men and munitions onto the islands. Its only hope was that the longer the task force was at sea, the longer there was for Britain to change its mind, or for the rest of the world to insist on a halt through diplomacy.

7. Diplomacy doublebluffing

There was, however, never any possibility of a peace treaty because neither side wanted one, for different reasons that they couldn't allow the world to know. The Galtieri government wanted to spin the diplomacy out to give them a chance to reinforce the islands, and to delay a British landing as long as possible in the hope that the weather would turn rotten. For its part, Britain could accept nothing less than repossession of the Falklands under pre-war conditions with no concessions at all to Argentina; but to justify force it had to show world opinion that it was seriously looking for a negotiated settlement. As there was no direct diplomatic contact between London and Buenos Aires, the president of Peru and the US secretary of state Alexander Haig acted as 'shuttle diplomats' in an attempt to broker a deal that neither side wanted.

8. First blood

The only thing that could have derailed the British strategy was a reversal of world (and with it US) opinion. This very nearly happened when political and military tactics came into direct collision. In order to keep the moral high ground, the British government needed to look as if it were the aggrieved party and reluctant to fire the first shot. It therefore faced a dilemma when the task force commander, Rear Admiral Sandy Woodward, feared he was being caught in a pincer movement by the Argentinian navy and ordered a nuclear-powered submarine to sink the cruiser, the General Belgrano. This action meant changing the rules of engagement quickly and Woodward short-circuited the normal route to and from Cabinet in order to get quick approval for his action. The Belgrano accounted for half of Argentina's casualties in the Falklands war: its sinking provoked criticism at home and some of Britain's wavering allies began to have doubts about who was in the right. But the much-feared Suez effect – whereby Britain would have been portrayed as an ex-colonial bully and forced back to port – didn't happen. This was partly because there wasn't time for the news to travel – this was before the age of the internet and mobile phone – but also because a second event overtook the first.

9. Taking casualties

Scoring a hit against the enemy plays well among a government's constituents – the electorate – but a military victory for the other side has the opposite effect. Two days after the Belgrano went down, two Argentinian aircraft hit the destroyer HMS Sheffield with Exocet missiles, damaging it beyond repair and killing 24 crewmen. There was a danger that public opinion in Britain would turn against the government and with three more Exocets still in Argentinian hands, the government could do little more than proceed as quickly as possible and hope for few losses.

10. Political fallout

The final stage was a brief land war. British troops overcame Argentinian resistance with significant loss of life on both sides but victory, naturally, vindicated the victors: British prestige was boosted and the 'Falklands Factor' helped Margaret Thatcher win an election the following year.

In Argentina, the debacle in the Malvinas had the opposite effect and contributed to the downfall of the Galtieri regime in favour of democracy.

Fathers of the House

By tradition, the MP with the longest continuous service in the House of Commons earns the title of 'Father of the House'.

Lloyd George was Father of the House until 1944, having served 54 years as an MP. Churchill spent 62 years altogether in the House of Commons but had two gaps, in 1908 and 1922-4.

Long-serving members who never got to be Father include Denis Healey (40 years) and Harold Macmillan and Harold Wilson (38 years apiece).

Years as Father	Name	Date entered House
1945 - 51	Earl Winterton	1904
1951 - 52	Sir Hugh O'Neill	1915
1952 - 59	David Grenfell	1922
1959 - 64	Sir Winston Churchill	1900, 1908, 1924
1964 - 65	Richard Austen Butler	1929
1965 - 74	Sir Robin Turton	1929
1974 - 79	George Strauss	1929, 1934
1979 - 83	John Parker	1935
1983 - 87	Sir James Callaghan	1945
1987 - 92	Sir Bernard Braine	1950
1992 - 2001	Sir Edward Heath	1950
2001 - 2005	Tam Dalyell	1962
2005 - present	Alan Williams	1964

Fault Lines

8 fundamental fault lines in both parties

> *"Every political movement, whether conservative or liberal, owes its success to its ability to maintain a coalition between the greedy and the idealistic."* Murray Kempton

> *"If…you have a two-party system where the differences between the parties are not fundamental, then you immediately reduce politics to the level of a football match. A football match may, of course, attract some very able players; it may also be entertaining; but it is still a game, and only the most ardent fans (who are not usually the most intelligent) take the game very seriously."* Julius K Nyrere, 'Democracy and the Party System' (from 'Freedom and Unity')

It's often said that the UK political system doesn't throw up coalition governments. But that is only because all governments are, in a sense, pre-formed coalitions. The two main parties are really just marriages of convenience. Like touring rock groups, they manage to keep their multifarious, competing egos in check when things are going well but can easily crack at the seems when no one wants to see them perform any more. Behind the scenes continually, and sometimes in public, the two parties argue within themselves as much as they argue with each other. And, surprisingly, both parties contend with more or less the same broad internal tensions. All politicians know that there is a danger in pushing their opponents' buttons (as they say in therapy-speak) in that the strategy can easily backfire.

Less tax, fewer services or more tax, more services?
The rich and successful will always vote for formula 1 whereas the have-nots clammer for formula 2.

Europe
The Labour Party keeps as quiet as it can on this issue because it knows that the Tories are even more deeply divided and therefore capable of doing themselves internal damage whenever the word is mentioned. The eurosceptics in the Conservative Party may well have scuppered their chances of winning the 2007/08 election by their determination to keep a pro-Europe candidate like Ken Clarke from the leadership.

Can you please all the people all the time?

Labour used to be a party charged with promoting the interests of one class over another. The Conservative Party also represented its own class, although it wouldn't have been gentlemanly to admit it. Now, both parties pretend to be serving the whole country, but can you pander to society's winners and losers at the same time? The truth is that MPs on both sides are still engaged in class warfare.

Education

The perpetual problems here are 1) what do you do with the most gifted pupils and the strugglers? Do you separate them or integrate them? Do you give resources to high achievers and abandon the sluggards to their fate? 2) how can you make sure all parents get what they want without letting money be the deciding factor? One section of the Labour Party still swears by comprehensive schools as the fairest way of offering everyone the same opportunity but New Labour has been busy creating choice. Among Conservatives the 11+ has never become a dirty word and the grammar school is remembered with nostalgia, though no one laments the passing of the secondary modern. But both parties are still groping towards an education system which is free for all without becoming a free-for-all.

Crime and security

Do you go for the quick votes by banging up more and more criminals or concentrate on trying to eradicate the causes of crime, a prolonged and invisible effort which wins few votes? Tony Blair came into office bent on dealing with both at the same time. And how authoritarian can a government be without infringing civil liberties?

Public or private ownership?

The Labour Party tore itself apart over Clause IV while Thatcher and Major were busy privatising everything they could, but the Conservatives also squabble over how far the state should extend its reach.

The NHS

It is a political taboo to suggest privatising the hallowed British insitution of the National Health Service, although some Conservatives would like to. Both parties are locked in an interminable struggle to offer healthcare to everyone who needs it without costs spiralling out of control.

Fictional Politics

10 portraits of politics from novels

Novelists and short story writers don't spend a lot of time on political themes but there are still some rich insights to be had from reading between the lines of some of the great authors.

📖 *Pickwick Papers* by Charles Dickens (1837). Chapter 13 is an account of riotous electoral campaigning that takes place before electoral reform in a place called Eatanswill. "It's not at all necessary for a crowd to know what they are cheering about. 'It's always best on these occasions to do what the mob do.' 'But suppose there are two mobs?' suggested Mr. Snodgrass. 'Shout with the largest,' replied Mr. Pickwick."

📖 The Palliser (or Parliamentary) Novels by Anthony Trollope – *Can You Forgive Her?* (1864) *Phineas Finn* (1869) *The Eustace Diamonds* (1873) *Phineas Redux* (1874) *The Prime Minister* (1876) and *The Duke's Children* (1879) – deal with the wealthy, industrious Plantagenet Palliser and his wife Lady Glencora. Trollope unsuccessfully contested an election himself (see p348) and only ever had an outsider's understanding of politics.

📖 *Brothers Karamazov* by Fyodor Dostoevsky (1880). Book Five includes the famous Parable of the Grand Inquisitor in which Christ returns to earth only to be imprisoned by the Spanish Inquisition. The Grand Inquisitor accuses him of giving humanity freedom which prevents people from being happy. The church, instead, offers them happiness through not having to make choices. The parable is often cited as a graphic speculation on one of the problems at the root of all political theory.

📖 *The Mayor of Casterbridge* by Thomas Hardy (1886). The rise and tragic, self-induced fall of a local self-made businessman and dignitary: a fable about the need to deal with closet-bound skeletons before they deal with you.

📖 *The Man Who Was Thursday* by GK Chesterton (1908). A novel about anarchists, spies and the desirability of keeping society in order. *The Napoleon of Notting Hill* (1904), in which London elects itself a king, is also interesting.

📖 *Corridors of Power* by CP Snow (1963), the 9th book in the Strangers and Brothers series (1905–1980), about an MP trying to influence policy on nuclear weapons, is mainly memorable for adding its title as a cliché to the English language. Snow was a scientist who joined the Wilson Labour government in 1964 but resigned in 1966.

📖 *A Very British Coup* by Chris Mullin (1982, later made into a TV series). A what-if story about how the Establishment would react if a left-wing Labour government were to take power and try to implement a truly radical programme.

📖 *First Among Equals* by Jeffrey Archer (1984) is about four rivals who want to be prime minister. Archer draws on his own experiences in the Commons and includes some real-life characters including Margaret Thatcher.

📖 *The Line of Beauty* by Alan Hollinghurst (2004, televised in 2006) is about life for a young homosexual man among the Thatcherite governing classes in the 1980s and how he is never quite accepted by them. "The 80s are going on for ever," declares one character blithely, while a typically self-serving civil servant sums up the mood in Whitehall: "The economy's in ruins, no one's got a job, and we just don't care, it's bliss." Thatcher appears in person.

📖 *A Parliamentary Affair* by Edwina Currie (1994) A woman struggling in the male environment of Westminster who falls for a whip. The book was published after her own affair with a whip, (John Major) had ended, but before she made it public. All her characters are Tories – the Parliamentary Labour Party has always been slightly less inhospitable to females.

Films

15 films for a political education

> *"Rick: You'll excuse me, gentlemen. Your business is politics, mine is running a saloon."* Casablanca (1942)

No two people would ever agree on the same list of best films on any given subject on any particular day. And when the subject is political films the choice grows even more controversial. Almost any film can be read politically but some are more political than others. What is certainly true is that not all films about politics and politicians bear a political message whereas many films which seem to have nothing to do with politics are pregnant with subversive meaning. All great art, of course, poses rather than answers questions. Here, therefore, are some politico-cinematographic posers.

❦ *Battleship Potemkin* (1925) Are the people revolting? (n.b. the question here is mimed.)

❦ *Snow White and the Seven Dwarfs* (1937) Is there any question of where our sympathies should lie when a spoilt, runaway princess flees from a dynastic struggle caused by vanity and jealousy and forcibly imposes herself on a group of communally-living, anarcho-syndicalist working-class men?

❦ *The Adventures of Robin Hood* (1938) How should a subject population (in this case the Saxons) respond to a repressive colonizing power (the greedily-taxing Normans)? A similar question is posed by Monty Python's *Life of Brian*.

❦ *Casablanca* (1942) What do you do if it is a choice between love and doing the right political thing?

❦ *Dr Strangelove* (1963) Aren't you glad that you can trust the people who hold power on your behalf?

❦ *From Russia with Love* (1963) Politically, who should we support: 1) a civil servant who is given an unlimited expense account courtesy of the tax payer but doesn't have to fill out a timesheet; who is free of the scruples of the Human Rights Act; and who has irresponsible amounts of casual sex with partners who he has no intention of forming respectful, long-term relationships with or 2) the corrupt, anonymous, accident-prone, unerrogenous, one-dimensional, employees of a vague, grey, fanatical, totalitarian organization that seeks to gain control over the whole world? Or neither?

🐾 *Planet of the Apes* (1968) Do animals (in this case, us) have rights?

🐾 *The Godfather* (1972) When the politicians are corrupt and inefficient, isn't it good to know you can rely on a Sicilian sense of honour?

🐾 *High Plains Drifter* (1973) Is it wise to entrust municipal affairs to a man with no name and no track record in office simply because of the hysterical fear of the populace?

🐾 *Apocalypse Now* (1979) Where do you stand when everyone is doing their own thing in the middle of chaos and no one has the greater good in mind? Oh, and by the way, your mission does not exist.

🐾 *First Blood* (Rambo) (1982) What could we achieve if the bureaucracts gave us the means to do our jobs and got out of our way?

🐾 *The Madness of King George* (1995) What happens when the stability of a nation hangs on the sanity of one man?

🐾 *Love Actually* (2003) Surely, politics is just a matter of doing the right thing, isn't it? Tony Blair, who recognised enough of himself in the idealised and idealistic screen prime minister (played by Hugh Grant) attempted to answer this question in a speech to the 2005 Labour Party conference: "Britain should also remain the strongest ally of the United States. I know there's a bit of us that would like me to do a Hugh Grant in *Love Actually* and tell America where to get off. But the difference between a good film and real life is that in real life there's the next day, the next year, the next lifetime to contemplate the ruinous consequences of easy applause."

🐾 *Goodbye, Lenin* (2003) Was there no one at all who had fun during the Cold War behind the Iron Curtain?

🐾 *The Motorcycle Diaries* (2004) How did the face of Irish-Basque Argentinian doctor Ernesto Guevara de la Serna end up as a poster on babyboom bedroom walls everywhere?

Free Speech

5 for a fair hearing

"The power of the press is very great, but not so great as the power of suppress." Lord Northcliffe 1918

One definition of a functioning democracy is a country in which you can say what you want, when and where and how you want, without fear of arrest. But in a modern society, freedom of expression involves more than defending the right of ersatz parliamentarians to declaim from a soap box in Hyde Park. It implies that there should be fair access to all channels of communication so that all shades of opinion are heard by all audiences, from the local to the national.

The issue of free speech is usually discussed as if it were synonymous with the freedom of professional communicators – that is journalists – to do their job. A more interesting question however, is how able is the common man to say what he or she wants to all fellow citizens? Anyone who is serious about 'open government' and increasing involvement in the political system needs to first question whether Britain is a society which not only permits but facilitates free speech.

Speakers' Corner

This space for impromptu orators in the north-east corner of London's Hyde Park can be laughed off as a tourist attraction, especially on Sundays, but its supporters describe it as "the first place on earth where free speech was guaranteed." There is a belief that an Act of Parliament of 1872 guarantees anyone the right to say whatever they want here (short of raising a mob to go and overthrow the government) but really free speech is allowed as a tradition rather than a legal right. Movements such as the Chartists, the Reform League, early socialists and the Suffragettes took advantage of this toleration to hold rallies here. But there are two dark sides to Speakers' Corner. One is the obvious implication that if free speech is allowed here it isn't allowed elsewhere in London (or the rest of the country) and many political campaigners have been prevented by the police from speaking in public, in places where crowds more naturally congregate. The other shadow is the alleged presence of plain-clothed police officers with recording devices who lurk among the bona fide listeners at Speaker's Corner. Confining free speech to a corner of a park makes it easy for the authorities to monitor incipient subversion of the state.

Even if Speakers' Corner is seen as a demonstration of pure democracy it is an ephemeral one; it is democracy dictated by the hours of the working week and by the British weather. Regulars at Speakers' Corner have proposed that there should be a permanent 'democracy wall' on the site on which anyone can post up his or her views.

Parliamentary privilege

Under the Defamation Act 1996 MPs cannot be sued for 'words spoken or things done in the course of... any proceedings in Parliament'. This applies to speeches, submissions or evidence given to the House or a committee, and it means that MPs can get away with more than mere mortals when they are inside the House of Commons. They can say things that, outside the House, would run a serious legal risk and this information can be picked up by the mass media and publicly aired. It's a convoluted route to free speech which is only open directly to 650 people but theoretically open to anyone, whether on the electoral register or not, who can find a willing MP to speak for them.

Television and radio

Access to local radio is fairly easy for any member of the public but national radio and television offer far more limited possibilities. There have been attempts at open access 'community programme-making' but these never result in prime time exposure on the main channels. The best that most people can hope for is to get through to a phone-in programme to make a point, get an email read out on air or join the audience for the BBC's *Question Time* and hope to be chosen to ask a question to one of the politicians present. Otherwise, free speech on the airwaves is a prerogative of journalists and their invited guests.

The press

Britain still has a flourishing print-media industry which has great freedom in what it does but as it is privately owned it has no obligation to allow its readers a platform. All papers publish readers' letters but these are selected and edited. Even so, it is a sign of a healthy press that the letters pages of the serious broadsheets are populated by specialists who know a great deal more about their subject than the journalists who write the rest of the paper.

Many papers nowadays conduct polls among their readers, although the questions are usually loaded so the results are of limited value. Recently, for instance, the *Daily Telegraph* (via its website) asked readers 'Which Labour laws should the Tories scrap?' (Many readers suggested the European Communities Act 1972, passed by a Conservative government.)

The internet

'Comment is free' could be the slogan of the internet and there is no shortage of it online. Anyone is free to leave an opinion, informed or not, on just about anything on hundreds of thousands of websites to which the world has 24-hour access.

The heirs of anarchism have found a natural home in this frontierless, stateless, virtual world which makes it easy to share information and the fruits of intellectual labour. It is wholly undiscriminating: the tenets of pacifism are disseminated as easily as recipes for terrorist bomb making.

The internet has the potential to nurture minority views to an audience which Speakers' Corner cannot reach and in an intimate way which is alien to television and the press. It can thus stimulate debate without anyone being able to control it. But it has drawbacks. It is a very fragmented media; it is a paradise for ranters; 'discussions' tend to end up as mind talking to like mind through a website with an overt political bent, which means that the power of the internet often reduces to a mechanism for stoking up prejudice and transmitting misinformation (the internet is to the conspiracy theory what damp, warm compost is to the mushroom). The fashion of 'blogging' (definition: talking in type, whether anyone is listening or not) is really nothing more than a technological extension of gossiping, boring your workmates at the office or preaching against the emperor down at the forum.

And, of course, to feel included in this communication revolution you have to have a computer (not everyone does or knows how to use one) and you have to enjoy staring at a screen for hours and communicating through a keyboard.

The internet seems to be settling down as a parallel universe to the existing mass media rather than a replacement for it. Television and the press increasingly refer to the stuff that bloggers and their e-hecklers chatter about as a means of generating free content which would otherwise have to be provided by professional journalists. And concerned citizens are still drawn more to a public meeting in the local village hall than to the feedback form on an MP's website which may or may not be read by anyone.

Government Change

10 handy methods if you're not sure what to do

Revolution
Throwing everything up in the air and making the best of it after the dust settles.

Counter-revolution
Putting things back the way they were.

Regicide
But you may have to answer to a higher authority; try hints at abdication and exile first.

Tyrranicide
Like regicide but with no morally ambiguous overtones to it.

Coup d'etat
Usually best carried out by military personnel with media studies degrees since it involves taking over the TV stations. A putsch is more or less the same thing in Suizadeutsch, if you are a Francophobe.

Civil war
Requires two roughly equal sides, at least at the outset.

Secession (independence movement)
If you start off with a 'them' to your 'us'.

Dismissal/appointment
Works if you've got a head of state but nothing else.

Regime change
Euphemism for military invasion on behalf of the opposition or whoever you fancy for the new administration. It needs a fair amount of military might and international cheek to pull this one off.

Elections
Bureaucratic, slow, inefficient and costly. More so if you have to rig the ballot – which is the only way to ensure the outcome you want.

Great Britons

4 surveys of those we love and loathe

The British are a race of list lovers, forever voting on who we love, hate or admire most. The enduring value of such surveys is debatable but the results provide a revealing snapshot of opinion at the time.

Great Britons

In 2002 the BBC carried out a poll to find out who the public considered the 100 greatest Britons of all time. 1.6m people voted. Below are the political figures who appeared in the top 100 with their rankings shown alongside.

Great figure	*Rank*
Winston Churchill	1
Oliver Cromwell	10
Margaret Thatcher	16
Emmeline Pankhurst	27
William Wilberforce	28
Guy Fawkes	30
Thomas Paine	34
Sir Thomas More	37
Aneurin Bevan	45
Enoch Powell	55
Tony Blair	67
David Lloyd George	79
Tony Benn	97

100 Britons We Love to Hate

In 2003 Channel 4 asked its viewers to vote for the contemporary public figures they least admired. Surprisingly there weren't many politicians on the list. Of course, the people nominated in such surveys tend to be those in the headlines at the time. Half of the people below had slipped from view a year later.

Hate figure	*Rank*
Tony Blair	1
Margaret Thatcher	3
Neil & Christine Hamilton	19
Edwina Currie	26
Peter Mandelson	49
Ken Livingstone	50
Alastair Campbell	57
Stephen Byers (& Jo Moore)	59
John Prescott	87
Iain Duncan Smith	99

G

Today's Personality of the Year

The Today Programme (see p319) has run a poll of listeners to find the most significant person of the year since 1982. Until 1991 there were two polls to find the Man and Woman of the Year. There was no poll in 1992 and 1993 – because there weren't any suitable candidates? – but the idea was resurrected in 1994 as the more politically correct, unisex *Personality of the Year*.

Margaret Thatcher won the accolade a record eight times. In 1982 Ken Livingstone, then leader of the GLC and reviled by the tabloid press (*The Sun* called him "the most odious man in Britain") surprised everyone by coming second to the Pope. In 1990, votes for the Hindu politician Lal Krishan Advani were discounted because there was evidence of a mass 'write-in' by his supporters. The same allegation was levelled at Labour and Conservative sympathisers in 1996 who were accused of trying to rig the ballot in favour of their respective leaders. Four thousand votes were disqualified and John Major eventually won.

The Key Figures of History

In *The 100: A Ranking of the Most Influential Persons in History* (1978, rev. 1992), American astrophysicist and author Michael Hart included the following figures from the world of politics – note that there are conspicuously more political thinkers than political players:

Influencer	Rank	Runners-up included:
Marx	27	St Thomas Aquinas
Adam Smith	30	Jeremy Bentham
Hitler	39	Bismarck
Cromwell	41	Churchill
Locke	44	Thomas Hobbes
St Augustine	54	Keynes
Calvin	57	Thoreau
Machiavelli	79	
Lenin	84	
Gorbachev	95	

Hansard

7 facts on the record

It hasn't been said or debated or decided if it's not in Hansard, the official version of what happened in the House of Commons and the House of Lords yesterday and the days before that.

Hansard is a report of both oral and written parliamentary proceedings, available to everyone from the MPs who dictated it to the rest of us who pay their salaries. It's certainly not bedtime reading and it is most useful to MPs themselves, researchers, journalists and historians; but, curiously, it can provide some compelling reading when searched online using keywords or even dipped into at random.

1. Until the beginning of the 19th century there was no official record of parliamentary debates. Things done were registered, but it wasn't seen as good form to write down what was said by MPs. Unofficial minutes of debates were, however, printed and distributed illegally. Parliament regarded their publication as a breach of its privilege.

2. Suppression of unofficial parliamentary reports came to an end in 1771, following a legal battle by John Wilkes MP. From then on it was assumed that newspapers had the right to report affairs in Parliament.

3. In 1803 the radical social reformer William Cobbett started printing Debates, the first attempt to report proceedings on an organised and regular basis. In 1812, financial trouble forced Cobbett to sell his business to Thomas Hansard. Hansard put his name on his publication in 1829.

4. In 1909, the House of Commons took control of Hansard but renamed it the Official Report. Colloquially, everyone continued to call it Hansard and in 1943 the Commons gave up the struggle and returned the name to the front cover. The word has slipped into the language as a generic name for parliamentary reports and many legislatures in the British Commonwealth call their official report of debates 'Hansard'.

5. Contrary to popular opinion, Hansard is not a verbatim report of what is said in Parliament. It is a report of what the MPs intended to say, edited "to remove repetitions and obvious mistakes". MPs are entitled to 'check' the transcript in the hour and half after they have finished speaking, and may request changes – though these should not extend to changes in meaning.

6. According to modern legend, applicants for a job on Hansard are given a tape of former Deputy Prime Minister John Prescott's speeches, and asked to interpret what he was trying to say. If they can do this, it is reasoned, they can do anything.

7. Hansard is printed overnight so that the previous session's debates (even if they finish in the small hours) are available in hard copy by 7.30 am and online by 8 am the next morning.

Heirs Apparent

6 leaders-in-waiting who never led their parties

Both the main political parties seems to have a knack for by-passing the obvious or best candidate for the leadership. It can happen for a number of reasons.

Sometimes the individual has been waiting for his or her turn for years and is thwarted at the last minute by an unhelpful turn of events.

At other times the candidate seems to have all the qualifications for winning an election and becoming an excellent prime minister but is so disliked by a section of his party that they would rather fester in opposition than promote him up the greasy pole.

Finally, there is the problem of departing party leaders or prime ministers anxious to secure their legacy. An essential part of this, it seems, is to sabotage the career of any would-be successor who may put their achievements in the shade or completely unravel them.

These eternal losers join an unofficial club of disappointed souls known as "the best prime ministers we never had."

- **'Rab' Butler**

  Richard Austen 'Rab' Butler took charge of government when both Eden and Churchill were ill in 1953, and stepped in again to negotiate the denouement of the Suez Crisis in 1956 so that Eden could rest. It was widely assumed he would succeed Eden as Prime Minister in 1957 but the Cabinet chose to support Macmillan. Butler was made Home Secretary and also party chairman. Macmillan, however, did everything he could to prevent Butler from becoming Prime Minister after him. Had Butler been chosen over Alec Douglas-Home, the Conservative Party might not have lost the 1964 election to Labour.

- **Denis Healey**

  Briefly a Communist in his youth, Healey drifted to the centre and then to the right of the Labour Party over his career which made him unpopular with the left. He was, however, a successful Chancellor of the Exchequer in the difficult economic circumstances of the 1970s. Following the 1979 election defeat, the party narrowly elected Michael Foot as leader. Healey would almost certainly have been a more successful opponent to Margaret Thatcher.

- **Michael Heseltine**

  If anyone seemed destined for the leadership of the Conservative Party it was Heseltine who had even sketched out his career to the top while at Oxford. He served under Thatcher but became increasingly hostile to her and was well placed in 1990 to take advantage of her unpopularity. He won enough votes in the leadership contest to force her from office but not enough to beat the uncharismatic John Major to the top spot. For the next five years many people speculated not on whether Heseltine would take over from Major but when. The uncertainty ended when Heseltine became Deputy Prime Minister in July 1995, the highest position he would achieve.

- **Michael Portillo**

  Adored by Thatcherites, loathed by the Labour Party, Portillo hesitated too long during the 1995 leadership contest and lost his seat at the 1997 election – thereby becoming the symbol of Tory humiliation. After returning to parliament somewhat chastened and softened in 1999, he stood for the leadership after the 2001 election but by that time had collected too much personal and political baggage to succeed.

- **Ken Clarke**

  A heavyweight politician with great media presence and a good track record as Chancellor of the Exchequer under Major, Clarke would have been a formidable election competitor to Blair but his euro-friendly views made him unacceptable to a well-dug-in section of the parliamentary party. He contested the leadership three times, in 1997, 2001 and 2005.

Impossibilities

Justifications for impotence and inertia

"*Politics is the art of the possible.*" Bismarck

Bismarck's terse summary of the business he was in might sound like a mere justification for pragmatism over principle but it hides a profound truth. Arguably, nothing else in this book matters if we can't answer the question: what is possible in politics?

Is anything possible for a politician who is strong enough to stand up to critics and bullies, popular enough to win elections, and lucky enough or astute enough to be in tune with the times? Or are there limitations which even the strongest, ablest, most popular, and most wilful leader cannot overcome?

In *The Political Animal*, Jeremy Paxman points out the dilemma of the Opposition spokesman who has previously been in ministerial office: how can he ridicule the government for being ineffective when he knows first-hand the constraints there are on any action?

Tellingly, there are far more quotes from politicians about how difficult it is to effect even minor legislative modifications than there are about the marvels of exercising power. Most of their criticisms are directed at the civil service but that may only be because it is an easy target: civil servants are not expected to make political comments, even to defend themselves.

If you are handed the reigns of a ministry, or even the prime ministership you will need to take the following forces into account before you decide on any action. But note: dealing with 12 different interest groups is fairly straightforward; the problem is they interact with each other and you have to be aware of all 144 permutations of the puzzle at the same time.

1. **Vested interests at home**

   Including business leaders, trade unions, pressure groups, charities and plenty of other tenacious groups capable of getting better press than you. This includes groups with a stake in the constitution including the Church of England and the monarchy.

2. **Vested interests abroad**

   Britain is part of a globalised world. Offend a multinational company and its board could decide to relocate causing massive job losses which could trigger one or more of the other forces to act against you.

3. **National security and defence**

   Damage Britain's defence capability or the 'interests of national security' and you will be hounded by people on all sides.

4. **International obligations**

   Will your decision meet Britain's treaty obligations (particularly in the European Union) and how will other political leaders (especially those in the White House) view it? Friendships need to be nurtured and disagreements managed if conflict and, worse, war is to be avoided.

5. **Your own party**

   They elected you; they can boot you out before you put your policy into practice, or stop you half way through. They need to be kept happy.

6. **The opposition**

   They can't do anything themselves but they can stir up criticism which will make your position untenable.

7. **The law**

   You can sometimes change this in parliament but to do so you may have to overcome any or all of the other constraints.

8. **The civil service and the rest of the public sector**

   Including the police. If they don't want to implement your policy, and with gusto, it will never fly.

9. **The public**

A fickle lot if ever there was one, which can be turned against you by the media or by a whispering campaign orchestrated by your closest rival. And even if the public voted for you and it lets you make the law because that's your job, what if there is mass resistance rendering it partially or wholly effective, as in the case of the poll tax and anti-hunting legislation?

10. **The City of London**

Lose the confidence of the currency speculators and money-lenders who keep business operating and consumers consuming and you may as well resign.

11. **The Treasury**

You need cash to do anything and there is only one source of the stuff. The Chancellor of the Exchequer and his team know that they will get someone's back up by raising taxes and they are not going to give you a blank cheque to go around upsetting people.

12. **The media (and the chattering classes)**

Journalists don't have any direct power, only influence over public opinion, but there's nothing they love more than to fill newspapers and TV bulletins with the face of an unpopular minister. You may say that you don't expect to be liked but if you are getting too much bad press someone else on this list will decide your time is up.

The Influential Unelected

Every society contains people who have influence over but not an overt role in the political system. In early 2007 the *Guardian Unlimited* website commissioned a panel to nominate the 50 most influential unelected people in contemporary Britain. The top 10 are below, the other 40 overleaf.

Top 10

1	Sir Terry Leahy	Chief executive, Tesco
2.	Mervyn King	Governor of the Bank of England
3.	Paul Dacre	Editor, Daily Mail
4.	The Queen	Monarch
5.	Simon Cowell	TV presenter and record co. executive
6.	Sir Richard Branson	Head of Virgin
7.	Sir Alex Ferguson	Manager, Manchester United FC
8.	Stephen Hawking	Physicist
9.	Kate Moss	Model
10.	Rowan Williams	Archbishop of Canterbury

Almost half the people in the *Guardian's* top 50 are quixotic celebrities and specialists with a point of view that happens to chime with public opinion today, but which may not tomorrow. It is the other half which is more revealing: they have been chosen not because of who they are personally but because of organizations they represent and if the *Guardian* were to draw up another list in ten years' time the same job titles would almost certainly be on it though the incumbents would have changed. *Note:* only 9 of the 50 are women.

But we should be cautious about how we interpret this information, remembering that there are different degrees of unelectedness, and accountability (or lack of it) is not as straightforward as it seems. MPs do not appear on the list (of course) because they are elected, but how much legitimacy is conferred by being confirmed in office once every five years by an unproportional voting system? CEOs of public companies do appear on the list because they are not elected, but they are, in a sense, accountable. If they don't perform, their shareholders get rid of them.

11-20 influential but unelected

11.	Jonathan Ive	Designer, Apple Computer
12.	Brendan Barber	General secretary, TUC
13.	JK Rowling	author
14.	Lord Winston	fertility expert and scientist
15.	Lord Goldsmith	Attorney General
16.	Sir Gus O'Donnell	Head of the civil service
17.	Sir Ian Blair	Metropolitan Police Commissioner
18.	Mark Thompson	Director General, BBC
19.	David Nicholson	Chief Executive, NHS
20.	Lord Rogers	architect

21-30 influential but unelected

21.	Lord Coe	Olympics organiser
22.	Max Clifford	publicist
23.	Lakshmi Mittal	steel magnate
24.	Sir David Attenborough	natural history expert
25.	Prince Charles	
26.	Jamie Oliver	chef
27.	Richard Madely	television presenters
	Judy Finnigan	
28.	Rebekah Wade	Editor, The Sun
29.	Sir Nicholas Serota	art historian and Director of the Tate
30.	Polly Toynbee	Guardian columnist

31-40 influential but unelected

31.	Trevor Phillips	Chair, Commission for Equality and Human Rights
32.	Wilf Stevenson	Director, Smith Institute
33.	Jonathan Ross	television presenter
34.	Sir Alan Sugar	founder of Amstrad
35.	Sir Andrew Lloyd Webber	composer
36.	Wayne Rooney	footballer
37.	Kate Barker	economist
38.	Stuart Rose	Chief Executive, Marks & Spencer
39.	Sir Philip Green	retail businessman
40.	Shami Chakrabarti	Director, Liberty

41-50 influential but unelected

41.	Michael Grade	Executive Chairman, ITV
42.	Sir Liam Donaldson	Chief Medical Officer
43.	David Bowie	singer
44.	Harvey McGrath	Chair of London First and Man Group
45.	Muhammad Abdul Bari	Secretary General, Muslim Council of Britain
46.	Jonathan Sacks	Chief Rabbi
47.	Dame Jane Campbell	disability rights campaigner
48.	Noel Gallagher	guitarist
49.	Sue Nye	Gordon Brown's special adviser
50.	David, Victoria Beckham	footballer and singer

http://politics.guardian.co.uk/homeaffairs/story/0,,2058199,00.html

One issue raised by this list is the extent to which elected politicians contribute to increasing or decreasing the numbers of the influential-but-unelected by pandering to party donors, appointing special advisers, granting access to government to employers and unionists, and handing out honours and knighthoods according to whatever criteria they think fit – surely a vital issue for British democracy.

Insults – Put Downs

10 artful political put downs

"Mr Gladstone speaks to me as if I were a public meeting."
Queen Victoria (attrib) c1890

"I do not object to the old man always having a card up his sleeve, but I do object to his insinuating that the Almighty had placed it there."
Henry Labouchere on Gladstone, quoted by Earl Curzon in 1913

"Honest in the most odious sense of the word."
Disraeli on Gladstone (attrib) c1860

"When they circumcised Herbert Samuel they threw away the wrong bit."
David Lloyd George c1918

"He has, more than any man, the gift of compressing the largest amount of words into the smallest amount of thought."
Winston Churchill on Ramsay Macdonald, speech in the House of Commons 1933

"Decided only to be undecided, resolved to be irresolute, adamant for drift, solid for fluidity, all-powerful to be impotent."
Churchill on Stanley Baldwin in a speech 1936

"He refers to a defeat as a disaster as though it came from God, but to a victory as though it came from himself."
Aneurin Bevan on Churchill speech in the House of Commons 1942

"A great many persons are able to become members of this House without losing their insignificance."
Beverley Baxter on the House of Commons 1946

"A piratical old bruiser with a first-class mind and very bad manners."
Lord Hailsham on Denis Healey, 1987

"Harold Wilson is going around the country stirring up apathy."
William Whitelaw c1983

Insults – Spectrum

A DIY diagram for sticking a label on your enemy

Instructions: Make an assessment of where you think your opponent
stands on the political spectrum and move two words to the left or
right as appropriate to find an insult that will hurt. Any of the words
below can be emphasised with a capital letter, thus 'Conservative' is
a more hard-edged insult than mere 'conservative'.

STTROGK*
far right
hanger and flogger
Monday Club member
reactionary
right-winger
Cambridge mafia
Conservative
conservative/Tory
moderate
centrist
liberal
social democrat
soft left
champagne socialist
Tribunite
socialist
red
hard left
loony left
Communist
Trotskyist
Bolshevik

*somewhere to the right of Genghis Khan

Insults – Rude Words

A primer in the art of the political taunt

10 adjectives to condemn (either friend or foe) with

Disloyal	Entrenched
Extreme	Fanatic
Fantasist	Fascist (or worse, Nazi)
Loony*	Machiavellian**
Raving	Two-faced

*as in 'loony left' and 'loony fringe' but also, to a lesser extent, 'loony right'. More mocking than 'extreme'.

**usually used by people who have not read *The Prince*.

10 activities no one wants to be accused of

Appeasement	Climbing down
Compromising	Expediency
Gerrymandering	McCarthyism
Pandering (to)	Selling out
Style without substance	U-turning

10 words that can compliment or insult, depending on who uses them to whom

Anarchist	Dogmatic
Maverick	Opportunist
Pragmatist	Rebel
Revisionist	Rogue
Troublemaker	Young Turk

Interviews – Saying Nowt

10 ways to avoid giving a straight answer to a straight question

Politics, it could be said, is the art of saying as little as possible. The more you give away, the more you commit yourself, and the more ammunition there is to use against you, especially when events take an unexpected turn – which they always do.

As a result the political interview on radio and television has become an uninformative sparring match between coy politician and jaded anchorman.

Your job as politician is to take up airtime by setting out a full programme of policies that no one could disagree with, while, in fact, saying nothing that would stand up in a court of law. The questions are irrelevant: the interviewer feels obliged to ask them but you aren't obliged to answer them.

Get on to the future as quickly as you can
You are not responsible for disasters that haven't yet happened. Tomorrow is full of hope and opportunity: everything can be better than it is today.

Take the moral highground
To answer a difficult question with a rehearsed sermon you need do no more than say, "There are serious issues raised by this..." Have ready a collection of words and phrases that no one can argue with: 'the family', 'working together', 'modernisation','freedom', 'reform', 'caring'. Just don't pause long enough on any of them for the interviewer to insist on a definition.

Collude
Take the interviewer into your confidence as if you are explaining the obvious truth to a simpleton. Make it clear that you sympathise with him for having to ask stupid questions on behalf of an audience which he obviously believes is stupid – whereas you and they know who is the really stupid one.

Plead the Fifth in the interests of national security
Make it clear that you are bursting to speak frankly but lives would be in danger if you did. Of course you can only use this one if you

are in charge of national security and the question wasn't "Are you competent enough to be trusted with the safety of the public?"

Blame your underlings
A tricky one to get away with since every chain of responsibility goes upwards rather than downwards but you might just be able to make out that "day-to-day operational matters" are beneath you and that it would be a waste of public money for you to micromanage staff you have every confidence in until the day they let you down.

Take over the interview
"With respect that is to ask the wrong question" or "We shouldn't waste our time talking about..." are good formulae if you want to set the agenda yourself.

Supply tomorrow's headline
Have a soundbite written and ready. Slip it in at the first vaguely appropriate opportunity. Once the interviewer has got that out of you, there's no point in grilling you any further.

Appeal to ordinary people
Show that you are more in touch with ordinary people than the metropolitan media-type who is interviewing you. "I think people/the public will understand..." and "Listeners will want to know what this means in practice..." Flatter the intelligence of the anonymous masses who you are really speaking to. Best of all is: "Ordinary people are fed up with..." because we all like to be told what we are fed up with.

Talk tough
Use words like 'strong', 'leadership', 'decisive'. Attack is the best form of defence, whatever you are or are not saying. Take a free swipe at the pusillanimity of your political opponents (unless they are in the studio with you and can fight back) or, if that fails, lambast the media or even the interviewer in person for his spineless cynicism.

Dispute definitions
If you have a few facts and statistics that no one can instantly check – best of all are figures that your advisers have dreamt up moments before you came on air – you can split any number of verbal hairs.

Islands

7 outposts of public administration

It seems a fairly obvious point that everyone in Britain is an islander, but some of us are more insular than others. Away from London the country breaks up into larger and smaller islands and peters out in bleak moorlands that hardly manage to raise themselves above the waves, craggy colonies of self-sufficient folk and rocks far out in the Atlantic. All these mini-territories have to be governed somehow and each has its own arrangements.

Jersey and Guernsey

The Channel Islands are crown dependencies, possessions of the Duke of Normandy, a title held by the monarch. Geographically, they are part of 'the continent' but official definitions usually place them obstinately in the British Isles. They are not part of Great Britain or of the UK and are half in and half out of the EU. They are self-governing and not represented at Westminster but the British government is still expected to look after their defence and foreign affairs and oversee law and order.

The islands are divided into the bailiwicks of Jersey and Guernsey (each presided over by a bailiff). Each is like a mini state. Jersey has a population of 90,000 and Guernsey 60,000 and yet there are fully functioning governments in miniature with parliaments and government departments. Legislation has to be given royal sanction by the monarch in the privy council. Acts of Parliament can only be applied in the Channel Islands by an order of the privy council.

Sark

Although part of the bailiwick of Guernsey, Sark has more archaic constitutional arrangements than the rest of the Channel Islands. Its system of government is promoted as one of its tourist attractions as if it were a medieval theme park, which in a political sense it is. The arrangement, until recent reforms introduced an element of democracy, was described (by one of its supporters) as one of noblesse oblige, where the hereditary landowners feel duty-bound to keep things running as they always have been.

The island is owned in perpetuity by the Seigneur as long as he or she can afford the annual rent of "one twentieth part of a knights fee" (£1.79) payable to Her Majesty's Receiver-General each Michaelmas Day. The Seigneur must also make sure that his tenants (don't say vassals) keep muskets at the ready with which to defend the Island. The Seigneur is the only person on the island who is allowed to own pigeons or an unspayed bitch.

There is a parliament, the Chief Pleas, which now has an element of democratic representation and a set of charmingly named officials to carry out administrative duties: the Seneschal (magistrate), the Prevôt (Sheriff), the Greffier (Clerk), the Treasurer, the Constable (in charge of policing) and the Vingtenier (subordinated constable). Over 10% of the island's population is involved in its administration, most of them part-time and unpaid.

Isle of Man

A crown dependency in which the monarch is head of state but represented by a Lieutenant Governor. The Isle of Man is part of the British Isles but not part of the UK or even of Great Britain, although its people are classed as British even if they call themselves Manx. The island has its own parliament, the Tynwald, which was founded by Viking settlers and out of which the political head of the island, the Chief Minister, is selected.

Outer Hebrides or Western Isles

This chain of islands separated from the rest of Scotland by the stormy channel of the Minch is governed by a unitary council in Stornoway which is officially known by its Gaelic name, Comhairle nan Eilean Siar. Like the rest of Scotland, the islands are represented by three levels of democracy: an MP at Westminster, an MSP in Edinburgh and an MEP in the European Parliament.

The Outer Hebrides consist of 15 populated islands, 50 unpopulated ones close by, and various isolated rocks including the Monach Islands (a nature reserve), the Flannan Isles (where three lighthouse men vanished without explanation in 1900), St Kilda (a UNESCO world heritage site), North Rona (the most remote island to have been occupied and not always shown on maps), Sula Sgeir (a nature reserve historically exploited for 'gannet farming') and Rockall, the remains of a volcanic plug far out in the north Atlantic about as insular as an island can get.

Orkney

The Orkney Islands Council is Britain's smallest local authority but its people could claim to be the best served. It employs 1800 staff to serve the needs of a population of 20,000 scattered over 20 inhabited islands (out of an archipelago of 70 islands altogether).

Shetland

The Shetlands Island council is the most northerly local authority in the UK, on the same latitude as Helsinki. It oversees a population of 22,500 people and 46,000 gannets. The isolated crafting communities of Fair Isle are administratively included with Shetland. Orkney and Shetland have a member of the Scottish Parliament each but share a Westminster MP.

Jobs

Some public sector positions not open to outside applicants

There is a parallel kingdom next door to the one in which the rest of us live in, where tradition reigns supreme. Along with the monarchy there exists a whole range of personnel whose functions were established in medieval times and have been adapted as the centuries passed. These staff members of the nation's super-civil service are only seen by light of day at ceremonial functions, particularly the state opening of parliament. On all occasions they observe a strict though complicated order of precedent.

The following is a selection of the most conspicuous positions not advertised at your local Job Centre.

Great Officers of State of England

1. Lord (High) Steward. Always held by a peer.
2. Lord High Chancellor, a member of the Cabinet.
3. Lord High Treasurer.
4. Lord President of the Council. Ministerial head of the Privy Council and Leader of the Lords.
5. Lord Privy Seal – a Cabinet post.
6. Lord Great Chamberlain. A hereditary post shared between three aristocratic families. Easily confused with the Lord Chamberlain who heads the Queen's household. Neither has anything directly to do with the Lord Chamberlain's Office either, previously the official censor.
7. Lord High Constable.
8. Earl Marshal. A hereditary position occupied by the Duke of Norfolk.
9. Lord High Admiral. A post held by the monarch.

Officers of Arms (members of the College of Arms, a branch of the royal household)

The officers of arms are appointed by the sovereign to undertake ceremonial duties and to keep a track of things heraldic, genealogical and armorial. They are organized into three ranks: kings of arms, heralds of arms, and pursuivants of arms.

All these people are paid a yearly salary by the Crown fixed in 1830 and ranging from £13.95 to £49.07. The appendage 'extraordinary' indicates a non-permanent (and non-salaried) appointment.

- ❖ Garter Principal King of Arms
- ❖ Clarenceux King of Arms
- ❖ Norroy and Ulster King of Arms
- ❖ Lord Lyon (Scotland)
- ❖ Richmond Herald
- ❖ York Herald
- ❖ Chester Herald
- ❖ Lancaster Herald
- ❖ Windsor Herald
- ❖ Somerset Herald
- ❖ Rouge Dragon Pursuivant
- ❖ Bluemantle Pursuivant
- ❖ Portcullis Pursuivant
- ❖ Rouge Croix Pursuivant
- ❖ New Zealand Herald Extraordinary
- ❖ Beaumont Herald Extraordinary
- ❖ Maltravers Herald Extraordinary
- ❖ Wales Herald Extraordinary
- ❖ Norfolk Herald Extraordinary
- ❖ Arundel Herald Extraordinary
- ❖ Fitzalan Pursuivant Extraordinary

Lord Lieutenants and High Sheriffs

The monarch has two representatives in each of the counties of England and Wales. The Lord Lieutenant is his or her personal representative. The Sheriff, meanwhile, oversees things to do with the judiciary and law and order within his respective shrievalty.

Sheriffs are nominated by the sovereign in the Privy Council by "pricking" the appointee's name with a bodkin. Some towns have their own sheriffs and there is still a Sheriff of Nottingham charged with civic duties to do with tourism and the promotion of business.

Kids' Politics

6 sources of information for the young

Children can't vote of course, and they don't generally know, or care, how political systems work. Mostly, they perceive adult authority as extending from parent to headteacher to prime minister in a continuum of incomprehensibly stupid rules. But they do think politically in the sense of questioning who wields power over them and how they perform; and they are frequently concerned about the issues of the day and what is not being done about them.

The adult world doesn't trouble itself much to nurture such incipient political awareness in the young but it does feed them messages through literature, films and television which must surely help to form their adult views.

Fairy Tales

Most children these days get their traditional fairy tales repackaged as cartoons but the original stories have hidden depths. In his classic study, *The Uses of Enchantment*, psychoanalyst Bruno Bettelheim explains what he thinks prepubescent readers or listeners take away from folk stories. Fairy tale lands are ruled by kings (and wicked queens) rather than elected burghers, and while these leaders may be judged for their wisdom or lapses into stupidity, the institution of monarchy is never called into question. The king represents a surrogate father-figure in the infant's imagination – and what are kings, prime ministers and presidents to grown-ups if not father figures we expect to rule wisely on our behalf?

Tintin

"I was fed the prejudices of the bourgeois society that surrounded me", remarked Hergé, Tintin's creator, when his character was accused of being euro-chauvinist, racist and having fascist sympathies. Today, the Tintin books look of their age and the overt and implicit political references are mere background to the stories: you could spend a childhood reading them without being brainwashed into believing that Belgian colonialism was a good thing. But for an adult reader it can add an extra layer of interest to read the Tintin books with a political overview in mind. The most explicit book is the early and primitive *Tintin in the Land of the Soviets* (1930) which is critical of Stalin's Russia. *King Ottokar's Sceptre* (1939) can be read as an allegory of the Nazis' tactics of aggressively annexing neighbouring countries. *The Calculus Affair* (1956), meanwhile, is a comment on the Cold War. More ambiguous is the character of General Alcazar (who appears in several of the books), would-be dictator of the fictional Latin American country of San Theodoros, with his dubious ethics. That Tintin befriends him is just one of many indications of his own lack of professionalism: as a reporter he is incapable of maintaining any sense of impartiality and is always getting sucked into adventures, thus becoming the story himself.

Asterix

One of the few pieces of supposed children's literature (although only adults will get the subtler jokes and allusions) which takes political sides at the outset, being a party political manifesto for the Brittany nationalist movement of the 1st century BC. On a broader level its message is that any small community can stand up to an oppressive state – if it has an unlimited supply of magic potion. It's worth noting that the otherwise utopian village which Asterix comes from is governed as a benign autocracy.

Blue Peter

The world's longest-running children's television programme has a brief to inform as well as entertain. Its presenters have visited Downing Street three times to meet the prime minister of the day and give viewers an idea of where power is exercised. First through the door of No. 10 was the legendary team of John, Peter and Lesley in 1974. Most recently, Konnie Huq met Tony Blair to put Blue Peter viewers' questions to him directly.

My Dad's the Prime Minister

Although ostensibly a comedy series for children's television, *My Dad's the Prime Minister*, co-written by Ian Hislop (editor of *Private Eye*), quickly became family viewing and is an indication of how the worlds of childhood and adulthood are becoming increasingly mixed up. It clearly symbolises a shift in the public perception of politics that took place in the Blair era. No longer do we want or expect the prime minister to be an aloof dignitary on a pedestal; instead, we've come to see him as just a man with human failings. And imagine if you had to live with him. For Dillon Phillips (aged 12), being the son of the prime minister is a curse rather than a dream (as previous generations would have thought): like every other dad, his is overworked, stressed, forgetful, proud, stupid, tyrannical and all the rest but on top of that he's also a politician, even at home. Dillon gets bullied at school for who he is and bullied in a different sense by his dad's spin doctor for whom he is just another pawn to be deployed in the game of clinging to power.

Harry Potter

Characters in JK Rowling's Harry Potter books hop between the everyday 'Muggle' world and a parallel reality in which sorcery is the norm. The Minister of Magic governs wizarding affairs in the other realm through a fairly conventional career-driven bureaucracy. He doesn't appear to be a member of either the Commons or the Lords; he doesn't attend Cabinet meetings; and he is not bound by the convention of collective responsibility. When he needs to tell the prime minister something – he gives the orders, rather than the other way around – he materialises with little warning in the fireplace of No. 10 Downing Street, as he does in the opening chapter of *Harry Potter and the Half-Blood Prince* (2005).

The Laws of Politics

30 infallible principles

As the sum of human incompetence grows, the more we are able to see how it forms a beautiful system governed by precise *a priori* rules such as the ones set out below.

A few of them have been crafted by established thinkers after lifetimes of study; others are the work of anonymous geniuses who merely observe political behaviour from the bottom of the heap and report back to us. Every day new laws are added to the canon and it can only be a matter of time before an enlightened university politics department gives up analysing election results and creates a chair of Anecdotal Political Wisdom.

Bureaucracy

Boren's Guide for Bureaucrats

When in charge, ponder; when in trouble, delegate; when in doubt, mumble.

Devised in the 1970s by James Boren, founder and president of The National Association of Professional Bureaucrats. Boren told *Time* magazine that NATAPROBU was dedicated to "optimize the status quo by fostering adjustive adherence to procedural abstractions and rhetorical clearances".

Career Building

Dirksen's* Three Laws of Politics

Get elected.
Get re-elected.
Don't get mad, get even.

*Everett Dirsken 1896–1969, Republican Senator of Illinois

Brown's Rules of Leadership

1. To succeed in politics, it is often necessary to rise above your principles.

2. The best way to succeed in politics is to find a crowd that's going somewhere and get in front of them.

Simon's Law of Destiny
Glory may be fleeting, but obscurity is forever.

Corruption

The Watergate Principle
Government corruption is always reported in the past tense.

Cameron's Pricing Arrangement
An honest politician is one who, when bought, will stay bought.

> Attributed to Simon Cameron, Abraham Lincoln's first secretary of war, elaborating on Sir Robert Walpole's remark in parliament in 1734, "I know the price of every man in this House."

Debate

Parker's Rule of Parliamentary Procedure
A motion to adjourn is always in order.

Representative Democracy

Walton's Law of Politics
A fool and his money are soon elected.

Diplomacy

Katz's Law
Men and nations will act rationally when all other possibilities have been exhausted.

Economics

Art Buchwald's Law
As the economy gets better, everything else gets worse.

Ethical Politics

Alinsky's Rule For Radicals
Those who are most moral are farthest from the problem.

Leadership

Gilmer's Law of Political Leadership

Look over your shoulder now and then to be sure someone's following you.

Evans' Law

If you can keep your head while all about you are losing theirs, then you just don't understand the problem.

Weiler's Law

Nothing is impossible for the man who doesn't have to do it himself.

Obligations of Office

Evanss' Law of Political Perfidy

When our friends get into power, they aren't our friends anymore.

Problem Solving

The Law of Diminshed Responsibility

When a politician gets an idea he usually gets it wrong.

Zymurgy's First Law of Evolving Systems Dynamics

Once you open a can of worms, the only way to recan them is to use a larger can.

Allen Ginsberg's Restatement of The Laws of Thermodynamics

You can't win.
You can't break even.
You can't even quit the game.

Freeman's Commentary On Ginsberg's Theorem

1. Capitalism is based on the assumption that you can win.
2. Socialism is based on the assumption that you can break even.
3. Mysticism is based on the assumption that you can quit the game.

Progress

Arthur C. Clarke's Law of Revolutionary Ideas

Every revolutionary idea evokes three stages of reaction:

1. It is impossible – don't waste my time.
2. It is possible, but it is not worth doing.
3. I said it was a good idea all along.

Cheop's Law

Nothing ever gets built on schedule or within budget.

Public Relations

Potter's Law

The amount of flak received on any subject is inversely proportional to the subject's true value.

Galbraith's Resignation Continuum

Anyone who says he isn't going to resign, four times, definitely will.

Parker's Law of Political Statements

The truth of any proposition has nothing to do with its credibility and vice versa.

Todd's First Two Political Principles

1. No matter what they're telling you, they're not telling you the whole truth.
2. No matter what they're talking about, they're talking about money.

Glyme's Formula for Success

The secret of success is sincerity. Once you can fake that you've got it made.

Special Advisers

Hiram's Law

If you consult enough experts you can confirm any opinion.

Van Roy's Second Law

If you can distinguish between good and bad advice, then you don't need advice.

Taxation

Morton's Fork

Rich or poor, the government will get your money.

John Morton was an adviser to Henry VII. The principle of his fork was that those who were ostentatious with their wealth could obviously afford to be taxed, whilst those who showed no outward signs of wealth must be hiding it, so they too could afford to pay tax.

Vision

Finnigan's Law

The farther away the future is, the better it looks.

Laws of Politics According to Inman

10 essential pieces of advice to stick on the office wall

1. Never stab a colleague in the back when it is much more rewarding to stab him in the front, in broad daylight, in public.

2. You can't fool all the people all the time unless you own the television stations.

3. Feed your grassroots with a regular forkload of manure.

4. What is sauce for the goose is gravy for the train, or: corruption is in the eye of the beholden.

5. Take the credit for success but ascribe failures to collective responsibility.

6. A stalking horse is never first past the post.

7. You can never be too tough but you can be too caring.

8. If you are worried about leaks, buy a pair of Wellingtons.

9. What happened is what you say happened in your memoirs.

10. Always tell people that you welcome a full and open debate but that it is either i) too soon for this because not all the facts are known or ii) too late because the decision has already been taken.

Laws of Politics According to Parkinson and Peter

3 indisputable laws of political nature

Serious students of politics should pay special attention to certain key text books which never seem to date. Below are useful extracts from two of them.

'Parkinson's Law' by C. Northcote Parkinson*

Parkinson's Third Law or the 'Coefficient of Inefficiency' concerns the optimum size of committees and in particular of the Cabinet.

"...the ideal size of a Cabinet council usually appears...to be five. With that number the plant is viable, allowing for two members to be absent or sick at any one time. Five members are easy to collect and, when collected, can act with competence, secrecy, and speed. Of these original members four may well be versed, respectively, in finance, foreign policy, defence, and law. The fifth, who has failed to master any of these subjects, usually becomes the chairman or prime minister."

With only three members a quorum is impossible to collect.

"Other members come to be admitted, some with a claim to special knowledge but more because of their nuisance value when excluded. Their opposition can be silenced only by implicating them in every decision that is made."

The more there are, the harder it is to collect them in one place and one time and:

"the far greater chance of members proving to be elderly, tiresome, inaudible, and deaf."

When a Cabinet grows over 20 strong it "suffers an abrupt chemical or organic change".

---

*'Parkinson's Law' by C. Northcote Parkinson, Penguin Books.

> "In the first place, the five members who matter will have taken to meeting beforehand. With decisions already reached, little remains for the nominal executive to do...all resistance to the committee's expansion comes to an end. More members will not waste more time; for the whole meeting is, in any case, a waste of time."

> "...with over 20 members present a meeting begins to change character. Conversations develop separately at either end of the table. To make himself hear, the member has therefore to rise. Once on his feet, he cannot help making a speech, if only from force of habit....Amid all this drivel the useful men present, if there are any, exchange little notes that read, 'Lunch with me tomorrow - we'll fix it then.'"

Parkinson's Fourth Law makes an observation about the lay-out of Parliament:

> "The British, being brought up on team games, enter their House of Commons in the spirit of those who would rather be doing something else .... the British instinct is to form two opposing teams ... The House of Commons is so arranged that the individual Member is practically compelled to take one side or the other before he knows what the arguments are ... the British system depends entirely on the seating plan. If the benches did not face each other, no one could tell truth from falsehood, wisdom from folly – unless indeed by listening to it all."

Whereas

> "the French form a multitude of teams facing in all directions...no one could tell (without listening) which argument was the more cogent....The semi-circular chamber allows of subtle distinctions between the various degrees of rightness and leftness. There is none of the clear-cut British distinction between rightness and wrongness."

'The Peter Principle' by Dr Laurence J Peter, Raymond Hull*

This states that:

> *"In a hierarchy every employee tends to rise to his level of incompetence. In time, every post tends to be occupied by an employee who is incompetent to carry out its duties. Work is accomplished by those employees who have not yet reached their level of incompetence...Hierarchies are therefore cumbered with incompetents who cannot do their existing work, cannot be promoted, yet cannot be removed...Capitalistic, socialistic and communistic systems are characterised by the same accumulation of redundant and incompetent personnel."*

Nevertheless there is still one question to answer: whether the world is run by clever men who are "putting us on or by imbeciles who really mean it."

---

* 'The Peter Principle' by Laurence J. Peter and Raymond Hull, Souvenir Press.

Leaders – the Also Rans

Party leaders who were never PM

Getting elected as party leader is one thing; winning an election is another. Sometimes it's not personal. The mood of the times is against you; your opponent is just too hard to beat; your party insists on promoting unpopular policies. It's just bad luck to be at the head of a party which is enduring a long spell in the wilderness as it regroups to face hard truths.

Sometimes, however, it's very personal, too personal. You get chosen by your party for all the wrong reasons and there's little you can do except go down gracefully at the next election. It can be especially hard to follow a strong and successful leader: the Conservatives are still trying to come up with a candidate who can live up to the legacy of Margaret Thatcher.

When out of office, parties have a tendency towards self-harm, choosing leaders who do not fit the minimum criteria.

The table on the pages that follow shows the fate that befell leaders of the three main parties who did not make it to No. 10.

Key

⊘	retired after losing election	☝	pushed out by own party
☘	died in office	⚱	voluntary retirement
☯	merger of parties	∦	scandal
☒	end or period of office		

CONSERVATIVE PARTY

Leader	Arr.	Dep.	Why	Comments
Austen Chamberlain	1921	1922	☺	Half brother of Neville, his support for Lloyd George deprived him of the chance to be prime minister.
William Hague	1997	2001	⊘	Having won the leadership as the default non-left-winger he was to become the second Conservative leader of the 20th century not to serve as prime minister.
Iain Smith	2001	Nov 2003	⊘	Famously and disastrously Duncan described himself as "a quiet man" in 2001.
Michael Howard	Nov 2003	Dec 2005	⊘	Could never quite shake off the curse of his colleague, Ann Widdecombe, that he had "something of the night about him", or the repeated showings of his 1997 interview with Paxman, in which he was asked, and failed to answer, the same question 12 times.
David Cameron	Dec 2005	NOT OUT		Elected leader over David Davis, the 5th to face Tony Blair. If he becomes prime minister he will be the 19th Old Etonian to achieve the highest office.

LABOUR PARTY

Leader	Arr.	Dep.	Why	Comments
Arthur Henderson	1931	1932	⊘	Elected on expulsion of Ramsay MacDonald from party.
George Lansbury	1932	1935	☺	A committed pacifist who resigned, aged 76, after being attacked by Ernest Bevin. His resignation was accepted with reluctance by Labour MPs.

Hugh Gaitskell	1955	1963	☠	Died suddenly of *lupus, erythematosus* a rare auto-immune disease (which also killed Ferdinand Marcos). There have been unfounded rumours that the KGB assassinated him.
Michael Foot	1980	1983	⊘	
Neil Kinnock	1983	1992	⊘	
John Smith	July 1992	May 1994	☠	Second post-war Labour leader to die in office and in opposition.
Margaret Beckett	May 1994	July 1994	⧖	Often referred to as 'acting' leader she was, as Deputy, technically leader till Blair's election.

LIBERAL/LIBERAL DEMOCRACTIC PARTY

Leader	*Arr.*	*Dep.*	*Why*	*Comments*
Herbert Samuel	1931	1935	⊘	
Archibald Sinclair	1935	1945	⊘	
Clement Davies	1945	1956	⊘	
Jo Grimond	1956	1967	⛰	Also served as interim leader in 1976 after Thorpe's resignation.
Jeremy Thorpe	1967	1976	✗	Alleged homosexual affair with Norman Scott was never proven but still forced resignation.
David Steel	1976	1988	☻	
Paddy Ashdown	1988/ 1989	July 1999	⛰	First elected leader of Liberal Democrats
Charles Kennedy	1999	5.1.06	♜	
Menzies Campbell	Mar 06 NOT OUT			

Left and Right Spectrum

Two methods to help you choose your team

The terms 'left' and 'right' date from before the French Revolution when supporters of the status quo sat to the right of the king in the Estates General and those who wanted change to the left. Although today the words are deployed *ad nauseam* in political discourse, they can confuse as much as define – especially when hurled as insults.

Some people would say that we should drop the classification since leftness and rightness became obsolete at the same time as the Berlin Wall came down; but others believe that in these times of political cross-dressing there has never been a greater need to assert the old divisions. Not in order to reignite ideological trench warfare, you understand, but to clear away the pretence that government is about achieving consensus, co-operation and compromise. British democracy is based on adversarial debate and if both parties try to espouse the same broadly fuzzy principles, what choice does that give the electorate?

In a wider sense, left and right represent philosophical traditions and clusters of beliefs about politics and even about the purpose of society and the meaning of life. But of course, few of us cleave obstinately to one side or the other and the words are most usefully used nowadays to mark out relative positions, say between two members of the same party (left-wing Conservative, right-wing of the Labour Party etc).

Any left/right summary is bound to be simplistic and contentious but the next three pages will, at least, provide you with the basis for a heated argument (see 'Debates' p64). If you think politics is more than subtle than the bipolar disorder so described, you might prefer one of the various 'three-dimensional' systems which have been devised for plotting the views of an individual or stance of a party or movement. The most elegant is the political compass, explained on page 182.

L ← —————— **THEORY** —————— → R

Human nature is basically co-operative. People are trustworthy, unselfish and generous unless you corrupt, starve or mistreat them through economic or social deprivation.	Human nature is basically selfish. People are not innately generous, trustworthy etc. – individuals may have these qualities but not everyone. Economic and social circumstances have nothing to do with how people choose to behave.
The future is the best guide to action: things can always be better because human beings have potential which can be tapped if you provide the right conditions.	The past (tradition) is the only reliable guide to action we have: we must heed its lessons. People don't change; they won't ever behave any better than they do now, whatever you do for them.
Societies can always be improved; we shouldn't be afraid to experiment; we can break the bounds of "the possible".	If it ain't broke don't fix it; everything has been tried before; further experiments mean further mistakes.
Ideology is respectable. It is fine to be an idealist and even a utopian (in the sense of working towards an ideal society).	All ideologies are suspect and frequently lethal. We should be pragmatic and sceptical. We have to be realistic: ideal societies do not and cannot exist; we should make the best of what we have.

L ← —————— **POLITICS** —————— → R

The status quo should be challenged. Breaks with the past are desirable. Revolution is a force for the good: it throws up new possibilities.	We should maintain the status quo at all cost. Stability and continuity are desirable. Revolutions never succeed and never improve anything; they just create chaos.
We should instinctively question authority and constantly re-evaluate the legitimacy of institutions: church, family, monarchy, police, military etc.	We should be instinctively obedient to authority. We must uphold the sanctity of institutions proven to work over time.
The only healthy political system is a republic.	A monarchy is preferable to a republic because it provides continuity and stability.
The state should benevolently intervene in people's lives to improve them. It should look after everyone "from the cradle to the grave".	The state has no business interfering in anyone's life for any reason. It is never benevolent. The individual has to rely on him or herself.
Bureaucracy is a necessary evil if the state is to provide services for people.	Bureaucracy is an unnecessary evil and should be eliminated wherever possible.
Politics should be driven by morality.	Politics should be driven by practicalities.

Power comes from collectivity. The individual is less important than the community.

Power comes from individuals; the individual is more important than the community. Collective endeavour is only ever a temporary alliance for a specific end.

L ◄─────────────── **ECONOMICS** ───────────────► R

Co-operation is good; competition is bad because it brings out the worst in people.

Co-operation is usually unrealistic, certainly in an altruistic sense; Competition is healthy: the survival of the fittest is the law of nature.

Central planning is the fairest way to allocate resources.

Central planning is the most inefficient way to allocate resources; the efficient way is to trust competing market forces.

State ownership is self-evidently the best way to organise key industries which work for the good of all e.g. transport and health.

State ownership is an evil which distorts markets which otherwise work efficiently and for the good of all.

In a mixed economy there must be extensive controls over business.

There should be as few regulations as possible to handicap business.

The interests of the working class should be promoted over those of more privileged, more articulate, more powerful social classes.

It is misleading to see politics in class terms. If anyone's interests are to be favoured by the state it must be the owners and managers of business who provide prosperity, security of employment, social provision etc.

Wealth should be redistributed through progressive taxation.

People have a right to keep what they earn.

L ◄─────────────── **SOCIETY** ───────────────► R

Hierarchies are bad. Equality and inclusivity are to be aspired to. Privilege should be legislated against.

Hierarchies and social divisions exist in all societies and are inevitable. People are not born, and cannot be made, equal. There must be privilege and inequalities if there are to be incentives.

Crime can only be understood by economic and social conditions. There are often extenuating causes ("society is to blame"). Punishment should take this into account.

Crime is just crime and should be punished appropriately. Punishment should be according to the crime's severity without looking for excuses for it.

No one is inherently bad or evil. The causes of bad behaviour (by individuals, organisations and states) should be understood and punishment should be only one option considered. Everyone should be offered the chance of rehabilitation.

Some people are inherently bad or evil and cannot be reformed. Everyone and every organisation is responsible for his/her/its actions. Bad behaviour should be punished, never rewarded by giving it attention or trying to understand it/justify it. Discipline is a first, not a last resort.

Comprehensive education is the only fair system. All children should get the same resources. Private education (the public school system) is anathema to a society of equal opportunity.

Education based on selection (grammar school/secondary modern model) serves everyone better, including working class kids: more resources should be given to high achievers. Parents who can afford to must have the right to pay for the education they choose for their children.

Everyone should have the same opportunities. We should encourage inclusivity even if we have to discriminate positively or practise "political correctness".

Everyone has the same opportunities but some people don't know how to take them, or simply don't want to. Political correctness is patronising; positive discrimination means unjustifiably discriminating against some people who have done nothing to deserve it.

Multiculturalism is to be encouraged. Minorities should be championed. The state should be on the side of the weak against the strong.

A society should defend its own culture including its language and dominant religion. Minorities must adapt to it. They should be empowered to help themselves.

Public service broadcasting is a good thing; ownership of the media should be regulated.

All media should be in private ownership, subject to competition without political regulation.

Freedom is a right guaranteed by the state.

Freedom means freedom *from* the state.

People have a duty to help society.

People can do what they want with their lives. Charity and compassion are for individuals to decide, not states.

L **INTERNATIONALISM** ──────────▶ R

We should think internationally, for the good of humanity as a whole, and create supranational organisations.

Humanity is too riddled with divisions to share common interests; we should be suspicious of international organisations and think nationalistically, forming non-permanent alliances between two or very few countries to pursue specific ends.

The Political Compass

The conventional political spectrum is rather subjective and one-dimensional and there have been various attempts to improve on it. One simple idea is the political compass which plots an individual or an organisation's views according to two simple criteria, attitudes towards authority and economic 'freedom'.

- A belief in the most extreme definition of personal freedom (unadulterated anarchism) scores -10 points while a belief in the need for totalitarian control of society scores +10.

- Someone who espouses an entirely planned economy (something close to ideal Marxism) would be marked as -10 and a no-holes-barred laissez faire capitalist would be +10.

Authoritarian left	Authoritarian right
Libertarian left	Libertarian right

-10	0	+10

L

Legacies

10 testimonials to a term in office

> *"The main essentials of a prime minister are sleep and a sense of history."* Harold Wilson

Given that almost all political careers consist of years of frustrating battles with your friends (and occasionally with your enemies), and inevitably end in disappointment, all you can hope is to leave something lasting behind you. Your legacy will be judged in different ways depending on who is doing the judging:

- Your contemporaries will be too steamed up about recent hurts and injustices to see any lasting good in what you have done, so you can forget them. They, of course, would have done much, much better with the majority and the goodwill you had. They will, at least, be magnanimous when writing your political and actual obituaries.

- The generation immediately after yours will quickly sift the truly enduring from the insignificant chaff that got you so het up so much of the time.

- Future generations will dispassionately reduce your performance on the stage of history to a walk-on, non-speaking part. If your hard-won legacy was reduced to insignificance by events shortly after you left office, they won't ever know anything about it. If by chance some great measure you steered through the House of Commons in the face of short-term public opinion and bullying vested interests, against all odds and at great personal cost to yourself, has lasted into their day, they'll simply take it for granted that its introduction was pain free.

In short, everyone who comes after you will wonder why you bothered. But before you start planning your legacy, note that few ministers and prime ministers manage to leave one at all. Which is still better than the third kind of legacy: universal vilification ensuring that you will never, ever be forgotten but for all the wrong reasons.

Over the page are listed the legacies, favourable and unfavourable, of recent prime ministers.

Balfour
The Balfour Declaration 1917 – Britain's approval of a plan to create a Jewish homeland in Palestine. It had as much to do with British expediency as generosity or altruism and in any case paid no regard to the interests of the Palestinians. But it did lead to the creation of the state of Israel, with all the problems that has entailed.

Asquith
Reform of the House of Lords.

Lloyd George
The 'People's Budget' (before he became prime minister, in collaboration with Asquith), winning World War I.

Churchill
Winning World War II.

Attlee
Nationalisation and the creation of the National Health Service.

Wilson
The Open University (the achievement of which he was most proud).

Heath
Britain's entry into Europe.

Thatcher
'Thatcherism' (privatisation of state industry, sale of council houses, crippling the unions etc) and winning the Falklands War.

Major
The Maastricht Treaty, leading to Britain's closer involvement with Europe (and to the near self-destruction of the Conservative Party).

Blair
The minimum wage, devolution for Scotland and Wales, a lasting peace settlement in Northern Ireland (unless we are speaking too soon), the overthrow of Saddam Hussein and the Iraq War.

The Lords

5 or 6 prototypes for a parliament of peers

> *"...a body of five hundred men chosen at random from amongst the unemployed."*
> Lloyd George

> *"a model of how to care for the elderly."*
> Frank Field, Labour MP 1981

> *"a good example of life after death."* Lord Soper (attrib.)

> *"useless, dangerous, and ought to be abolished."*
> Henri Labouchere 1882

Bizarrely, the House of Lords is at once the most staid political institution in Britain and the one which has seen the most evolution. That is, at the time of writing. It is about to take its third lurch forward in 100 years and no one knows what it will look like in the future. The only thing which will perhaps remain constant is that no one loves it unless they are privileged enough to sit in it or have the prospect of doing so.

Lords Mark I – 'Nothing in Common' – The year dot to the 14th century

The Lords was the original parliament which grew out of the witans, advisory councils to the Saxon kings. In the 14th century the kings' advisers divided themselves into lords (us) and "commoners" (them) and a long tussle began between the two parts of the same legislature. The House of Lords' membership consisted of the Lords Spiritual (or Spiritual Peers), being the top clergymen of the Church of England, and the Lords Temporal (the aristocracy of Britain). Although the word 'peers' means equals there were five ranks: dukes, marquesses, earls, viscounts and barons.

Lords Mark II – 'The Conservative Chamber' – 14th century to 1911

Over the next five centuries the power of the Commons grew while the House of Lords trod water as the repository of superior birth, privilege and reward. In 1876 the Lords of Appeal in Ordinary, better known as the Law Lords, joined the existing peers. The House of Lords had begun as a conservative institution and in the 19th century became a Conservative one, resistant to any reform instigated by the Liberals. It even posed as a virtuous bastion against the 'tyranny' of the House of Commons. When Lloyd George tried to get his populist 'People's Budget' through Parliament the Lords opposed it as a matter of routine. Its attitudes had become anachronistic, however, and it was emasculated by the Parliament Act of 1911 which took away its veto over public spending and left it with a delaying power only.

Lords Mark III – 'Delay and Decay' – 1911-1958

By the time Lloyd George had finished with it the House of Lords was toothless but still influential. The 1911 act was supposed to be the first step towards complete abolition of the political powers of a hereditary aristocracy, but the House of Lords survived with the same composition as before and evolved a new role for itself. It creaked with its weight of inherited privilege but served several purposes nonetheless: it was still the highest court of appeal, it still accommodated the upper hierarchy of the Church of England, and it still served as the venue for the opening of Parliament – the 'commoners' being sent for to hear what the sovereign had to say. Other than that it provided a forum for party-free discussion and the examination and revision of laws (its delaying power was further reduced by an act in 1949), as well as being a talent bank for the government to make personnel deposits into and withdrawals from.

Lords Mark IV – 'Life Means Life' – 1958-1999

In 1958 Macmillan's government passed legislation allowing the creation of an unlimited number of life peers. Over the next 40 years almost a thousand life peers were appointed to the Lords, including the first women to sit in the House - hereditary peeresses only became equal in rights to their menfolk in 1963. Meanwhile, the movement for reform was building. The Wilson government considered taking away the voting right from the hereditaries in 1968 but the proposed bill foundered in the House of Commons. Labour policy in the 70s and 80s was to abolish the House of Lords altogether but by 1997 the party had come to accept the principle of reform.

Lords Mark V – 'The Hybrid House' – 1999-2007

The Lords posed a problem for Blair's 'New' Labour ministers when they were elected in 1997. Clearly leaving it to rumble on unchanged wouldn't fit with their modernising image but what to do about it? Until 1999 it was the largest regulatory body in the world with 1,200 people entitled to sit in it, the majority of them by accident of birth.

The solution they came up with was the House of Lords Act (1999) which removed the right of hereditary peers to sit in the Lords but, as a compromise, allowed 92 of their number and 26 archbishops and bishops, to remain on an interim basis, alongside the 480 life peers. For the first time in its history, appointees outnumbered annointees in the House of Lords. The hereditary lords departed surprisingly quietly but not without protest.

Lords Mark VI – 'The Definitive Model' – 2007- Eternity?

But now what? Does Britain need a second chamber at all? And if it does, should it be made up of members elected by the public or should prime ministers still be able to promote people to the second chamber as a reward for service or because they have especially useful talents? If there is to be a mix of elected and appointed members, in what proportions? In February 2007 the government drew up a white paper on Lords reform and put it to an 'advisory' vote in the House of Commons which accepted that at least 50% of the Lords' membership should be elected. It is possible, although unlikely, that the House of Lords will become a 100% elected body in which case, wouldn't we be faced by a future of eternal strife between two competing chambers of equal democratic legitimacy? For this reason, few people believe Britain will ever have a wholly elected second chamber.

Lost Deposits
5 financial facts about electoral failure

Before the 1872 Ballot Act enabled a candidate to vote for himself, eight candidates managed to win no votes at all in British general elections and by-elections. Now, every candidate is assured of one vote at least, unless he or she spoils his own ballot paper.

The next challenge for a candidate is to keep his or her deposit. To discourage the proliferation of frivolous candidates, anyone standing for election has to pay a deposit (currently £500) which is only returned to those who poll at least 1/20th (5%) of the votes cast in the constituency. If the candidate fails to reach this threshold, the Treasury rings up another successful sale in the name of democracy.

- In the 1983 election Labour set a record for the two major parties by losing 119 of its deposits. Previously, the post-war record was held by the Conservatives who forfeited 28 deposits in October 1974.

- 1987 was the first election in which neither major party lost a single deposit.

- In 2005, 1,385 candidates lost their deposits, a gain to the Treasury of £692,500.

- The two parties that tried hardest and fared worst in 2005 were the Greens who lost 135 out of their 145 deposits, and UKIP which fielded 496 candidates and lost 458 of its deposits – failure rates of 93% and 92% respectively.

- The last resort of a desperate candidate is to demand a recount but only very occasionally does this make the difference between keeping and losing a deposit.

Marxist Pin-Ups

The 10 top ten posters to hang on the wall on the left

Political scientists have long been aware of a contradiction inherent in Marxism: its adherents bore even their own comrades to death with their polysyllabic rhetoric yet still have far more sex-appeal than anyone on the right wing of politics. Or, to put it bluntly, if the Communist bloc didn't invent Viagra, it's because they didn't need it.

Karl Marx – German philosopher, revolutionary library card holder
Distinguishing features: hidden by beard and sideburns.

Lenin (Vladimir Ilyich Ulyanov) – Russian revolutionary
Distinguishing features: preserved intact in Moscow; have a look for yourself.

Trotsky (Lev Davidovich Bronstein) – Ukranian revolutionary runner-up
Distinguishing features: goatee beard, hunted look.

Picasso – Spanish painter and sculptor
Distinguishing features: stripy smock, all facial features on the same plane facing the viewer.

André Breton – French founder of Surrealism
Distinguishing features: insouciant pose.

Che Guevara – Argentinian revolutionary
Distinguishing features: moustache, beret and faraway look.

Mao Zedong – Great Chinese Forward Leaper
Distinguishing features: inscrutable expression, receding hairline (sometimes covered by a proletarian cap).

Jean-Paul Sartre – French existential philosopher and writer
Distinguishing features: worried, intellectual expression.

Fidel Castro – Cuban revolutionary and revolutionary president
Distinguishing features: military uniform, cigar.

Groucho Marx – Founder of alternative school of Marxism
Distinguishing features: ironic smirk; could be confused with Trotsky (because of the moustache) or Castro (because of the cigar).

Menu

What to order if you want to eat with political attitude

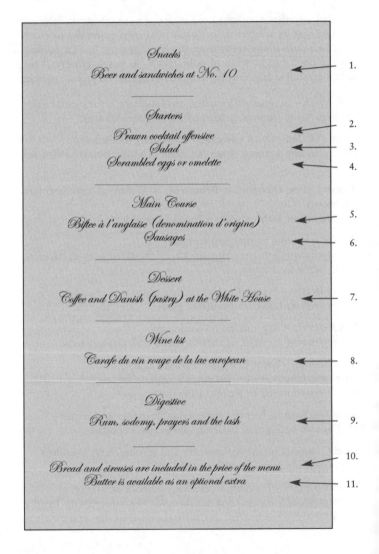

Snacks

Beer and sandwiches at No. 10   1.

Starters

Prawn cocktail offensive   2.
Salad   3.
Scrambled eggs or omelette   4.

Main Course

Biftec à l'anglaise (denomination d'origine)   5.
Sausages   6.

Dessert

Coffee and Danish (pastry) at the White House   7.

Wine list

Carafe du vin rouge de la lac european   8.

Digestive

Rum, sodomy, prayers and the lash   9.

Bread and circuses are included in the price of the menu   10.
Butter is available as an optional extra   11.

[1] Harold Wilson had a habit of inviting trade unionists to No. 10 Downing Street so that he could talk them out of industrial disputes. Marathon talking sessions were punctuated with pub-like rounds of beer and sandwiches.

[2] In 1992, John Smith, shadow chancellor embarked on a charm offensive of lunches in the City of London to convince financiers that they had nothing to fear from a Labour government. "Never have so many crustaceans died in vain," remarked Michael Heseltine.

[3] Acronymous (almost) nickname for the Social and Liberal Democrats. SLD, formed in 1988, later simplified to Liberal Democrats, which would make them now just "lads".

[4] When health minister Edwina Currie warned in 1988 that "most of the egg production in this country, sadly, is now affected with salmonella" she was but a hen's hop from resignation. Eggs, of course, are the weapon of choice for political hecklers – causing Norman Tebbit to remark, "Those who scream and throw eggs are not the real unemployed. If they were really hard up, they would be eating them." Robespierre justified the bloodshed of the French Revolution by saying "You can't make an omelette without breaking eggs." Anthony Eden elaborated, "If you've broken the eggs, you should make the omelette".

[5] In 1990, at the height of the BSE scare John Selwyn Gummer, Minister for Agriculture, Food and Fisheries, was photographed feeding a beefburger to his 4 year-old-daughter to prove that the beef was safe to eat. It has been alleged that the photograph was staged and a civil servant took a bite out of the burger. But don't let any of this put you off your lunch.

[6] Harold Wilson scornfully referred to the Heath government as being "custodians of the national sausage" in a 1974 speech attacking its inability to keep food prices under control. The "threat to the British sausage" (rules about the ingredients it may or may not contain) is regularly trotted out by eurosceptics as an example of Brussels meddling in the affairs of member states.

[7] The US equivalent of beer and sandwiches at No. 10.

[8] No party will run dry if the booze comes from the European wine lake, a mythical claret-red expanse the size of a small country which is fed by the run-off from myriad unprofitable plonk producers in southern Europe.

[9] Winston Churchill's summary of the traditions of the navy.

[10] If there is no bread, you can always eat cake.

[11] As Josef Goebbels said, "We can do without butter but, despite our love of peace, not without arms. One cannot shoot with butter, but with guns . . . but I ask you, would you rather have butter or guns?...Let me tell it to you straight: preparedness makes us powerful. Butter merely makes us fat."

Middle England

8 ways to programme your GPS system before you go in search of it

Middle England is like Tolkein's Middle Earth: we know everything about it except where it is. That doesn't stop politicians and journalists talking to it or about it, and often referring to it as an inexhaustible well of all things good or bad in Britain.

Rather than think of it as a geographical term it is better understood in a sociological or demographical sense: the 'Middle English' are a people without a specific home that you can pinpoint on a map. These people are (lower) middle class, white (there are no immigrants among them), heterosexual, hard working and responsible.

Eight co-ordinates for finding the inhabitants of Middle England:

1. *Daily Mail* readers are often characterised as being from Middle England. Upwardly mobile and staunchly moral, they don't consider themselves to be tabloid readers; they aren't part of the Establishment; they aren't party activists; they certainly aren't liberals or socialists (they despise the *Guardian*). What unites them is that they feel hard done by and ignored, and that manners have gone to pot.

2. The 'Silent Majority'. Middle England, we are told, is continually muttering about its moral indignation but never loud enough for the microphones of the media to pick it up. In the 19th century the phrase referred to the dead.

3. 'Mondeo man'. This demographic concept was supposedly invented in 1997 when Tony Blair saw a man polishing his Ford Mondeo. He is a 30-something middle-income homeowner who could vote Labour or Tory, and will choose whoever would best preserve his way of life.

4. 'Worcester Woman'. A provincial urban/suburban woman identified (by pollsters) as a swing voter in 1997 and in subsequent elections. She has consumerist views and a shallow interest in politics, and is thus easily persuaded by spin doctors.

5. Anyone who identifies with John Major's vision of classless Britain: "What does this England mean to me?" Major once

asked the Conservative Party conference. "I shall tell you. It means lukewarm beer, the sound of cricket ball against willow, old dears cycling to church, rosy-faced bobbies patrolling every suburban high street – and, once a week or so, really getting stuck into a curry." He also said "Fifty years on from now, Britain will still be the country of long shadows on cricket grounds, warm beer, invincible green suburbs, dog lovers and pools fillers."

6. 'Essex Man'. In anthropological terms, this Thatcher supporter of the materialist late 80s probably evolved into Mondeo Man.

7. In the pubs and clubs and on the doorsteps. Almost every politician at some time or other quotes the real, hard-working, tax-paying, law-abiding people he or she finds in such places who are eager to pour out their grievances and place their naïve trust in anyone who will listen.

8. 'Pebbledash People'. A concept invented by ICM pollsters for the Tories in 2001 as the group they had to win over: married couples of white-collar workers, 35 to 50 years old, living in semi-detached (pebbledashed) suburban houses.

Non-residents of Middle England

Perhaps the surest way to identify Mr and Mrs Utterlynormal is to exclude everyone among the 50 million inhabitants of the England who they would regard as *not* being one of their own. Which means anyone who:

belongs to

.... the 'Westminster village'

.... the chattering classes

.... the royal family

.... the aristocracy

.... the landed gentry

.... the Establishment

.... the upper ranks of the civil service

.... a trade union

lives in

.... London or the Home Counties
.... sink housing estates; the lumpen proletariat
.... anywhere except suburbia or the rural-urban fringes

is

.... a single mother
.... on any state handout
.... suffering from a modern medical syndrome such as 'yuppy flu'
.... a political party activist
.... Scottish, Welsh or Irish but living in England
.... not white
.... white but foreign
.... an owner or directory of a large company
.... an upper ranking army, navy or RAF officer
.... voluntarily unemployed
.... a hippy, squatter, new age traveller, hunt saboteur, animal rights
       activist*, hoody or pacifist (including Quakers)
.... a Mormon or Jehovah's Witness
.... a local dignitary with airs and graces

works in

.... the media
.... social work
.... a comprehensive school
.... the arts in the widest sense (incl. all artists and showbiz people)

has

.... more than average inherited wealth

goes

.... on demonstrations – although a one-off demonstration on a
       'safe' single issue (such as cruelty to animals) is acceptable.
.... fox hunting (supporting fox hunting is alright*)

---

*Note: Middle England is divided about animal rights. It is against cruelty to animals, naturally, but probably pro-fox hunting because of those awful hairy people they have seen on the television protesting against it.

Middle Ways

Attempts to steer down the central reservation

For some politicians the mythical 'middle way' (or third way) is the only goal worth striving for and, by coincidence, the only way to get enough votes to attain power. To others, both right and left of centre, merely to talk of some muddled compromise is to opportunistically sell out.

Not all politicians believe in courting the centre ground but there is a common belief that this is where the swing voters in marginal seats hang out. What they want exactly, is never certain. Their mood seems ever shifting, and with it the solidity of the centre ground. (See p192)

Two warnings

> *"We know what happens to people who stay in the middle of the road. They get run down."* Aneurin Bevan

> *"... in politics the middle way is none at all."* John Adams

Churchill's call

> *"What we require now is not a period of turmoil, but a period of stability and recuperation. Let us stand together and tread a sober middle way."* Election address, 11 Nov 1922

Inter-war national governments

A crisis, particularly a war, can lead to the formation of 'a government of national unity' and a suspension of hostilities between parties in the search for co-operation against a common problem.

However, attempts to steer a middle course in the national interest usually provoke antagonism from those outside government who think it is careering off in one direction or the other. Both Lloyd George (beginning in 1916, but particularly in 1918) and Ramsay MacDonald (in 1931) thought they had hit on a winning centrist formula but found that their respective power bases slipped from underneath them.

'The Middle Way' (1938) by Harold Macmillan

The future prime minister's exposition of a Keynsian economy with social provision extending to a minimum wage (which not even Labour would talk about seriously until 50 years later) made him unpopular with die-hard laissez-faire Conservatives. Even his nanny is supposed to have concluded, "Mr Harold is a dangerous pink."

Butskellism

A consensus identified by *The Economist*, being a composite word made from the surnames of the incoming and outgoing Chancellors of the Exchequer, Butler and Gaitskell. After the war, the Labour government had created a mixed economy and a state-run system of education and health. When the Conservatives took over in 1951, they accepted this arrangement and it wasn't questioned until Margaret Thatcher came to power in 1979.

'The Third Way: Renewal of Social Democracy' (1998) by Anthony Giddens

A seminal book by the director of the London School of Economics often described as Tony Blair's "guru". New Labour sought a new third way which could build a consensus after Thatcherism and the end of Marxism.

The Third Sector

In May 2006 the government appointed a Minister for the Third Sector, the third sector being defined as "non-governmental organisations which are value-driven and which principally reinvest their surpluses to further social, environmental or cultural objectives. It includes voluntary and community organisations, charities, social enterprises, cooperatives and mutuals."

The Monarchy

10 political powers vested in the hereditary head of state

Britain is a constitutional monarchy, which means that it has a queen or king as head of state who reigns but does not rule. It would be more accurate to call the system a conventionalised monarchy, since it is precedent and force of habit rather than a written document that dictates how things are.

By custom, the monarch delegates ruling to a team of ministers drawn from parliament who are largely left to get on with things as and how they see fit. This leaves the monarch politically neutral – 'above politics' – and he or she is expected not to interfere in the workings of the government. But it would be wrong to regard the monarchy as a mere symbolic figurehead uninterested and disinterested in politics.

The British monarch has the right or power to:

1. **Vote**
    There is no legal reason why the monarch and the royal family should not vote in general and local elections like everyone else. In practice, they don't vote so as to preserve their neutrality.

2. **Order the dissolution or prorogation (suspension) of parliament**
    It is assumed that he or she will only do this on the request of the prime minister. Parliament hasn't been directly dissolved by a sovereign since 1818. Parliament is prorogued by the monarch at the end of each session.

3. **Summon and open Parliament**
    The only time when Parliament can meet without being summoned is when a monarch dies – then members are obliged by law to reassemble. In normal circumstances, the members of the House of Commons must be called to Westminster and they cannot get down to business until they have heard a speech by the monarch in the House of Lords.

4. **Nominate the prime minister**

   The winner of a general election (the leader of the majority of MPs) is, by tradition, given the top job but if the election produces a hung parliament the monarch may intervene and invite one of the party leaders to form a coalition government. This almost happened in 1974.

5. **Hold confidential meetings with the PM and other ministers**

   The Queen has met with the prime minister of the day once a week since the start of her reign. She is considered to have a constitutional right to be consulted about affairs of estate, to encourage her ministers where she sees fit or to warn them where appropriate. She hence has more direct input into the political system than any voter in Britain.

6. **Veto an act of parliament**

   The monarch must approve every act of parliament for it to become law. The Royal Assent was last withheld by Queen Anne in 1707 but the right to use it still exists.

7. **Approve decisions taken by the Privy Council**

   The Privy Council is, as the name suggests, the monarch's 'private' council and can be thought of as an unelected constitutional by-pass. It is Britain's oldest legislative assembly and is responsible for several executive and judicial functions. It has 400 appointed members although not all of them attend meetings which are held wherever the monarch happens to be. Ministers use it to issue orders and proclamations which do not have to be debated in parliament.

8. **Appoint officials**

   These include a diverse range, from members of the royal household to the governors of Britain's last colonial possessions (see p20). In practice, such appointments are normally made by or on the advice of ministers.

9. **Distribute honours and awards**

   Honours are usually made on the advice of ministers. The Queen has conferred over 387,700 during her reign and held 540 investitures. Many are, of course, for achievements unrelated to politics but there is a close, and sometimes unhealthy, relationship between politics and the honours list. It is far from being a fair and meritocratic system for rewarding efficient or honest political behaviour: many posts in government and the civil service come almost with the routine promise of a knighthood as part of the remuneration package.

10. **Exercise similar powers in the 15 other Commonwealth realms**
In many former colonies, the British monarch is head of state, an unseen presence serving much the same function as a president but in times of emergency empowered to authorise extraordinary measures by proxy. An interesting precedent was set in Australia in 1975 when an impasse in parliament led to the elected, serving prime minister being replaced by an opponent on the orders of the Governor-General, the Queen's representative as head of state. 'The Dismissal' serves as a salutary reminder of the residual powers of the monarch to resolve a constitutional crisis either in Britain or in the Antipodes.

Mouldbreaking

8 attempts to upset the party balance

Britain is, and always has been, a two-party political system with Labour and the Conservatives taking it in unequal turns to govern. This is how things are meant to be. The House of Commons is arranged for confrontation between two sides and the voting system makes it difficult for minority parties to get a look in.

While this arrangement produces, as a rule, stable governments rather than coalitions, it also effectively disenfranchises anyone who doesn't support either of the two main parties – especially when the two parties espouse very similar policies.

In frustration, and believing themselves to have significant support from the electorate, many politicians have dreamed of upsetting this cosy power-alternating system but no one has yet found a way to do it. Typically, an up-and-coming smaller party attracts protest voters during its first election who subsequently slink off back into the night whence they came.*

The only way that things could ever change would be for a small party to hold the balance of power after an indecisive election and use its influence over its dominant coalition partner to insist on the introduction of proportional representation.

The Liberal Party/Liberal Democrats

Britain's third political force was one of the big two parties until Labour rose as the voice of the working class in the early 20th century. Both of the major parties live in fear of going through the same freefall as the Liberals experienced in the election of 1924 when the party lost 118 of its 158 seats (75%).

Labour looked as if it was on the same course during the Thatcher years but the Conservatives came even closer to disaster when they dropped 171 seats in the 1997 general election – a fall of 50%.

---

* *Note to mouldbreakers*: it's easy to say what you are against, not so easy to become the protagonist. Minor parties spend their energies and money exposing weaknesses of the main parties, revealing trends in public opinion, lancing boils. Their problem is to move from pressure group to political party.

After its fall from grace, the Liberal Party limped along for the next few decades, espousing worthy policies and enjoying the freedom to speak with the frankness of those who know they won't have to form the next government. In the indecisive atmosphere of 1974, and during a pact with the Callaghan government, the Liberals smelled power but it came to nothing. Later the Liberal Party absorbed the SDP (see below), although there is still a rump of members who opted out of the merger, and who see themselves as the authentic torchbearers of British Liberalism.

Social Democratic Party (SDP)

Roy Jenkins, in his Dimbleby Lecture of 1979, called for an end to the "queasy ride on the ideological big dipper" which British politics had become. Two years later he was one of a group of disenchanted Labour MPs, the so-called 'Gang of Four' (the others being Shirley Williams, David Owen and Bill Rodgers), who set up what they hoped would be a political movement occupying the slightly-left-of-centre ground which Labour had vacated in its lurch (as they saw it) towards the extreme left. The SDP fought two elections in partnership with the Liberals but their appeal never translated into seats and they eventually merged with their allies to form the Liberal Democrats. Nevertheless, the SDP came close to breaking the mould and its leaders, far from being ostracized and cast into oblivion for their pains, all had successful subsequent careers.

UK Independence Party (UKIP)

Campaigning under the slogan "Let's get our country back" UKIP is arguably an idea born to fail as it was conceived in opposition to something rather than as a stand-alone political idea. Critics have called it a refuge for disgruntled, eurosceptic Tories. It was formed in 1993 with the aim of getting Britain to pull out of the EU but only began to draw mass support a decade later. Perhaps understandably, given its name, it had its biggest success in the European elections of 2004 when it secured 12 MEPs, although two of them subsequently declared themselves independent. It fielded 497 candidates in the 2005 general election but lost all but 45 deposits. Under a system of proportional representation, however, it would have done well and leant more credence to its claim to be Britain's fourth largest party.

Veritas

The media-loving Labour MP Robert Kilroy-Silk stood successfully as UKIP candidate for the European Parliament before announcing the formation of his own party, Veritas, at a golf club in January 2005. He did badly as a candidate in the subsequent general election, was challenged for the leadership and driven out of the party to become an independent MP. Veritas – 'the straight talking party' – continues without him but so far has not made much of a mark on British politics.

Respect

The party which goes by the acronym of 'Respect Equality Socialism Peace Environmentalism Community and Trade Unionism' was founded in 2004 in response to the numbers of people willing to demonstrate their dislike of the Labour government but unwilling or unable to do much about it through the ballot box. It could be said to have occupied what was always the traditional working-class, left-wing campaigning ground of the Labour Party until New Labour shifted towards the centre. Respect, for instance, favours renationalizing private industries and promoting comprehensive education.

Referendum Party

Founded by Sir James Goldsmith as a single-issue party to warn of the dangers of the emerging 'federal European super-state' of the EU and to call for a referendum over Britain's continuing membership, the Referendum Party fought its first and only election in 1997. It fielded a candidate in every constituency where there was not already a eurosceptic standing for one of the two main parties. It polled well but failed to win any seats. Even some of its supporters argued that it had somewhat sabotaged its own cause by depriving the Conservatives of seats and thereby boosting Tony Blair's winning majority. The Referendum Party briefly held a seat in parliament from March 1997 until the election, that of the Thatcherite ex-Conservative MP George Gardiner. Gardiner lost his seat in the general election and Goldsmith's death shortly after, in July, caused the Referendum Party to fold. Its heirs have subsequently formed a pressure group known as the Democracy Movement.

Natural Law Party

Formed in 1992 and fielding 310 candidates in that year's general election, the Natural Law Party decided not to contest the 2001 election and ceased to be a registered political party thereafter. Its source of motivation was Maharishi Mahesh Yogi's Transcendental Meditation and its aim was to align politics everywhere with the 'natural law' of the universe. Its main proposition was to form a government of national unity which would set about creating a "crime-free, problem-free, pollution-free" world and its first step once in power would have been to create a group of 7,000 'yogic flyers' to:

> "*prevent negative trends within our society, and ... protect the nation against destructive influences either within the country or coming from beyond its borders. In fact, with such a group of Yogic Flyers, Britain will hold the balance of power in the world and prevent the birth of an enemy for all nations through the ability to nourish every nation.*"

Nationalism

Nationalist parties in Scotland, Wales and Northern Ireland (and parts of England even) pose regional challenges to the two-party status quo. Elections to the Scottish Parliament in May 2007 resulted in the Scottish National Party forming the largest party in the assembly, ending the Labour Party's dominance of Scottish politics and inviting the possibility of independence for Scotland in the future.

MPs' Qualifications

To stand as an MP you must be:

✓   a British or Commonwealth citizen

✓   over 21

✓   literate – you'll have to fill in an application form

✓   numerate – you must be capable of keeping a record of your election expenses, keeping them under the maximum limit permitted and declaring them to the Electoral Commission after the election.

You must not be:

✗   a prisoner serving a sentence of more than 12 months

✗   bankrupt

✗   convicted of treason under the Forfeiture Act of 1870

✗   a civil servant or a member of a quango

✗   a member of the police force

✗   a member of the armed forces

✗   a judge

✗   a government-appointed company director

✗   convicted of an electoral offence

✗   a peer who is entitled to sit and vote in the House of Lords

✗   a bishop who is entitled to sit and vote in the House of Lords

✗   homeless: you have to provide an address on the registration form

✗   a republican, or at least not one incapable of telling a lie, as you will be required to swear to or affirm an oath of allegiance to the reigning monarch

You'll also need to:

✓   find a proposer and seconder in the constituency where you are going to stand, together with eight 'assenters' to your application.

✓   cough up £500 in cash or in the form of a banker's draft as a deposit. This gives you the right to send an electoral address to all voters in your constituency free of charge. (You can stand in more than one constituency as long as you can afford the deposits but if you are elected in both you will have to choose to serve only one.) If you get less than 5% of the votes cast in the election your deposit money is forfeited to the Treasury.

MPs' Loyalties

An MP's 12-way loyalty

> *"Most MPs are deeply ambivalent about their primary role .....
> MPs come to Westminster not as independents but as
> partisans."* Robin Cook

Who do – or *should* – MPs listen to when they cast their vote in the
House of Commons? The answer is not that easy: it comes down to
shuffling a list of allegiances into order of priority.

Self-interest
Cynics would say this is what motivates all politicians. At its noblest
it comes down to the ambition to achieve high office ostensibly to
serve the public better. At its most tawdry, it translates into looking
after personal financial interests and paying back friends.

Constituency and constituents
An MP is elected to serve a constituency but is expected to decide for
himself on issues rather than merely bear pre-approved policies to
parliament. Should he or she try to speak for all constituents, the
majority of them, disempowered minorities among them or merely
the marginal voters (while not offending hard-core supporters) who
will get him or her re-elected? What if voting on behalf of
constituents means voting against the party, or vice versa (e.g. where
a cut in public spending would increase unemployment in the
constituency)? "I have 70,000 employers," Tony Benn remarked in
1983 "That is the basic relationship."

The whip
MPs are under continual pressure to do what the party whip tells
them to. Some are habitual rebels but most know it is in their career
interests to obey. (See 'Backbench Rebellions', p11)

Sponsorship
Some MPs openly represent outside interests that have helped their
campaigns, such as trade unions or businesses whose boards they sit
on. Such interests have to be openly declared. Studies suggest,
however, that sponsors are rarely able to exert an undue influence on
an MP's voting record.

Conscience
Some MPs, especially those with a specified religion, have strong personal ethics which can dictate the way they vote, whatever a majority of their constituents think. The most extreme test case is always the abolition or retention of the death penalty.

Government
A hundred or so MPs have a major or minor involvement in government and this dictates their stance on many issues.

Pressure group pressure
Many groups outside Parliament try to exert influence over MPs and some MPs openly support certain campaigns.

The Constitution
As it is unwritten, some strict parliamentarians see it as their duty to uphold what they think is correct whenever the government tries to create a new precedent.

Party
Every MP belongs to a party but what does the party mean? Should he (or she) cleave to the views of the party as a whole (as perceived), to the constituency party which got him elected, to the parliamentary party, to the bureaucrats in party HQ, to the resolutions passed at party conference, to the promises in the manifesto for the last election, to the instructions of the party leader or to a faction which he belongs to within the party?

Ideology
An idea an MP believes in can override personalities and conditions of the day.

The national interest
Several MPs name this as their most important motivator: they claim to be thinking of what is in the long term interests of the country as a whole, whatever the short term consequences.

International interest
A few MPs aim to vote altruistically for what's best for the world or even for humanity – or at least to include this in their mental calculations.

Newspeak and Doublethink

7 steps to full fluency

(from George Orwell's *1984*)

Newspeak is the language of the Party which rules over Oceania and is designed to meet the needs of Ingsoc (English Socialism).

Its purpose is to "make all other modes of thought impossible". A heretical thought is "literally unthinkable".

Its vocabulary provides a way of expressing every meaning that a Party member will ever need "while excluding all other meanings and also the possibility of arriving at them by indirect methods".

Newspeak is based on English but includes many invented words whose purpose is "not so much to express meanings as to destroy them." Most are compound words, such as *prolefeed*: "rubbishy entertainment and spurious news which the Party handed out to the masses."

The words *honour, justice, morality, internationalism, democracy, science, religion* and countless others do not exist in Newspeak and there are no equivalents for them. A citizen of Oceania would not be able to understand any of the concepts embraced by these words.

An important concept in Newspeak is *doublethink* which is "a system of mental cheating": "the power of holding two contradictory beliefs in one's mind simultaneously, and accepting both of them."

The process of applying doublethink is at once conscious and unconscious. "To tell lies while genuinely believing them" but at the same time be aware of tampering with reality is pure doublethink, with "the lie always one leap ahead of the truth."

Thus the Party is able to deliver its three slogans without fear that anyone will question them or misunderstand them:

WAR IS PEACE

FREEDOM IS SLAVERY

IGNORANCE IS STRENGTH

Nicknames

10 alternative appellations

> *"One half of politics is beyond parody, and the other half's too dull to contemplate ... the more grotesque, larger-than-life politicians seem to be dying out. Perhaps having too much character is a liability."* Rory Bremner, *Radio Times* 2007

In families, schools, offices and regiments, nicknames are semi-affectionate substitutes for what is written on a person's birth certificate, or else a comment on his or her physical characteristics. Sometimes no one can remember how they arose.

In politics, nicknames serve a different purpose. They are invented by enemies, journalists and satirists to ridicule the bearer. They are contrived and artificial; and they must mean something. They are meant for wider public consumption, not the convenience of a closed circle of acquaintances.

The following are nicknames of prime ministers and other politicians but some were only ever used by their inventors.

Arthur Balfour	*Pretty Fanny* A nickname acquired at Eton. Later, when he had proved his political mettle: *Bloody Balfour*
David Mellor	*Minister of Fun* He was actually Secretary of State for National Heritage which included being responsible for sport and the arts.
Dennis Skinner	*The Beast of Bolsover*
Harold Macmillan	*Mac the Knife* Ultimately derived from Brecht and Gay. *Supermac* (see p36)
Harold Wilson	*The Houdini of Politics*

Herbert Asquith	*The Sledgehammer*
	Squiff/Squiffy
	When he split with Lloyd George his followers were known as *Squiffites*.
Jim Callaghan	*Sunny Jim*
Lord (Sir) Keith Joseph	*The Mad Monk* (after Rasputin)
Margaret Thatcher	The 20th century politician who has been given the most nicknames:
	The Iron Lady
	Mother (her nickname inside the Conservative Party)
	Tina (from "there is no alternative")
	That Bloody Woman
Michael Heseltine	*Tarzan*, on account of his mane of blond hair.
Neville Chamberlain	*The Coroner*
	Following a remark by Aneurin Bevan that "in the funeral service of capitalism … the cortége is now under the somber and impassive guidance of the undertaker."

Outmoded political systems

12 experiments to cross off the list

Greek City State

Pros: optimum system for small 4th century BC Hellenistic cities without bellicose neighbours.

Cons: only suitable for small 4th century BC Hellenistic cities without bellicose neighbours.

Roman Empire

Pros: I'll tell you what the Romans did for us...

Cons: encourages fiddlers and backstabbers and creates envy among barbarians.

Divine Right of Kings

Pros: the ultimate meritocracy – God decides who deserves to rule.

Cons: if you get a mad or bad king you have to depose him (but he may be back with his friends), appoint a regent (constitutionally iffy), execute him (for which you will never live down the guilt) – or do what he says.

Mongol horsepower

Pros: quick and efficient justice system; minimal bureaucracy.

Cons: here today, gone tomorrow; not tolerant of left-wing dissenters.

Byzantine Empire

Pros: excellent career structure for bureaucrats.

Cons: dismissal of emperor usually involves nose chopping, eye-gouging, horrible death or at best permanent exile. Truly unfortunate retirees may have their skulls made into drinking bowls.

Ottoman Sultanate

Pros: ruler gets a private harem without having to endure the intrusion of a tabloid press.

Cons: succession has to be ensured by killing all your sons except one.

Totalitarian communism

Pros: everyone's dacha is equal (although some are more equal than others); art can be produced just the way you like it.

Cons: have to build lots of walls and barbed wire fences; later there are rusting nuclear submarines to deal with.

Fascism

Pros: motorways get built and trains run on time; everyone gets to wear a uniform; ruler is universally loved – or else.

Cons: relies on having an unlimited supply of political enemies and ethnic and religious minorities to persecute, and countries to conquer.

One-party state

Pros: no point in rigging elections; no more arguments.

Cons: not the kind of place where you can say you've got another party to go to.

Military junta

Pros: at least you know whose side the army is on.

Cons: people disappear.

A Party League Table

The results since 1945

Team	Played	Won	Drawn	Lost	Average % of vote	Seats scored	Years in government
Con.	17	8	0	9	41.9	4,944	34yrs 8m.
Lab*	17	8	1	8	35.7	5,315	27yrs 4m.§
Lib	17	0	1	16	13.6	329	0
Other	17	0	0	0	8.8	272	0

* including 'New' formula (invented *c.* 1994)

§ to August 2007, not out

(e)Petitions

10 steps to importuning the Prime Minister online

Before the internet was invented, getting together a petition and handing it in to No. 10 Downing Street was a laborious process – and that was the whole point: the effort of amassing all those signatures and the willingness of so many people to bother signing was proof of the strength of feeling behind the cause.

Now you can compile a petition online without getting up from your desk or stopping passers-by on the street. And Downing Street, far from recoiling from the prospect of popular protest, provides the facilities.

How's that for stealing your righteous thunder?

1. Since November 2006 you have been able to create your own petition or sign an existing one at petitions.pm.gov.uk

2. The system is run for Downing Street by mySociety, a politically neutral charitable project also responsible for the website TheyWorkForYou.com

3. In the first three months 3,381 petitions were activated and 2,555,972 signatures collected from 2,110,710 signatories.

4. 1 in 6 petitions are rejected for one of several reasons, usually because they are unclearly worded or because they are too specific to certain individuals such as the one which reads:

   "End the rules of male primogeniture with regard to succession to the Earldom of Stirling via a Resettlement-by-Letters Patent to the current Lord Stirling."

   submitted by Earl of Stirling of Clan Alexander

5. There are no 'sign against' petitions because the system is not intended to be an ad hoc referendum but to mimic the conventional petitioning system. There is nothing to stop you setting up a counter petition against a proposition you disagree with.

6. If your petition is validated it stays on the site for 12 months. People signing must have a verifiable email address.

7. The first such petition to get over a million signatures was against road pricing policy. This was launched in February 2006 and by the time it closed on 20th February 2007 had 1,810,982 signatures.

8. Other popular petitions have called for:
   - the repeal of the Hunting Act 2004
   - the scrapping of plans to introduce ID cards
   - the scrapping of inheritance tax
   - the reduction of the period of classifying census data from 100 years to 70 years
   - the government not to replace Trident
   - the government to keep the teaching of creationism out of schools
   - a law to forbid companies using premium rate telephone numbers when they could use an ordinary number
   - the removal of speed cameras from Britain's roads

9. Some petitions don't attract any signatures or only one in addition to the creator.

10. The system is of course widely suspect (you could, in theory, create multiple email addresses to generate false signatures) and is not binding on the prime minister. It is a lazy, blunt way of raising a petition but perhaps it is a step in the direction of responsive democracy. It is certainly easier than standing outside a supermarket for days on end or assembling a million people with banners to march through the streets of London.

Pilgrimages

10 revolutionary routes for fellow travellers

These routes are a little harder to follow than those given in conventional travel guides since each involves a journey through time as well as space.

Route 1: Northern Pride

Start: Jarrow, County Durham on 4 Oct 1936
Finish: Marble Arch, London on 31 October 1936
Mode of travel: not by ship

Northerners rarely make incursions into the cosy political life of the capital but in 1936 a mass march from Newcastle came to protest at the closing of a shipyard and the 70% unemployment caused. Prime Minister Stanley Baldwin refused to see the marchers and wasn't much interested in the petition they handed in. Modern Jarrow, a suburb of Newcastle, is home of the tourist attraction formerly called the Venerable Bede and at the heart of what job-creators might dub 'Call Centre Country' but still seems as far from London as it did in 1936.

Route 2: Two Different Ways to Get to the Same Place

This route has a choice of starting points:

Start 1: 1 North Parade, Great North Road, Grantham, Lincolnshire on 13 October 1925
Start 2: Pantry Street, Worsborough Dale (south of Barnsley), West Riding of Yorkshire on 11 January 1938
Finish: Congress House in London on 3 March 1985
Mode of travel: on your bike

Margaret Thatcher was born and lived her early years in the flat above her family's grocery shop in the centre of Grantham. Her father, alderman and lay preacher Alfred Roberts, taught her the importance of individual responsibility and individual effort leading to individual reward. It can't have been easy for her to empathise with the experience of Britain's coal miners who had been a thorn in the side of almost every government since trade unions were first organised but who she knew she would have to face down to in order to pursue her policy of liberalising markets.

In the 1980s, the National Union of Mineworkers (NUM) was led by **Arthur Scargill**, son of a devout Communist miner, who had grown up in industrial West Yorkshire to believe in the virtues of community solidarity as the only way to stand up to the bosses (and Conservative governments).

When Margaret Thatcher became Prime Minister in 1979, two world views were set on a collision course and finally collided in 1984 when the year-long miners' strike started (see p298). After a bitter and violent dispute, and the vilification of Scargill in the mainstream press, the NUM was forced to concede defeat in March 1985. Thereafter, the Thatcher government had the upper hand in its relations with the unions.

Route 3: A Night to Remember or to Forget

Start: Pourtbou, Catalonia, February 1939
Finish: Enfield Southgate constituency election count, night of 1 May 1997
Mode of travel: ambition

Luis Gabriel Portillo was a lecturer in law at the University of Salamanca when the Spanish Civil War broke out in 1936. He joined the Republican cause and served in the peripatetic ministry of justice as it retreated first to Valencia and then Barcelona. No one with an official position in the defeated government wanted to stay behind as Franco took over the country, and Portillo joined the exodus over the border into France. He settled in England, married and 14 years later had a son who not only grew up to be a Conservative politician but was anointed to take over the mantle of Thatcher amid the ruins of the Major government. The electoral defeat of Michael Portillo junior in the early hours of 2 May 1997 has come to symbolise the transition point from one kind of Britain to another.

Route 4: Sovereignty Special

Start: Palazzo dei Conservatori, Piazza del Campidoglio, Rome on 25 March 1957
Finish: Maastricht, Limburg, Netherlands on 7 February 1992
Mode of travel: gravy train

The European Union was born when the heads of six nations signed the precognitively blank Treaty of Rome in 1957 – only the front and back page had been printed. It was an economic agreement but those who had devised it knew that it was the first step towards a future political union. That dreamed-of integration seemed to become a reality with the signing of the Maastricht Treaty in 1992. Get from Rome to Milan's handsome Mussolini-built station, and you can catch a handy train, the Vauban, that crawls around the perimeter of France via Strasbourg (home of the Europarliament) and Luxembourg (home of the European Court of Justice and other EU institutions). Change in Brussels for Maastricht or hang around and get yourself a cushy job.

Route 5: A Conventional Circle

Start: Winter Gardens, Blackpool, October 1977
Finish: the same, 24 years later, almost to the day (as if you'd never left)
Mode of travel: door to door, handing out leaflets, smiling, patting babies heads etc.

William Hague famously gave his first speech to a Conservative Party conference at the age of 16, winning the admiration of Margaret Thatcher. In October 2000, he spoke to the Party (and the country) at Bournemouth as its leader but failed to win over voters for the election held in June 2001. He resigned immediately the result was known and appeared back at his starting point 24 years later, almost to the day, having passed the leadership on to Iain Duncan Smith who would be equally unsuccessful.

Route 6: The Social Democratic Shuffle

Start: Narrow Street, Limehouse E14 on 25 January 1981
Finish: Upper Street, Islington N1 in late May 1994
Mode of travel: swimming with the incoming tide (you hope)

The starting point is the house of Dr David Owen where the formation and aims of the Social Democratic Party were announced in the 'Limehouse Declaration' (appealing for a new start for British politics and a classless, more equal society). The SDP failed to establish itself as an alternative to the Labour Party during the 1980s and Labour simultaneously failed to get itself out of its trough of opposition.

Things only began to change when two men met over a meal at Granita restaurant in Islington shortly after the sudden death of the Labour leader John Smith on 12 May 1994. Between them, apparently, Tony Blair and Gordon Brown hatched a deal or 'fairness agenda' whereby each would achieve his ambition to be prime minister.

Although the SDP had long since merged with the Liberal Party, its spirit was resurrected in New Labour.

Route 7: On Murdoch Mile

Start: Fleet Street on 24 January 1986
Finish: 'Fortress Wapping' at clocking-on time the next morning
Mode of travel: midnight flit

Buoyed by the government's defeat of the miners the year before, and by new legislation restricting strike action, Rupert Murdoch decided to take on the print unions that had come to dictate working conditions in Fleet Street. He secretly prepared a factory in Wapping with new technology and waited for a pretext to shift production there. When the printers went on strike after protracted negotiations, Murdoch gave his staff an ultimatum to move east under new contracts or find new jobs. Printers and journalists who didn't want to accept the terms besieged 'Fortress Wapping' for the following year but the balance of industrial relations power had shifted against them and the fight was lost.

Route 8: Thrice Lord Mayor

Start: County Hall on 31 March 1986
Finish: City Hall (further down the Thames, near Tower Bridge) on 4 May 2000
Mode of travel: On foot along the South Bank

It took Ken Livingstone 14 years to move house, from being leader of the Greater London Council to being appointed the first mayor of London. Between 1986 and 2000 a lot of politically polluted water flowed down the Thames. Livingstone has managed the unique feat of being reviled by the Thatcher government and dismissed with scorn by the leadership of New Labour, and yet winning respect from most Londoners. Having been a kind of mayor for the city until 1986 and an official one from 2000, he was elected in 2004.

Route 9: A Recommended Career Map

Start: Eton College, Windsor (Berkshire) from the age of 13 (boys only; put your name down as soon as you are born; ask a grown up to make a cheque out for £24,990 per year)

Finish: Downing Street in about 40 years time

Mode of travel: luxury elevator from an upper floor to the highest floor

This express career route – why bother with any other? – calls at Oxford – where you'll probably want to be President of the Union and might want to join the Bullingdon Club if only for the connections you will make – Conservative Party headquarters (to get allocated a safe seat), Westminster (for as brief a time as possible on the backbenches) and Whitehall. If you're lucky with the constituency you are given you will barely have to leave the Home Counties in your life. Most travellers who come this way only get to ministerial office but mustn't grumble.

Route 10: Getting Away from It All

Start: Downing Street, on the evening of 25 October 1962 (or sometimes in the near future?)

Finish: 100ft beneath Corsham limestone quarry, Wiltshire in the early hours of the morning

Mode of travel: classified until the last minute. Either military helicopter or in deathly-silent motorcade leaving London by stealth.

Should you find yourself prime minister, or an essential member of the government, when nuclear war is judged imminent by the White House (such as might have happened in the middle of the Cuban Missile Crisis) you will be whisked to a bunker somewhere, safe from the rain of weaponry which is about to vaporise at least a third of the British population. Underground you will join 6,000 other lucky winners of the lottery of political life and live a weirdly restricted existence for 90 days before having the chance to experience a nuclear winter first hand. Today, the Corsham bunker is disused but the government must have somewhere similar lined up to go. If any communications system is still functioning on the intoxicated morning after, the prime minister will be in charge of four redundant nuclear submarines which were supposed to serve as a deterrent. For the rest of us it will be the end of politics as we know it – and of travel for some time to come.

Plays

10 dramatic discourses on political themes

> *"The greatest films are those which show how society shapes man. The greatest plays are those which show how man shapes society."* Kenneth Tynan

> *"I, as a Socialist, have had to preach, as much as anyone, the enormous power of the environment. We can change it; we must change it; there is absolutely no other sense in life than the task of changing it. What is the use of writing plays, what is the use of writing anything, if there is not a will which finally moulds chaos itself into a race of gods."* George Bernard Shaw

Before film and television, the theatre was the only place to bring politics alive for an audience and it still offers an immediacy which the other two media cannot match.

The Acharnians by Aristophanes (425BC)
An anti-war satire which ridicules the Athenian establishment of the day. This and his other plays are open to various political interpretations.

An Enemy of the People (or A Public Enemy) by Henrik Ibsen (1882)
Ibsen was never afraid to upset convention and ask awkward questions. He explained the idea underpinning this play in a letter: "Never in any circumstances shall I be able to belong to a party that has the majority on its side…The minority is always right – this is to say, the minority that is leading the way towards some point at which the majority has not yet arrived."

Saint Joan by George Bernard Shaw
A mature, complex work, some would say masterpiece, by a literary figure who had strong views and often expressed them. Shaw was a Fabian socialist who was involved in the formation of the Labour Party, a pacifist and an apologist for Stalin's Russia (although Stalin didn't think much of him). None of his plays is overtly political – he was too good an artist to write mere agitprop – but many are suffused with the political experiences of individuals in the wider sense. Saint Joan looks at the fate of Joan of Arc in the hands of the Church and the Law and how people acting from what they sincerely

believe to be honorable motives can put a woman to death for promoting visionary ideas. Shaw's thoughts on politics are set down frankly in his prose writing, such as *The Intelligent Woman's Guide to Socialism and Capitalism* (1928) and *Everybody's Political What's What?* (1944).

The Threepenny Opera by Bertolt Brecht (1928)

One of the earliest and probably best known of Brecht's works – all of which are strongly political – which was written before he was driven out of his native Germany by the Nazis. It looks at the perennial themes of Brecht's theatre: class inequality, property as a form of theft and social exclusion.

Les Mains Sales (Dirty Hands) by Jean-Paul Sartre (1948)

Sartre's play was criticised by both left and right at the time of its first production because it exposed the messy nature of all politics. It explores the interface between the personal and political and whether expediency or truth is the more important guide to action.

The Crucible by Arthur Miller (1952)

Miller uses the 1692 witch trials in Salem, Massachusetts, as an allegory for McCarthyism (1948-1956). Transcending polemic, it draws universal conclusions about how any campaign of persecution can – or does inevitably? – become detached from reality.

Look Back in Anger by John Osborne (1958)

The play that created the 'angry young man' and shocked audiences with its realism. Indicative of a new post-war political mood, the embittered central character is driven by an instinctive rejection of authority and a frustration that there are no longer any causes worth fighting for.

A Man for All Seasons by Robert Bolt (1960, filmed in 1966)

A dramatisation of Sir Thomas More's refusal to endorse the divorce plans of Henry VIII. Bolt shows what happens when an individual's conscience comes up against authority which will do or say whatever is needed to get its way.

Death and the Maiden by Ariel Dorfman (La Muerte y La Doncella, 1991, filmed by Roman Polanski in 1994)

A former political prisoner meets the man who she believes raped her under a now-fallen repressive regime. Is it really him? And what should she do if he is unwilling to confess his guilt and repent?

Stuff Happens by David Hare (2004)

Britain's most stridently political living playwright takes on the causes of the Iraq war. The play is unusual in that it attacks real, still-serving politicians for real, still-controversial events, and thus comes as close to being agitprop as British theatre ever does. Hare is one of the few prominent political figures to call publicly for the abolition of the monarchy.

P

Prime Minister: Qualifications

Have you got what it takes? Take this self-assessment test to see if you are the next PM

> *"More than any other position of eminence, that of Prime Minister is filled by fluke."*
>
> Enoch Powell

In theory, anyone in Britain could grow up to be prime minister. In practice, it's not that easy.

To have a chance you have to join one of the two main political parties, improving your odds from 1 in 60 million to 1 in 500,000. But more than being a member you'll need to be active and make your face known – a process which eliminates:

- ⊘ introverts
- ⊘ full-time carers
- ⊘ people on low pay
- ⊘ most single parents

Your next steps are to get selected for a safe parliamentary seat, stand as an MP (having complied with the various criteria, for which – see pp224-230) and get yourself elected.

Your only remaining hurdle is to become leader of your party, which will give you a 1 in 2 chance of becoming prime minister if you make it to a general election and can stop your colleagues tearing each other to pieces in public over policies they can't agree on.

But before you do any of the above you'd be wise to read the job requirements below – it might save you a lot of wasted time and tears. There is a set of unofficial minimum conditions for the post of prime minister which only a few people in Britain fulfil. In fact, only one person in Britain fulfils them all.

According to C. Northcote Parkinson, a job advert should be written to attract only one candidate – the right one. This is the checklist that party whips and spin doctors use to make sure they have chosen the next man who will be king.

Minimum Requirements (preliminary stage)

CAREER REQUIREMENTS	# of potential candidates
You must be an MP for either the Conservative or the Labour Party. If you can't sign up to the doctrines of one or the other, you are automatically ineligible. If you pass this first test you are one of 533 people who have been shortlisted by central party machineries and local selection committees stuffed with self-important people, but most of all by their own self-confidence or talent for self-deception.	533
You must have been a party member and an MP long enough to convince influential people that you are committed to the long term. You'll need to be a veteran of at least two general elections. It is probably safe to knock out a token 20%, or 106 candidates, on grounds of potential fugacity.	427
You'll need enough political friends to vote for you or at least enough people who don't particularly dislike you and see you as the least offensive choice. A damaging remark from one of your colleagues could finish your candidacy. Deduct 10% of MPs with a grudge held against them or an unresolved feud.	385
You must have an untarnished reputation. Although experience of office is desirable it can be a liability if you have been associated with any controversial policies in the past. A few years in opposition is a good way to keep a positive political virginity. Deduct 10 ex-ministers who have been around so long they have gone past their sell-by date.	375

P

PHYSICAL ATTRIBUTES	# of potential candidates

You mustn't be too young or too old. The minimum age is 43 (possibly negotiable by a year or two); and the absolute maximum age is 77 at the next general election – but these days anyone over 60 looks old. 10% of Labour MPs and 17% of Conservative MPs are under 40 so we can eliminate about 50 candidates on grounds of youth. 19% and 18% respectively are over 60 so we must tactfully ask 58 MPs whether they should be thinking of retiring instead of running a country.   267

You must be male. The chances of a woman candidate getting through to the final round of a PM ballot are slim, although there has been one famous exception – just one. The safest assumption is that 20% of MPs will be tacitly disqualified because of their gender.   214

You must be white. There are very few non-white MPs – just 15 in both major parties – and we might have eliminated them all by now. But just to round things down…   210

You must be in a reasonable state of physical and mental fitness. No one disabled has yet made it to be prime minister. Any story of mental illness will be picked up on by the whips when you first enter parliament. And anyone perpetually wheezing, limping or snoozing just wouldn't be taken seriously. We can't know how many MPs would fail a medical exam but we're probably underestimating if we eliminate 40 candidates.   170

You'll need a good head of hair. Churchill was the last bald man to be elected and only then because of an extenuating war record. Who knows how many men are too bald to be prime minister? Another 10% of the target age group seems a generous assumption.   153

BACKGROUND AND EDUCATION   *# of potential
candidates*

You must be middle class even if you were born working   149
class. The job of an MP is, by definition, middle class so it
is impossible to put yourself forward for leader of a party if
you are lumpen proletariat. Until the end of the 19th
century, being an aristocrat was a prerequisite of the job;
since the demise of Alec Douglas-Home, however, it has
been assumed that being upper class is the kiss of death to
a candidacy. Middle England wants someone it can talk to.
Let's assume two more candidates drop out for trying to
insist that they are still working class; and two more for the
aura of snobbery and privilege that hangs around them.

You must be educated, neither over- nor under-...   149
Surprisingly, you can be self-taught and still become prime
minister, as long as you fulfil all the other requirements.
You cannot, however, be wholly uneducated and uncouth.
An Eton education has looked good on a CV in the past but
some people regard it as a disadvantage in these days of
supposedly classless Britain. On average a university
education will give you a better chance but it is not essential
to have a degree.

...but certainly not intellectual. If you like to read and   135
think, keep it to yourself or you'll go the same way as
Michael Foot. As Frank Zappa said (in another context)
"Don't ever let them know that you're smart/ the universe
is no place to start." We need to remove the 10% most
brainy people left in the race.

You must be at least mildly religious, best of all a   130
Protestant. There is no constitutional faith requirement but
Britain has never had a Catholic prime minister and only
one Jewish prime minister. The Prime Minister advises the
Monarch on the appointment of Church of England bishops

and it would be hard to do this unless you were at least nominally Protestant (71% of the population). Discreet agnostic views are acceptable; atheism is not. Let's assume that 5 more candidates drop out for questions of conscience.

SEXUALITY & MARITAL STATUS   *# of potential*
                                                       candidates

You must be heterosexual. Britain has never had an openly   117
homosexual or bisexual prime minister. 5% of men and 1%
of women in Britain are estimated to be exclusively
homosexual, athough 13% consider themselves bisexual
with a strong "preference" for homosexuality. If we take
off 10% to allow for non-vote-catching sexual orientation
we're probably safe: 13 candidates (whether out of or still
in the closet) need not apply. *Note:* sexual ambiguity may
be acceptable but only if you can keep it ambiguous.

Preference will be given to candidates who are married   59
with a family... There's an outside chance of a bachelor
making it in the absence of anyone better – Heath managed
it – but in these media-intrusive days, it is better to have a
family or journalists will never stop speculating whether
you are – see above. Single parents and divorcees are
almost certain to be rejected – imagine an MP having to put
off a summit meeting because "it's my turn with the kids
this weekend." 50.7% of the population are married so let's
assume 58 of our candidates fail this test.

...and that means *faithfully* married. There mustn't be   54
any adultery or deviant sexual practices behind your
bedroom door – unless you are sure they won't be made
public until after you've left office. Westminster is
notorious for adultery: long, anti-social hours away from
home and the availability of young female staff mean that
at least 10% of candidates will have an infidelity to hide.

DISQUALIFICATIONS	*# of potential candidates*

You must not have a drink or drugs problem or any other personal vice (unless you can keep it hidden). The whips will make sure another 5% don't put their names forward. Youthful experimentation is probably acceptable these days and might even increase your appeal to younger voters. But anything blackmailable in your history means instant disqualification.

52

You must not hold any extreme political views. You must not, for instance, have been critical of the USA at any time in the recent past. You will need to be mildly pro-European but the less you say about the EU in your speeches the better. You'll need to be able to convince a majority of your party that you share their views on a majority of subjects. Deduct, say, 5 MPs with big mouths.

47

You cannot be a declared republican as you will have regular dealings with the monarch of the day and exercise power on his/her behalf. Perhaps 5 candidates will have a sycophancy shortfall.

42

You mustn't have any other undesirable baggage. If you are or have been associated with any particular vested interest group (e.g. a private company or any contentious pressure group) its opponents will undermine your candidacy. You may have had a profession before you went into politics but it should have been brief and uncontroversial. You certainly shouldn't have ever had any dodgy business dealings which could return to haunt you. Your spouse, children and immediate family should be similarly free of scandal – at least until after you become prime minister. Remove 5 more candidates for past lapses in judgement.

37

TALENTS	*# of potential candidates*

Gift of the gab. This can be taught to some extent but you must have a natural talent for making speeches to large and small audiences and always saying something that fits the occasion in public and in private conversations. Quiet men should not apply. You must sound like you use words like "moral, responsibility, unity, purpose, caring, compassion, tough" all the time. An ability to make people think you have said something significant when you have said nothing at all will guarantee you the post. If you stumble or misuse the English language, or come across incoherent during interviews, deduct yourself from the race. You must be able to lie convincingly in the national interest. Take away ten tongue-tied contestants.   **27**

The media must love you. You've either got charisma or you haven't, however good your political skills, and a desperate party will put the charm factor above all other considerations. If you can smile a lot and look sincere – whether you are or not doesn't matter – and don't fall down on any of the above points, you've got the leadership in the bag. Being dour but effective may be considered a handicap. A quaint, photographable pastime like playing the guitar (but not reading books – see above) will be of help. Charm can even distinguish between the last two candidates in a party leadership race. The clinching factor in David Cameron's victory over David Davis in the Conservative Party leadership election was the latter's 'poor' performance at the party conference as judged by journalists.   **4**

FINAL CONSIDERATIONS	*# of potential candidates*
You must (of course) **want the job.** And you must want it badly enough to say and do what it takes to get it. You'll need to be scheming and ruthless even if you "allow" your friends to put your name forward. Appearing hard to get or indifferent to the honour being offered you by the party can kill off your chances even if your CV is impeccable. Just to become leader you are going to make a lot of enemies and you will need to know how to placate them. As prime minister you will lose most of your friends and may be loathed by most people in the country. In Downing Street you will age rapidly as you realise the limits to your power, what secrets the state withholds from the public, what it means to send troops to possible death and so on, Probably no more than half of our potential candidates will want to put their names forward for a job that makes high demands in return for high status.	2
Finally, **the electorate must like you** or dislike you less than it dislikes the other man.	1

NUMBER OF QUALIFYING CANDIDATES   **1**

Note: All this is just to get into No. 10. You might be the perfect candidate for the job but turn out to be no good at it; then people are really going to hate you.

Prime Ministerial Curiosities

10 facts about particular or peculiar prime ministers

- *Palmerston* and his wife were renowned for their unpunctuality. He even made Queen Victoria late for dinner and it was said of them that "the Palmerstons always miss the soup."

- *The Earl of Rosebery* suffered from insomnia and in an attempt to lull himself to sleep would ride around London during the night in a primrose-coloured carriage.

- One theory for the origination of the phrase "Bob's Your Uncle" is that the *Marquess of Salisbury*, Robert Gasgoyne-Cecil, gave his nephew a job in his government.

- *Arthur Balfour* inherited £1 million when he turned 21, making him one of the wealthiest young men in Britain at the time.

- *Churchill* was born in a ladies toilet in Blenheim Palace in 1874, having arrived prematurely while his mother was at a dance.

- *The Earl of Aberdeen* bought a sculpted foot of Hercules from the Parthenon in Athens and had it brought home. Its present whereabouts is unknown.

- *John Major's* father worked in an itinerant troupe of variety performers which toured the music halls of Britain.

- *Ramsay Macdonald* liked to consult a medium after the death of his wife Margaret. He supposedly received messages from her and sometimes replied.

- *Earl Grey* gave his name to a distinctive blend of tea which is flavoured with bergamot oil.

- *Perceval's* recreations included studying Biblical prophecy.

Prime Ministers by 3s, 4s, 5s and 6s

4 curious but inconsequential coincidences

3 prime ministers who had American mothers

Churchill, Macmillan and Grafton

4 prime ministers who fought duels (duelling was outlawed in the 1840s)

Earl of Shelburne in Hyde Park on 22 March 1780, before he became prime minister. He was injured in the groin.

William Pitt the Younger on Putney Heath on 27 March 1798 against a fellow MP.

Canning on Putney Heath on 21 September 1809 against Castlereagh, who he was trying to have removed from the government. Canning had never fired a pistol before and missed his mark. Castlereagh shot him in the thigh. There was outrage that a rivalry within the Cabinet should be settled in this fashion. Both men stood down from office after the incident and the ill-fated Spencer Percival became prime minister.

Wellington in Battersea Park on 21 March 1829. Wellington was accused by the 10th Earl of Winchelsea of double dealing over Catholic emancipation legislation, a charge which enraged the Duke. Wellington fired at his opponent's legs and (deliberately?) missed. Winchelsea then fired into the air and apologised.

5 prime ministers who had four administrations apiece

Gladstone – Salisbury – Asquith – MacDonald – Baldwin

6 pairs of prime ministers who had the same birthday

Addington and Asquith (15 February)
Chatham and Perceval (11 May)
Wilmington and Peel (2 July)
Portland and Bonar Law (30 October)
MacDonald and Chamberlain (9 November)
Aberdeen and Baldwin (14 December)

Prime Ministerial Firsts

10 pioneering achievements

1. The **first person to hold the office** of prime minister was Sir Robert Walpole who was appointed in 1721.

2. Disraeli was Britain's first, and so far only, **Jewish** Prime Minister

3. Balfour was the first PM to **own a car**.

4. Campbell-Bannerman was the **only PM to die in office** and in 10 Downing Street (in 1808), a place he once described as a "rotten old barrack of a house".

5. Andrew Bonar Law was the first and only PM to have been **born outside Britain**.

6. When Chamberlain flew to Germany for his meeting with Hitler in 1938 it was the **first time he'd been on a plane**.

7. Margaret Thatcher was the **first and only woman** prime minister.

8. Tony Blair was the first prime minister to **have a child while in office**: Leo Blair was born on 20th May 2000.

9. Tony Blair was the first prime minister to be **questioned by police** (in 2007) about a criminal offence: the accusation that the Labour government had been giving out honours in return for cash donations. (Lloyd George was also caught up in an honours scandal – see p29.)

10. Alec Douglas Home was the first PM born in the 20th century and the **first and only peer to renounce his title** in order to sit in the Commons – by convention during the 20th century it became unacceptable for a prime minister to sit in the House of Lords.

Prime Ministerial Superlatives

5 lists of records not strictly to do with politics

The youngest prime ministers (age on taking office)

William Pitt the Younger	24
Duke of Grafton	33
Marquess of Rockingham	35
Duke of Devonshire	36
Lord North	37

Youngest prime minister of the 20th century

Tony Blair, 43, the youngest since the Earl of Liverpool in 1812, who was 42.

Shortest periods in office

George Canning	119 days (became prime minister 10th April 1827, died of pneumonia 8th August)
Viscount Goderich	130 days (1827-8)
Bonar Law	209 days (1922-3), shortest of the 20th C.
Duke of Devonshire	225 days (1756–7)

Longest periods in office

Sir Robert Walpole	20 years, 314 days (1721-42)
William Pitt the Younger	18 years, 343 days (1783–1801 and 1804–6)
Earl of Liverpool	14 years, 305 days (1812-27)
Lord North	12 years, 58 days (1770-82)
Margaret Thatcher	11 years, 209 days (1979–90), the longest tenure in 200 years
Tony Blair	10 years, 57 days (May 1997 to June 2007)

Prime Ministers who had the most children

Earl Grey	17
Grafton	16
Perceval	12
Bute	11
Lord Grenville	9

Prime Ministers' Names

26 good names for a boy and one for a girl

These days we're used to thinking of the premier as one of us, an ordinary bloke with an abbreviated Christian name which, we suppose, he uses down the pub. In the past, prime ministers weren't so pally. Many were aristocrats who were known in their lifetimes – and who are known to history – only by their titles. But each of them still has a name by which he was called in the nursery or by his mother, father and siblings. These are the prime ministers of Great Britain, in order, by their given names. Statistically, the name *William* gives you the best chance of becoming prime minister (there have been eight of them, ahead of four *Henrys* and four *Roberts*).

Robert	*Charles*	*Anthony*
Spencer	*William*	*Harold*
Henry	*Robert*	*Alec*
Thomas	*John*	*Harold*
William	*Edward*	*Ted (Edward)*
John	*George*	*Jim (James)*
George	*Henry*	*Margaret*
Charles	*Benjamin*	*John*
William	*William*	*Tony (Anthony)*
Augustus	*Robert*	*Gordon*
Frederick	*Archibald*	
William	*Arthur*	
William	*Henry*	
William	*Herbert*	
Henry	*David*	
William	*Andrew*	
Spencer	*Stanley*	
Robert	*Ramsay* (first name James)	
George	*Neville* (first name Arthur)	
Frederick	*Winston*	
Arthur	*Clement*	

Prime Ministerial Success

The 20 most successful premiers

In 2004, the *Political Studies Association* commissioned MORI to carry out a survey into the views of 139 experts and academics specializing in politics or modern British history to find out which prime ministers of the 20th century (up to Tony Blair) had achieved the most and the least in their tenures of office. The results, in descending order of efficacy, were as follows:

1.	Clement Attlee	Labour	1945-51
2.	Winston Churchill	Conservative	1940-45, 51-55
3.	David Lloyd George	Liberal	1916-22
4.	Margaret Thatcher	Conservative	1979-90
5.	Harold Macmillan	Conservative	1957-63
6.	Tony Blair	Labour	1997-2007
7.	Herbert Asquith	Liberal	1908-16
8.	Stanley Baldwin	Conservative	1923-24, 24-29, 35-37
9.	Harold Wilson	Labour	1964-70, 74-76
10.	Lord Salisbury	Conservative	1895-1902
11.	Henry Campbell-Bannerman	Liberal	1906-8
12.	James Callaghan	Labour	1976-79
13.	Edward Heath	Conservative	1970-74
14.	Ramsay MacDonald	Labour	1924, 1929-31, 31-35
15.	John Major	Conservative	1990-97
16.	Andrew Bonar Law	Conservative	1922-23
17.	Neville Chamberlain	Conservative	1937-40
18.	Arthur Balfour	Conservative	1902-05
19.	Alec Douglas-Home	Conservative	1963-64
20.	Anthony Eden	Conservative	1955-57

Attlee came out on top because of his welfare state reforms and the creation of the NHS which built the postwar consensus that would last until the reign of Margaret Thatcher. Churchill and Lloyd George both rank highly because of their wartime leadership.

Margaret Thatcher and Tony Blair polarized opinions, attracting some of the best and worst scores – academics, too, have their poltical allegiances – but both still come high up the chart.

Chamberlain, tainted with the policy of appeasement, comes near the bottom but is beaten in disgrace by Balfour who was defeated in an election landslide, Douglas-Home who was probably a capable man at the wrong time, and Eden whose reputation went down with the Suez crisis.

Respondents to the survey said that the main ingredients of a successful premiership were, in descending order of importance:

Quality	nominated by % of respondents
leadership skills	64%
sound judgement	42%
good in a crisis	24%
luck	23%
decisiveness	23%
stable parliamentary majority	18%
good quality colleagues	18%
understands the problems facing Britain	16%
integrity	11%
practises Cabinet government	10%
charisma	9%
in touch with ordinary people	8%
ruthlessness	6%
poor state of the opposition	5%
strong convictions / ideology	4%
high-level ministerial experience	3%
understands world problems	2%
understands economics	1%
down-to-earth	1%
honesty	1%

Prime Ministerial Psychology

A clue to their motivation

> *"He is a man suffering from petrified adolescence."*
> Aneurin Bevan on Churchill (attrib.)

In The Fiery Chariot: A Study of British Prime Ministers and the Search for Love (1970) Lucille Iremonger examined the family backgrounds of British prime ministers between 1809 and 1937 to see if she could discern any particular pattern that might explain their motivations to succeed in politics. Remarkably, she discovered that 15 of the 24 prime ministers who served during that period had lost one or both parents when they were children: 62% compared with a modern day average of 1% of adults.

Jeremy Paxman, in *The Political Animal* was so intrigued by Iremonger's findings that he extended the research to the present day. He concluded: "There were fifty-one Prime Ministers from Sir Robert Walpole to Tony Blair. Twenty-four – almost half the total number – had lost their fathers before they reached the age of twenty-one."

The broader characteristics which Lucille Iremonger identified among prime ministers were: a childhood deprived of affection, unusual sensitivity, an outstanding mentor, extreme self-discipline, an overdeveloped religious sense, aggression and timidity, and overdependence on the love of others.

Date*	Name of PM	Parental death
1809	Spencer Perceval	8 when father died
1812	Earl of Liverpool	one month when mother died
1827	George Canning	1 when father died
1827	Viscount Goderich	4 when father died
1828	Duke of Wellington	12 when father died
1830	Earl Grey	
1834	William Lamb, Viscount Melbourne	

* date when they became prime minister

1834	Sir Robert Peel	15 when mother died
1846	Lord John Russell	9 when mother died
1852	Earl of Derby	
1852	Earl of Aberdeen	7 when father died, 11 when mother died
1855	Viscount Palmerston	
1868	Benjamin Disraeli	
1868	William Gladstone	
1885	Lord Salisbury	9 when mother died
1894	Earl of Rosebery	3 when father died
1902	Arthur Balfour	7 when father died
1905	Henry Campbell-Bannerman	
1908	Herbert Asquith	7 when father killed in cricket accident
1916	David Lloyd George	17 months when father died
1922	Andrew Bonar Law	2 when mother died
1923	Stanley Baldwin	
1924	James Ramsay MacDonald	
1937	Neville Chamberlain	6 when mother died
1940	Winston Churchill	driven by father's death at 45
1945	Clement Attlee	
1955	Anthony Eden	lost father as a teenager
1957	Harold Macmillan	
1963	Alec Douglas-Home	
1964	Harold Wilson	
1976	James Callaghan	9 when father died
1979	Margaret Thatcher	
1990	John Major	18 when father died
1997	Tony Blair	11 when father had serious stroke

Prime Ministers: In and Out of Office

"A halo only has to slip nine inches to become a noose."
                              Iain Macleod on political careers

A total of 52 prime ministers have occupied 10 Downing Street, 20 since 1900.

Only two PMs in modern times have retired at their own chosen time and in their own chosen way: Harold Wilson in 1976 and Tony Blair in 2007. Churchill almost managed it but in the end he had to give way because he was petering out mentally and physically and everyone knew it.

The table opposite shows how the last 24 prime ministers were prompted to call for the removal van.

Key	
◔	retired after losing election
♥	pushed out by own party
↻	election defeat but he'd be back
⌂	voluntary retirement
✚	retired through ill health
☠	died in office

---

*After 1918, David Lloyd George was a coalition PM, not a Liberal MP.

**Ramsay MacDonald was leader of a coalition not a Labour government from 1931

Leader	Party	Term	Age first PM	Time in office	Reason resignation
Balfour	Con	1902-1905	53	3 yrs, 145 days	⊘
Campbell-B	Lib	1905-08	69	2 yrs, 122 days	☠
Asquith	Lib	1908-16	55	8 yrs, 244 days	☝
Lloyd George*	Lib	1916-22	53	5 yrs, 317 days	☝
Bonar Law	Con	1922-23	64	209 days	✚
Baldwin I	Con	1923-24	55	7 yrs, 82 days	⊘
Macdonald I	Lab	1924 briefly	57	6 yrs, 289 days	⊘
Baldwin II	Con	1924-29			⊘
Macdonald II**		1929-31 & 1931–35§			☝
Baldwin III		1935-37			⚓
Chamberlain	Con	1937-40	68	2 yrs, 348 days	⊘
Churchill I	Con	1940-45	65	8 yrs, 240 days	↻
Attlee	Lab	1945–51	63	6 yrs, 92 days	⊘
Churchill II		1951–55			⊘
Eden	Con	1955–57	57	1 year, 279 days	✚
Macmillan	Con	1957–63	62	6 yrs, 281 days	✚
Douglas-Home	Con	1963-64	60	362 days	⊘
Wilson I	Lab	1964-70	48	7 yrs, 279 days	⚓
Heath	Con	1970–74	53	3 yrs, 259 days	⊘
Wilson II		1974-76			↻
Callaghan	Lab	1976-79	64	3 yrs, 29 days	⊘
Thatcher	Con	1979-90	53	11 yrs, 209 days	⊘
Major	Con	1990-97	47	6 yrs, 154 days	⊘
Blair	Lab	1997–2007	43	10 yrs, 57 days	⚓

Prime Ministers: Birth, Background, Education and First Job

It may seem a bit gauche to ask a prime minister what he did for a living before climbing to the top of the greasy pole, but why not?

Key: O = only child   B=bachelor   2x= married twice

Leader	Born in	Father	Education	Previously	Other
Balfour	Scotland	MP	Eton and Cambridge	Philosopher	B
Campbell Bannerman	Scotland	Lord Provost	Glasgow High School, Glasgow Univ. Cambridge	Warehouse-man and draper	
Asquith	Yorkshire	Clothing manuf.	City of London School and Oxford	Barrister	2x
Lloyd George	Manchester*	Teacher & farmer	Village school, self-taught	Solicitor	2x
Bonar Law	Canada	Clergyman	Glasgow High School	Banker then iron merchant	
Baldwin	Worcs.	Industrialist	Harrow and Cambridge	Finance Dir. in family ironmongery	O
Macdonald	Scotland	Farm labourer	Church of Scotland school and evening classes	Teacher and clergyman's assistant	O
Chamberlain	Birmingham	Cabinet Minister	Rugby and Mason College	Estate manager, manufacturer	

*although born in Manchester he was Welsh

242

Churchill	Blenheim Palace	Tory politician	Harrow & Sandhurst	Soldier	
Attlee	London	Solicitor	Haileybury and Oxford	Lawyer	
Eden	Durham	Aristocrat	Eton and Oxford	Soldier	2x
Macmillan	London	Publisher	Eton and Oxford	Publisher	
Douglas-Home	Mayfair	Earl	Eton and Oxford	None	
Wilson	Yorkshire	Industrial chemist	Grammar school and Oxford	Academic, economist, civil servant	
Heath	Kent	Carpenter	Grammar school and Oxford	Civil servant	B
Callaghan	Hampshire	Naval petty officer	Secondary school	Civil service (tax officer), union official Royal Navy	
Thatcher	Lincs.	shopkeeper	Grammar school and Oxford	Research chemist (preserving ice cream)	
Major	Surrey	Travelling showman	Left school at 16	labourer, insurance broking clerk, banker	
Blair	Edinburgh	Barrister and lecturer	Fettes and Oxford	Barrister	

Prime Ministers: Props

7 inseparable personal possessions

In some developing countries, symbols associated with tribes or parties are used on ballot papers to enable the illiterate to vote. A similar system has long been in informal use in Britain where several prime ministers have chosen a particular object to carry with them at all times in public as a symbol of their power, with which to rally followers and strike voodoo fear into the hearts of enemies. We haven't yet got to the state of putting our polling-day crosses beside pictograms but with plummeting levels of literacy it may not be long before every politician feels obliged to carry a personal totem.

Chamberlain	*umbrella*
Churchill	*cigar*
Eden	*homburg hat* (like a bowler but with an upturned brim)
Wilson	*pipe* he was named 'Pipe Smoker of the Year' in 1975) and Gannex raincoat (manufactured by Joseph Kagan, raised to the peerage in Wilson's resignation honours list and later jailed for fraudulent accounting)
Heath	*yacht* ('Morning Cloud') and *organ*
Thatcher	*handbag*

P

Poetry

10 or 20 political lessons in verse

> *"I've never read a political poem that's accomplished anything.*
> *Poetry makes things happen, but rarely what the poet wants."*
> Howard Nemerov (US poet laureate)

> *"Poetry makes nothing happen."*
> WH Auden, In Memory of WB Yeats

In the days before the mass media and satire, one good way to ridicule a political opponent was to write a poem about him. The Romantics were good at hit-and-run poetry, as was Rudyard Kipling. Other poets have addressed political themes with more subtlety. Good literature is rarely pure polemic (or vice versa) so most political poetry raises questions rather than writes constitutions.

The poems with the most lasting impact tend to be those written with passion and humanity. They may emanate from one side or other of the political divide, but their conclusions suggest rather than dictate. Free of the constraints of other art forms, poetry is able to speculate on more than one contradictory truth at the same time.

Not many poems have been written specifically about politics but many poets have been politically committed and their work can offer rewarding insights into the processes of politics and political thinking. The postwar Labour Prime Minister, Clement Attlee, was himself an amateur poet.

The Masque of Anarchy by Shelley (1819)

The poet's response to the Peterloo Massacre on 16th August 1819 in which cavalry charged a supposedly peaceful crowd which had gathered in Manchester to hear a speech on parliamentary reform. The poem criticized several members of the government by name:

> *"I met Murder on the way –*
> *He had a face like Castlereagh"*

Vision of Judgement by Lord Byron (1821)

Byron had a savage tongue and pen which he sometimes used to show his contempt for politics but he also sat for a time in the House of Lords and defended the Luddites. The preface to this poem prepares the way for a demolition of the characters of George III and the Poet Laureate Southey who Byron believed to have sold out and become a sycophant. His next best known political piece is Canto XIV of *The Age of Bronze* (1823), sometimes known as *The Landlords' Interest* for its scathing attack on the political hypocrisy of the propertied classes.

Waiting for the Barbarians by C.P. Cavafy (1904)

Political life in the city is on hold as the barbarians will be arriving any minute and they'll be taking over. But what do we do when we realise the barbarians aren't coming after all?

Gehazi by Rudyard Kipling (1919)

One of the 'greatest hate poems' written in the English language, the five stanzas of Gehazi draw a parallel between a corrupt character in the Old Testament and Sir Rufus Isaacs, one of three members of Asquith's Liberal government who were accused of using high political office to make money out of speculating on shares. There was an unsavoury hint of Tory anti-semitism to Kipling's very personal attack. The Conservative Prime Minister, Stanley Baldwin, was Kipling's cousin.

The Cantos by Ezra Pound (1924-1962)

Pound was an influential Modernist poet whose work is difficult to separate today from his biography because of his sympathy for Mussolini and his espousal of anti-semitism. During the war he broadcast fascist propaganda and after, it was for a while incarcerated by the American forces occupying Italy.

Jerusalem by William Blake (1804-10)

The stirring, alternative English national anthem capable of bearing any connotation loaded on it. During the First World War it served as a patriotic hymn and today the Women's Institute uses it as a symbol of national female pride. What Blake meant by "dark satanic mills" and the rest has been and always will be endlessly debated.

Politics by W.B. Yeats (1938)

Written shortly before the poet's death, *Politics* is a deceptively simple poem of 12 lines at once about looming war and the bittersweet wisdom of ageing. More overtly political is *Easter 1916.*

September 1, 1939 by W.H. Auden (1939)

Written in the first days of World War II, one of Auden's best-known poems speculates on the causes and the effects of the conflict on various levels. It contains the line, "We must love one another or die".

The Nation by Roy Fisher (1984)

A wry observation of the follies of obsessive nationalism and patriotism: festivities on "national day" are "constrained by the national debt" while "the national method of execution" is meted out to those who have succumbed to "the national vice."

Winter Ending by Adrian Henri (1992)

Adrian Henri's poem was used as the preface to the Labour Party manifesto in the 1992 general election and ends with the lines:

> *"the cold blue landscape of winter*
> *suddenly alive with bright red roses."*

Political Correctness

Some subjects on which you should choose your words carefully

> *"A chair is a piece of furniture."*
>
> Anne Widdecombe 2007*

It sounds like something you wouldn't want to argue with: don't we all like to be right so who wouldn't want to be correct politically? But this term, imported from the USA in the 1980s, has become a weapon of abuse, principally because it assumes that you can only be politically correct (PC) if you are on the moralising left of politics.

It is based on the notion that words can hurt as much as sticks and stones, and we should therefore police our own language and that of our less moral neighbours so as not to cause offence to minorities. In practice, this means that some self-appointed thought police, acting no doubt with the best of intentions, feel justified in waving a three-pronged fork across every committee table and over every political document that is to be signed.

But there is a serious point being made. Proponents of political correctness say that it is important for minority groups to be able to choose the names that are used to identify them, just as we all prefer one forename or nickname over another, and that some words in the language are too loaded with hate and derision to have any useful meaning left in them and should therefore never be uttered again in public.

Critics of political correctness say the whole idea of a 'fixed code' of what you can and cannot say inhibits the variety of the language, curbs self-expression, creates social schisms, promotes artificial equality, instigates witch hunts, engenders discrimination against anyone who happens to belong to the 'dominant' culture (those who are white, male, middle class, Church of England etc) and amounts to forcible self-censorship which is no less pernicious than actual censorship.

---

*referring to New Labour plans to neutralise the word "chairman" in future legislation.

The three main targets of political correctness

Homophobia

It is only about forty years since almost every homosexual in Britain was still in the closet out of fear for his safety. Disparaging remarks and cruel jokes were accepted at all levels of society, fostering an atmosphere of repression and hypocrisy. Unfortunately, with the breath of PC air that has made it safer and more acceptable to be a declared homosexual the words 'gay' and 'queer' have been lost to the main body of the English language.

Racism

No culture is superior to another, according to PC, although curiously it seems to be acceptable to show mainstream western culture as culpable for the ills of the world.

Sexism

The position of women in society has changed enormously since the peak of feminism which tried to make us all perfectly equal. There have been clumsy attempts to neuter the English language (s/he, chairperson etc) and while they haven't become universally accepted they have acquired a certain respectability so that only proudly unreconstructed men will snigger these days when a woman calls herself 'Ms'.

Other minorities protected by political correctness

The religious

While religious minorities (now called 'faiths') kept their beliefs to themselves, there was no problem of extending political correctness to them; but in the era of faith-incited terrorism the issue has become more complex. Causing unnecessary offence to anyone who believes in God is to be avoided but should every religious person have the right to impose his/her definition of blasphemy on the rest of society?

The mentally ill

There's a lot more mental illness around these days and the politically correct approach is to accept that there are infinite gradations between sanity and insanity. Interestingly, the non-PC word 'mad' is starting to be used in Britain in its American sense of 'angry'. The sting of manic depression, meanwhile, has been blunted by re-naming it 'bi-polar disorder'.

The disabled

The English language has, admittedly, helped itself in the cruellest sense to words that have specific medical meanings in order to use them as insults: 'cripple', 'spastic' and so on. Even some words that don't seem particularly abusive – blind, deaf – are now to be avoided in favour of the concept of being 'sense-impaired'. The notion of being 'challenged' (as in 'height-challenged' for a short person) owes more to jokes directed against political correctness than to political correctness itself.

Children

As children have acquired rights (undeniably a good thing) so adults have become more confused about how to handle them. What should a teacher do with a pupil who is persistently disruptive if he can't use corporal punishment? And should strangers tell other people's kids how to behave on the bus? The current vogue is to understand children's problems rather than to discipline them: don't say 'bad' say 'behavioural problems'; don't say 'lazy' or 'rude' say 'suffering from attention deficiency syndrome'.

The poor

Always with us, but clearly not the way they were in Victorian times or even in the 1950s, when there were still lawless slum quarters rather than lawless, run-down housing estates. To be politically correct in the 21st century, we need to refer to relative rather than absolute poverty, and to be concerned with inequalities within society.

The workers

Ever since the employment exchanges became job centres and started looking like shops, job titles have similarly been going up-market. Hence we have refuse collectors instead of dustbin men and sex workers instead of prostitutes.

Politician Quotes

12 pronouncements on those who play politics

"A politician is a person with whose politics you don't agree. If you agree with him, he is a statesman."   *David Lloyd George 1935*

"A politician is an animal that can sit on a fence and keep both ears to the ground."   *HL Mencken*

"A statesman is a politician who places himself at the service of the nation. A politician is a statesman who places the nation at his service."   *Georges Pompidou 1973*

"Those who coldly condemn everyone else's absurdities while clinging to the notion of their own seriousness are destined to become politicians. (While those who do the opposite are fated to be satirists. Which, one might wonder, is the more absurd?)"
     Michael Bywater, Lost Worlds

"Vote for the man who promises least; he'll be the least disappointing."   *Bernard M. Baruch, presidential advisor*

"He stands for what he thinks people will fall for."
     Anonymous definition of a politician

"Mothers all want their sons to grow up to be President but they don't want them to become politicians in the process." *JFK (attrib.)*

"My choice early in life was either to be a piano player in a whorehouse or a politician. And to tell the truth, there's hardly any difference."   *Harry S. Truman 1962*

"I'm often amazed at the way politicians – who spend hours poring over opinion poll results in a desperate attempt to discover what the public thinks – are certain they know precisely what God's views are on everything."   *Simon Hoggart*

"The penalty that good men pay for failing to participate in public affairs is to be governed by others worse than themselves."
     Bernard Weatherill

"Politicians use statistics in the same way that a drunk uses lamp-posts – for support rather than illumination."   *Andrew Lang*

Politics is...

"the art of looking for trouble, finding it whether it exists or not, diagnosing it incorrectly, and applying the wrong remedy."
Sir Ernest Benn

"a field where the choice lies constantly between two blunders."
John Morley MP

"the Art of the Possible." *RA (Lord) Butler*
but probably originally said by Bismarck

"not the art of the possible. It consists in choosing between the disastrous and the unpalatable."
JK Galbraith

"the diversion of trivial men who, when they succeed at it, become more important in the eyes of more trivial men."
George Jean Nathan

"nothing more than a means of rising in the world."
Dr Johnson

"the systematic organisation of hatreds."
Henry Adams

"the art of preventing people from busying themselves wth their own business."
Paul Valéry

"a blood sport."
Aneurin Bevan

"the art of making the inevitable seem planned."
Quentin Crisp

"the art of preventing people from taking part in affairs which properly concern them."
Paul Valéry

Postmodern Politics

50 vital expressions to avoid being old-fashionedly modern

If you long to return to the certainties of Edwardian Britain, don't read on; otherwise, undo your psychic seat belt and prepare to enter the fog of postmodernism.

Modernism, the last big thing, was unremittingly in-your-face but at least it came to an end. Postmodernism, however, in which everything that has gone before is infinitely and purposelessly recycled, promises no such easy escape. You can think of the postmodern world as like being trapped in a prison cell with an inmate who only knows two or three jokes and insists on telling you them over and over again in an expressionless voice. The only people not laughing at postmodernism, you see, are the postmodernists.

Of course, postmodernism is a term mostly applied to art and architecture but its proponents see it as more than just another cultural trend. It is rather a way of viewing the world; a 'mood'; or 'condition'. Sceptics prefer to see it as a malaise, the socio-political equivalent of ergot poisoning. Either way, it has been earnestly applied to politics by a number of distinguished academics; and it is far too self-important to be pinned down by any simple definition. The point of being a postmodern is to appear to know just a fraction more than everyone else, as if you are seeing the whole amusing world from above without having to belong to it.

If you want to become a postmodernist yourself, and apply for a slice of public funding that goes with it, you'll need to be able to talk in the right way. The words in the two lists overleaf comprise the entire vocabulary of postmodern political philosophy. They can be combined in endlessly creative ways to give the impression of muttering profound insights while not saying anything of substance at all. Marxist sociologists will feel especially at home with postmodernism as it allows them to talk in the same long-winded but incomprehensible way as they used to do before perestroika – but note, you can't be earnest and postmodern; a barely detectable smirk of irony is essential to get the accent right.

But one word of warning: do not try postmodernism if you want to enjoy anything ever again. If you assimilate these words into your everyday speech you will not be able to watch a film, listen to a piece of music, admire a building or consider a political proposition in the same way as you did before; instead, you will find yourself 'reading' these 'constructs' for their inchoate 'meanings' even if you know they can 'tell' you nothing.

Adjectives*

binary
conceptualised
constructionist

context-dependent
contingent
demystifying
diffuse
digressive
discursive

dissolved
experienced
fetishistic
founding
indeterminate
intersubjective

invalidated

knowing, as in the "knowing subject"
metaphorical

originating
overarching
referent
reflectionist
self-referential

synchronic

unrepresentable (often to be found within systems of representation)

Nouns

agency
assemblage
boundaries, most being *'supposed'* rather than *'verifiable'*
circulation
constituencies, but not those of MPs
construct
displacement
fictions (as in all facts are)
gradations, often going towards supposed boundaries
hybridity
identity
knowledges (always plural)
linkage
multiplicity
narrative: usually overarching but often founding, never grand
normality (as in the absurd idea that there is such a thing)
policing, but not of course in the obvious sense
reading (except when referring to the printed word)
redrawing (of categories)
signage
simulacrum
surfaces
totality (always use in the sense of incompleteness)
uncertainty (There is no postmodern translation for the word 'certainty')
unpacking (and repacking)

*(any of these can be made into a noun by putting 'the' in front)

Power is...

"a dangerous thing to leave lying about."

Edmund Burke

"the simple, indestructible will of the people."

Fidel Castro

"the ultimate aphrodisiac."

Henry Kissinger

"like a seafront; when you achieve it, there's nothing there."
Harold Macmillan

"like a woman you want to stay in bed with forever."

Patrick Anderson

"so apt to be insolent and Liberty to be saucy, that they are very seldom upon good terms."

Lord Halifax

"not happiness."

William Godwin

Predictions

8 erroneous enunciations

> *"Since the dawn of man every politician has been torn between a wish to say something memorable, and a terror of saying something which is remembered. They do not want to sound too significant but they don't want to give hostages to fortune."*
>
> Matthew Parris, 'Read My Lips'

No one remembers you for saying what, with hindsight, looked like an obvious reading of the present and future, but no one is ever going to forget when you get things back to front.

> *"Those who imagine that Germany has swung back to its old imperial temper cannot have any understanding of the character of the change. The idea of a Germany intimidating Europe with a threat that its irresistible army might march across frontiers forms no part in the new vision...they have no longer the desire themselves to invade any other land."*
>
> Lloyd George, Daily Express, September 1936, having visited Nazi Germany

> *"I've seen the future and it works."*
>
> Lincoln Steffens, American journalist, after visiting the Soviet Union in 1919.

> *"If the British public falls for this...it will be stark staring bonkers."*
>
> Quentin Hogg (Lord Hailsham) Conservative press conference, 12 October 1964, about the manifesto that would soon win Labour the general election.

"We can predict with mathematical certainty that in terms of industrial development, of technological advance and of mass consumption, the planned Socialist economy, as exemplified in the Communist States, will prove its capacity to outpace and overtake the wealthy and comfortable Western economies."

> Richard Crossman in 'Labour in the Affluent Society' (1960)

"Go back to your constituencies and prepare for government."

> David Steel to the Liberal Party conference, Lladndudno 11 Sep 1981. He was emboldened by the formation of the SPD and an alliance with his own party but neither would earn a stake in government in the next election.

"He will never get to the top in English politics, for all his wonderful gifts; to speak with the tongue of men and angels, and to spend laborious days and nights in administration is not good if a man does not inspire trust."

> Herbert Asquith, of Winston Churchill

"The chancellor's position is unassailable."

> Margaret Thatcher confirming that Nigel Lawson was secure in his post as Chancellor of the Exchequer. It's not quite fair to call this a prediction as it was she who would soon undermine Lawson by consulting her own economic adviser and forcing his resignation.

"The British won't fight."

> Leopoldo Galtieri, president of Argentina, April 1982, to US secretary of State Alexander Haig. The following month the British did.

Progress, and the lack of it

8 good reasons to keep things the way they are

In hindsight, many great social leaps forward look like inevitable courses of events, even predestined. Can anyone really have believed the abolition of the slave trade to have been a disreputable cause? Well, yes.

For every William Wilberforce (and every Florence Nightingale, Elizabeth Fry or Emmeline Pankhurst) there is a battalion of furrowed brows to be seen behind the barricades. Having the moral imperative on your side does not guarantee that you will win the argument.

The following quotes from Hansard during the arguments over slavery constitute an action charter for professional delayers of progress.

Argument 1 – Those who stand to benefit don't want change

> *"The negroes in the West Indies do not desire the abolition; for they consider any obstacle to the importation of new slaves as a prolongation and increase of their present hours."*

Welbore Ellis, 1797

Argument 2 – They aren't ready for it

> *"Emancipating those who are not sufficiently enlightened to understand and feel the blessings of liberty would be like putting a sword into the hands of a madman."*

Sir Robert Peel, 1794

Argument 3 – In fact, they are happy the way things are

> *"There does not exist a more happy race than the slaves in our colonies if any trust is to be placed in outward appearances which universally indicates cheerfulness and contentment."*

Thomas Hughan, 1807

Argument 4 – Always has been like that, always will be

"I have heard a great deal of kidnapping slaves and of other barbarous practices. I am sorry for it, but it should be recollected that these things are the consequence of the natural law of Africa. I acknowledge it is not an amiable trade but neither is the trade of a butcher and yet a mutton chop is, nevertheless, a very good thing."

Sir Richard Grosvenor, 1791

Argument 5 – Who are we to interfere?

"They [slave merchants] only buy slaves whom the African states thought proper to dispose of. The African states are as competent to transport such offenders as we are those whom we send to America or Botany Bay."

John Fuller, 1804

Argument 6 – If we don't do it, someone else will

"If this Bill were to pass, the trade would be carried on by other nations and the miserable slaves would therefore be again exposed to all the miseries from which the wise and humane regulations under which the trade has been conducted by British merchants have relieved them." *

Sir William Young, 1804

Argument 7 – Besides, it won't do us any good …

"The Bill [abolishing the trade] will terminate all spirit of adventure, all incitement to industry, all thirst of emulation, for hitherto it has been the hope of overseers to rise in the world . . . by saving a portion of their wages to purchase two or three negroes which they let out to the planter for hire."

Sir William Young 1796

---

*At the time British ships accounted for well over half the slaves transported annually. Death rates in transit were as high as 25%.

Argument 8 – It may even jeopardise our survival

"Our existence depends on the strength of our Navy and the strength of our Navy is chiefly derived from the slave trade."

Earl of Westmoreland 1807

Conclusion

Did the world come to an end?

Did British trade cease?

Did the British navy dwindle to nothing?

Was slavery merely taken over by less scrupulous nations?

Did slaves voluntarily beg to hand back their freedom to their ex-masters?

Did any emancipated slave regret the rash humanitarian actions of the British parliament?

When the Bill abolishing the slave trade was passed in 1807, the leader of the House of Lords, Lord Grenville thanked all who had passed this obviously good measure with so little opposition:

"I congratulate the House on having now performed one of the most glorious acts that have ever been done by any assembly of any nation in the world."

The Aboliton Act of 1807 did not, of course, end the slave trade at a stroke. Traders, bankers shipbuilders and manufacturers found it easy to circumvent the act.

Psephological Shockers

8 interesting statistics about an iniquitous system

> *"All voting is a sort of gaming, like checkers or backgammon, with a slight moral tinge to it."*   Thoreau

'First-Past the Post' (FPTP) is the second most popular voting system in the world after party lists. It is, however, misnamed. It could be better thought as 'the one who is ahead of the rest' or 'least far from the post' (of 50%). It is also, more aptly, called 'winner takes all'.

1. Only one government in modern times has had more than 50% of the votes cast. That was in 1931. No party since 1945 has governed with a majority of votes cast. The Conservatives came closest with 49.6% but since then things have been getting worse and no government since 1970 has even had 45% of the votes.

2. No government has ever received the support of more than 50% of eligible voters (as opposed to those who actually vote) since universal adult suffrage was introduced. Labour won a mere 21% of eligible votes in 2005. Even Margaret Thatcher at the height of her power was endorsed by only 33% of the electorate.

3. The first problem is getting people to turn out. Voting in the United Kingdom is voluntary, not – as it is in some countries – obligatory, and a proportion of the electorate opt out. Others who are eligible to vote, may not be able to: either their names have been missed off the register (the inaccuracy level is estimated at 4%), or they are ill on the day, or they are on holiday and have failed to arrange a postal or proxy vote.

    Turnouts have been falling, on average since the 20th century's highest in 1910 (86.8%). The lowest was in 2001 (59%). Abstainers are classed as positive (they decide not to vote because they think it will be a waste of time or legitimise a system they don't believe to be democratic) and negative (can't be bothered or forget). The weather has some impact on turnouts. Labour is traditionally thought to suffer more from low turnouts than the other parties.

4. Turnout matters because if it falls too low it can have an odd implication. It could be argued that abstainers regularly win elections, turning democracy on its head. In 2005, 17 million people abstained, against 9.6 million people who voted for the winning party, Labour.

5. Even if you leave aside the problem of participation/non-participation what you get from a general election is not a result proportional to the votes cast. The British electoral system does not claim to be based on proportionality but the whole point of a general election is that the result should reflect the 'will of the people' in some accurately measurable way.

   In 2005 the Blair government won 35.2% of the vote – only one percent higher than Kinnock's losing share in 1992, 34.4%, and less than Callaghan's losing total in 1979, 36.9%. It was the lowest number of votes cast for Labour since the war except for 1983 but the party attained a majority of 65 seats.

   Conversely, a party can lose an election even if they win more overall votes. In 1951, Labour won more votes than the Conservatives but fewer seats. In February 1974, the same happened to the Conservatives, but the other way round.

   It is certainly not proportional representation; perhaps it should be called iniquitous representation.

6. Only three MPs elected in 2005 secured the votes of more than 40% of their constituents. George Galloway won his seat with a mere 18.4% – 35.9% of the votes cast on a 51.2% turnout.

7. In theory a party can get a minority of votes cast in each constituency and still win all 635 seats. Likewise you can get 20% of the votes in all of them and not win a seat. Electoral history is littered with stories of minor parties which failed to turn popularity into parliamentary seats because the system has no way of gauging support for 'non-winners'.

8. The Electoral Reform Society describes FPTP as "very wasteful". Votes for a losing candidate count for nothing and votes in excess of the total a candidate needs to win are effectively useless. 70% of votes or 19 million votes in 2005 could be classed as wasted.

The Public Sector

A small guide to the very large state

It might seem easy to define the public sector of the economy as everything that isn't the private sector. In practice, the two intertwine like mating octopi so that it is difficult for the non-expert to tell which body part belongs to which animal. This is a beginner's guide to the tentacled state.

1. The state has a direct involvement in a large number of activities within its territory, including (but not exhaustively):

    the running of central government with all the bureaucracy and quangocracy entailed

    the running of the devolved governments and their bureaucracies

    the running of local authorities and their bureaucracies

    administration of Britain's last foreign territories (see p20)

    the workings of the European Union

    the National Health Service

    the armed forces

    education

    public transport

    the infrastructure and regulation of private transport (e.g. the rail and road networks)

    broadcasting (the BBC)

    the emergency services

    the regulation of privatized industries

    the supervision of health and safety standards

    town planning

    law and order

    national security

    the postal service

    the arts and sport

    skills training

    food standards control

    the encouragement of regional development

    the management of a portfolio of 'national assets' including parks, ancient buildings and a lot more

    the supervision of fair play in the financial services industry

2. The picture of what is and is not in the public sector is complicated by:

    -   public-private partnership initiatives, in which private sector expertise and capital is used for public sector projects.

    -   state subsidies given to the private sector e.g. to the rail operators.

    -   certain branches of government raising some of their own money e.g. the BBC's commercial operations.

    -   The enormous variety of agencies and other quangos that are half in, half out of the conventional structure of the state.

3. Britain's total public sector expenditure is 508 billion pounds.

4. The number of people employed by the public sector is 5,855,000 or 20.4% of the country's workforce, which means that 1 out of every 5 workers is employed by the state. (The highest the proportion has reached in recent years was 23.1% in 1992 under John Major.)

5. Over 1.3 million of these people work for the NHS (22% of all public sector workers; or almost 5% of all workers in Britain) which is believed to be Europe's biggest employer and the fourth biggest employer in the world after the Chinese Army, Indian Railways and Wal-Mart.

6. 65% of public sector workers are women (compared with 41% in the private sector).

    -   72% are over 35 years old (62% cent in the private sector).

    -   57% have been working for the same employer for 5 years or more (45% in the private sector workers).

    -   41% work part time (30% in the private sector).

    -   13% are disabled (about the same in the private sector).

    -   7% describe their ethnicity as 'non-white' (about the same in the private sector).

7. 554,000 of these people are officially classed as civil servants, employees of 'the Crown', which means, in essence, they work for central government departments which report to ministers of the government. The word 'Whitehall' is often used as shorthand for these ministries together.

8. The numbers of civil servants goes up and down (mostly up)

Year	# employees	Key event of the year
1914	70,000	Outbreak of Word War I
1939	347,000	Outbreak of World War II
1945	1,114,000	End of World War II
1949	784,000	mid-way through Attlee government
1955	719,000	Churchill–Eden handover
1970	701,000	Heath becomes prime minister
1974	694,384	Wilson becomes prime minister again
1976, 1 April	747,614	Highest postwar level (discounting 1945)
1979	733,176	Margaret Thatcher comes to power
1990	556,584	Thatcher leaves office
1997	516,000	Tony Blair wins election
2006	554,000	Blair's last year in office

The civil service has changed as it has grown. In 1914 it was 'Balkanized', that is each department had a different structure. It was homogenised after the First World War and brought under increasing central control. The civil service changed radically in the 1980s (under Margaret Thatcher) when privatisation of previously state-run industries, contracting out work and the creation of 'next steps' agencies caused numbers of civil servants to fall.

9. The biggest departments of central government are:

Department	Staff
Defence	57,000
HM Revenues and Customs	43,390
Home office	43,190
Work and pensions	40,500
Constitutional affairs (DCA)	13,410
Transport	11,300

Quangos (and Gocos)

A beginner's guide to everyday agency-spotting

It sounds like some loveable little marsupial, but a quango – Quasi-Autonomous Non-Governmental Organization – does not so much hop as sit and wait for brickbats to be thrown at it.

Like some genetically-engineered strain of super-resistant organism, the quango has no natural predator to keep its numbers down and because it breeds so rapidly no one is quite sure how many there are. This is partly because there is officially no such thing as a quango and also because there are greater and lesser degrees of quangosity – some bodies are entirely public-funded and shielded from the scrutiny of elected politicians while others are only partly subsidised and kept under half a watchful eye by parliament. One recent official report puts the population of quangos at around 1,000 but a professional quango-hunter has estimated that there are over 2,500. Either way, the species is well-fed with taxpayer's money.

Governments create quangos for noble and ignoble reasons. They can be a way of carrying out public administration without constant political interference; but they can equally be a way of disguising civil service spending and staffing by outsourcing work.

If the cheery creature you see through your binoculars falls into one of the categories below, chances are it's a quango. This classification is vastly simplified. Government business is now farmed out to a convoluted flowchart of institutions which is hard enough for the civil service to keep track of, never mind the rest of us. Note: quangos are slippery creatures and any one of them may fall into more than one category at the same time.

1. **Non-Ministerial Department (NMD)**

    A hybrid institution, being a politically headless department in which the staff are civil servants – not, therefore, a true quango. There may be some policy input from a minister but an NMD is otherwise run by a commissioner or board and left to get on with its own affairs.
    Examples: HM Revenue and Customs, Office of Fair Trading.

2. **Executive Agency**

The 147 executive agencies, including those controlled by devolved governments or administrations, were set up after a report in 1988 which recommended breaking up the civil service. They have 'customers' rather than taxpayers. They are divided into research, regulation, internal service delivery (serving government itself) and external service delivery (serving society or the public).

> *Examples:* Job Centre Plus (annual budget £3 billion; 85,000 staff), Prison Service Agency (46,000 staff), Patent Office, Companies House and the Met Office.

3. **Non-departmental public body (NDPB)**

Also known unofficially as an 'Arm's Length Body' as they are deliberately kept out of the clutches of a minister and department so they can function independently. There are over 640 of them.

> *Examples:* Environment Agency, Medical Research Council.

4. **Public Corporation (PC)**

A semi-commercial hybrid body that earns at least some of its money from commercial activities. Some of them are charmingly classified as GoCos: Government owned companies. PC quangos are also spawned by the famous public-private partnerships.

> *Examples:* Audit Commission, Ofcom, British Nuclear Fuels, BBC.

5. **Ad hoc Advisory Bodies, Task Forces, Working Groups, Reviews**

The mayfly of the quango genus, such organisations are set up to provide expert advice quickly. After they have delivered it, they generally die. Average life expectancy: 2 years.

6. **Ombudsmen and regulators**

The referees of the political and economic world. Don't ask who adjudicates disputes with adjudicators.

> *Examples:* Information Commissioner, Competition Commissioner.

7. **NHS Bodies**

The National Health Service has its own sub-classification of quangos:

- Special Health Authorities
- NHS Trusts
- Primary Care Trusts
- Strategic Health Authorities

8. **Police Authorities**

There are 43 bodies of 17-23 appointed members apiece which oversee the performance and behaviour of the police in England and Wales.

Reith and Dimbleby

28 disquisitions by people in important positions

The Reith Lectures

In line with the BBC's remit to contribute to the cultural life of the nation, each series of Reith Lectures addresses an issue of contemporary relevance. Some lectures can be heard at www.bbc.co.uk/radio4/reith

1948   Bertrand Russell, *Authority and The Individual*

1949   Robert Birley, *Britain in Europe*

1951   Lord Radcliffe, *Power and The State*

1952   Arnold Toynbee, *The World and The West*

1954   Sir Oliver Franks, *Britain and Tide of World Affairs*

1961   Margery Perham, *The Colonial Reckoning*

1962   Prof. George Carstairs, *This Island Now*

1966   JK Galbraith, *The New Industrial State*

1970   Dr Donald Schon, *Change and Industrial Society*

1973   Prof. Alistair Buchan, *Change Without War*

1974   Prof. Ralf Dahrendorf, *The New Liberty*

1975   Dr Daniel Boorstin, *America and The World Experience*

1977   Prof. A H Halsey, *Change In British Society*

1983   Sir Douglas Wass, *Government and the Governed*

1986   Lord McCluskey, *Law, Justice and Democracy*

1988   Prof. Geoffrey Hosking, *The Rediscovery of Politics*

1998   John Keegan, *War In Our World*

1999   Anthony Giddens, *Runaway World* (globalization)

2002   Onora O'Neill, *A Question of Trust* (trusting public institutions)

2004   Wole Soyinka, *Climate of Fear*

The Dimbleby Lectures

Created in 1972 in memory of the legendary documentary broadcaster Richard Dimbleby who died in 1965, the annual Dimbleby Lecture gives an opportunity to a guest speaker to talk about business, the arts or politics. Eight of the lectures have been on political themes, or at least been delivered by politicians.

1976   *Elective Dictatorship*
        Lord Hailsham, Former (and later, again) Lord Chancellor.

1979   *Home Thoughts from Abroad*
        Roy Jenkins, President of the European Commission. A telling view of the British political scene of the moment, two years before Jenkins jointly founded the SDP.

1980   *Misuse of Power*
        Lord Denning, Master of the Rolls.

1994   *Security and Democracy – Is There a Conflict?*
        Stella Rimington, Director-General of MI5.

1997   *Public Life, Public Confidence*
        Lord Nolan, Former Law Lord.

1998   *Principles of Peace*
        George J. Mitchell, Former US senator and chair of the talks leading to the Belfast Agreement.

2001   *The Struggle For The Soul of The 21st Century*
        Bill Clinton, Former President of the United States of America.

2003   *The Path towards a New World (The Future of Europe and Co-operation between Britain and France)*
        Dominique de Villepin, French Foreign Minister, the first lecturer to be actively serving in government at the time.

Secrecy (Freedom of Information)

A few good reasons not to know what you should know and several iffy ones.

Every government in the world would like to carry on its business away from the prying, critical eyes of public opinion but to do so is to miss the point of democracy. Whereas a little operational confidentiality is understandable – we wouldn't want the prime minister to feel he has to interrupt work and make a press statement every half an hour – the public has a right to know what is being done in its name. There is clearly a balance to be struck, but the default setting of the state is secrecy.

Successive administrations in Britain have made a convention of keeping whatever they feel uncomfortable about in the locked filing cabinets of Whitehall but the public can never know whether it is being deprived of information for its own good or to save someone self-important from being held up to public ridicule.

The Freedom of Information Act (FOIA) was a long time due when it was passed in November 2000 (and even more so when it came into force on 1 January 2005). In line with a Labour manifesto promise, it enables anyone to shine a light into any corner of a now transparent government and civil service. Or does it?

On the box it says that the:

> *"FOI applies to information whatever its age... The 30 year standard closure period no longer determines access to records; instead, information is assumed to be 'open' right from the start unless one of the exemptions set out in the Act applies. Anyone, anywhere in the world, can send a written request for information (a letter, fax or email) to an FOI authority. The FOI authority must say whether it holds the information, and if it does, provide it."*

So far, so good. But the act has 88 sections and includes numerous exceptions to the general rule of disclosure. Any branch of government (including quangos, hospitals, schools and universities) may apply for exemption, that is non-disclosure, that is to keep secrets secret, for one of the following reasons:

- interests of National Security.

- matters to do with defence.

- safeguarding Britain's international relations.

- not upsetting relations between the regional governments of the United Kingdom.

- cases in which disclosure would be detrimental to the British economy including giving away trade secrets.

- anything to do with law enforcement: ie where disclosure would prevent the police and the courts from doing their jobs.

- the auditing of public accounts.

- the protection of parliamentary privilege.

- formulation of government policy and anything which might prevent the government from carrying out its job effectively e.g. where information might undermine the principle of collective responsibility within the cabinet.

- communications with the monarchy, the Royal Family and the Royal Household.

- information about the workings of the honours system.

- information which would pose a health or safety risk to anyone.

Also … a request can be turned down because of the cost of compiling the information required.

But … some of the grounds for exemption – not all of them – can be challenged if the disclosure of information can be proved to be in the public interest.

And so … appeals to do with the workings of the act can be taken to the Information Commissioner, an independent regulator.

The Department of Constitutional Affairs publishes statistics on the implementation of the Act every quarter. Of all 'resolvable' requests received during Q4 of 2006, 59% were granted in full, i.e. 41% were *not* granted in full. Of the 864 rejected requests sent to review, the original decision (not to disclose) was upheld in 665 (77%) of cases.

Secretaries

7 members of staff who may not sit on your knee and take shorthand

Secretary is the most flexible job title in government and the civil service. People at both the very bottom and very top of their careers are called 'secretary' and it is to a secretary you must turn whether you want some routine filing done, coffee served or someone sent to prison for the rest of their natural life.

Cabinet Secretary: head of the home civil service.

Diary Secretary: an unheard of, unglamorous job, until John Prescott was revealed to be having an affair with his.

Home, Foreign, Defence, Health Secretary etc.: (secretaries of state) government ministers in charge of their respective departments. The title of First Secretary of State is often conferred on the Deputy Prime Minister, making him the ultimate personal assistant.

Parliamentary Private Secretary (PPS): MP chosen by a minister as an unpaid assistant. A junior role in government.

Permanent Secretary: the top civil servant in any department, working for and with but ultimately answerable to the secretary of state. Often referred to as a mandarin.

Political Secretary: assistant to the prime minister or other top politician.

Private Secretary: assistant to the Queen, the Prime Minster, chief whip or a top civil servant.

Shakespeare's Politics

10 tips from the bard

Who needs political advisers when you have a copy of The Complete Works of Shakespeare to hand? It's all in there.

Antony and Cleopatra: Don't let your pecker dictate policy.

Coriolanus: Sticking to your principles is suicide: compromise!

Hamlet: Don't go mad, get even.

Henry IV: Some battles you have to win if you want to have a second term (part II).

Julius Caesar: Don't trust your friends. They'll (literally) stab you in the back if they can.

King Lear: Truth is more useful than flattery.

Othello: Sometimes you really can blame a scheming, jealous underling for everything that goes wrong.

Richard II: Power corrupts but absolute power gives you insomnia.

Richard III: Always devise an exit strategy before you stage a showdown.

Romeo and Juliet: A plague on both your parties.

Slogans

10 minimalised messages that struck home or sank like a stone

A good slogan which sums up the situation is more effective in politics than any amount of pontificating. The Conservatives have historically come up with slogans damning the Labour Party more often than vice versa.

'Vote early and vote often'
An apocryphal piece of corrupt electoral advice thought to have originated in Ireland a long time ago.

'Be Thankful Only One of Them Can Win'
A bumper sticker during the Nixon v Kennedy presidential election 1960, but some voters would say that it applies to every election.

'Labour isn't Working'
The ingenious caption to a 1978 Conservative Party poster devised by Saatchi and Saatchi which showed an infinite line of unemployed people. Thatcher's victory in 1979 owed a lot to it yet unemployment increased even further during her time in office, peaking at just over 3 million in 1986.

'Capitalism should be replaced by something nicer'
A placard at a May Day demonstration in London, *c.* 2000.

'Don't vote – it only encourages them.'
A pithy war cry for anarchists, abstainers and apathetics.

'New Labour, New Danger'
Later, no one in the Conservative Party would own up to having authorized this personal attack on Tony Blair in 1997. It showed the would-be future prime minister with glowing red demonic eyes. The concept backfired because it was felt to be too personal an attack.

'Are you thinking what we're thinking?'
Michael Howard's theme for the 2005 general election. Obviously, the public wasn't and some of the billboards were defaced to read 'Are you drinking what we're drinking?'

'Whoever you vote for, the government still gets elected.'
Either a timeless anarchist slogan or a piece of Zen political theory.

'Britain will Win with Labour'
The Labour Party's slogans generally lack the imagination and impact of the Conservatives', this rallying cry for the 1987 election being a prime example of doomed prophecy.

'Yesterday's Men.'
Labour Party slogan for the 1970 election, implying that the Conservatives were an out-of-date, spent force. The Conservatives won the election against the odds and the BBC cruelly used the phrase as a title for a documentary ridiculing the out-of-office Labour Party. (see p.16)

Socialism is...

"... a philosophy of failure, the creed of ignorance, and the gospel of envy, its inherent virtue is ...the equal sharing of misery."

Winston Churchill

"... the religion people get when they lose their religion."

Richard John Neuhaus

"... the same as Communism, only better English."

George Bernard Shaw

"... an excellent way of sharing misery, but not a good way of sharing abundance."

Lord Hailsham

"... the standard bearer of the second-rate."

Sir Gilbert Longden

"... not dead but brain-dead."

Norman Tebbit

"... workable only in heaven, where it isn't needed, and in hell where they've got it."

Cecil Palmer

whereas communism is...(or should that be was...?)

"... not love. Communism is a hammer which we use to crush the enemy."

Mao Tse-Tung

"... like Prohibition, it's a good idea, but it won't work."

Will Rogers

"... like one big phone company."

Lenny Bruce

and a communist is...

"... one who has nothing and wishes to share it with the world."

Anon

"... a socialist without a sense of humour."   *George Cutton*

"... one who hath yearnings/For equal division of unequal earnings."

Ebenezer Elliott

Songs

30 suggestions for a political karaoke

> "We learned more from a three-minute record, baby, than we ever learned in school."   Bruce Sprinsteen, No Surrender

> 'Don't worry about the government.'
>   Talking Heads song title, 1977

Pop songwriters usually concern themselves more with boy meets girl/loses girl and its variations than with politician gets ministerial job/loses ministerial job. But pop has something to say about politics amid its endless profusion of bland, meaningless, pretentious and arcane lyrics. It doesn't usually show a knowledge of current affairs but it might reveal how youth perceives those in power.

As with poetry, a song which is strong on polemic and poor on nuance is unlikely to last beyond the era in which it was written. The best political songs, therefore, are those that explore the subject matter rather than preach about it and whose messages are not obvious at first hearing.

Animal rights

'Meat is Murder'

(song and album title) The Smiths, 1985

Anti-war

"Ev'rybody's talking about
Bagism, Shagism, Dragism, Madism,
Ragism, Tagism
This-ism, That-ism, is-m, is-m, is-m
All we are saying is give peace a chance."

Give Peace a Chance, The Beatles, 1969

Class war

"For a strong and healthy working class,
Is the thing that I most fear.
So I reaches my hand for the watering can
And I waters the workers' beer."

The Man Who Waters the Workers' Beer, Paddy Ryan 1938

The cold war

"No one likes us
I don't know why.
We may not be perfect
But heaven knows we try.
But all around even our old friends put us down.
Let's drop the big one and see what happens."

Political Science, Randy Newman, 1972

Conflict mediation

"Hey hey I saved the world today
Everybody's happy now
The bad things gone away
And everybody's happy now
The good thing's here to stay
Please let it stay."

I Saved the World Today, Eurythmics, 1999

Consumer society

"We live in a greedy little world
That teaches every little boy and girl
To earn as much as they can possibly
Then turn around and spend it foolishly
We've created us a credit card mess
We spend the money we don't possess
Our religion is to go and blow it all
So it's shoppin' every Sunday at the mall."

Ka-Ching! Shania Twain, 2003

Direct action

"Think the time is right for a palace revolution
'Cause where I live the game to play is compromise solution."

Street Fighting Man, The Rolling Stones, 1968,
inspired by anti-Vietnam war demonstrations

Education

"We don't need no education
We don't need no thought control."

Another Brick in the Wall, Pink Floyd, 1979

Elections

"I called my congressman and he said, quote
"I'd like to help you son, but you're too young to vote."

Summertime Blues, Eddie Cochran, 1958

Feminism

"Now there was a time when they used to say
That behind every great man
There had to be a great woman
But in these times of change you know
That it's no longer true.
So we're comin' out of the kitchen
'Cause there's somethin' we forgot to say to you (we say)
Sisters are doin' it for themselves.
Standin' on their own two feet
And ringin' on their own bells."

Sisters are Doing it for Themselves
Eurythmics with Aretha Franklin, 1985

Financial markets on politics

"Do the Wall Street shuffle,
Hear the money rustle,
Watch the greenbacks tumble,
Feel the Sterling crumble."

The Wall Street Shuffle, 10cc, 1974

Gay Rights

"Sing if you're glad to be gay,
Sing if you're happy that way."

(Sing if You're) Glad to be Gay, Tom Robinson, 1978

Human rights

'Bring Him Back Home.'

(song title) Hugh Masekela 1987. The song which
summed up the campaign to free Nelson Mandela
who was released from prison three years later and
became president of South Africa.

Individualism

"The shoes on my feet I bought it
The clothes I'm wearing I bought it
The rock I'm rockin' I bought it
'Cause I depend on me
If I wanted the watch you're wearin' I'll buy it
The house I live in I bought it
The car I'm driving I bought it
I depend on me."

Independent Women, Destiny's Child, 2001

The iron curtain

"And if there comes a time
Guns and gates no longer hold you in
And if you're free to make a choice
Just look towards the west and find a friend."

Nikita, Elton John and Bernie Taupin, 1986

Law and order

"All day long they work so hard
Till the sun is goin' down
Working on the highways and byways
And wearing, wearing a frown
You hear them moanin' their lives away."

The Chain Gang, Sam Cooke, 1960

Manifestos

'Things Can Only Get Better.'

D:Ream (song title, 1993)
New Labour's campaign theme in 1997.
Prescott infamously danced to this song
after the election.

Monarchy

"God Save the Queen…fascist regime."

God Save the Queen, The Sex Pistols 1977
expressing an undercurrent of alienation at the time of Queen
Elizabeth II's Silver Jubilee Year.

National Health Service

"It's the kidney machines that pay for rockets and guns."

Going Underground, The Jam, 1980

Nationalised industries

"Within weeks they'll be re-opening the shipyards
And notifying the next of kin
Once again
It's all we're skilled in
We will be shipbuilding."

Shipbuilding, Elvis Costello, August 1982
three months after the Falklands War

Planning policy

"They paved paradise
And put up a parking lot
With a pink hotel, a boutique
And a swinging hot spot."

Big Yellow Taxi, Joni Mitchell, 1970

Prime ministerial and presidential government

"Oh can't you see
That your democracy
Is just a game you play
No matter what you say."

Every Bomb You Make, Sting 1984.
An adaptation of the Police's *Every Breath
You Take* (1983) written for television's
Spitting Image and peformed with modified
lyrics at the Live 8 Concert in London in
2005. The words were specifically directed
at the leaders of the G8 countries.

Racial equality

"We'd rather die on our feet,
Than be livin' on our knees...
Say it loud, I'm black and I'm proud."

Say It Loud, I'm Black and I'm Proud, James Brown, 1968

Redistributive taxation

"Don't ask me what I want it for (Aahh Mr. Wilson)
If you don't want to pay some more (Aahh Mr. Heath)
Cos I'm the taxman, yeah, I'm the taxman."

Taxman, the Beatles,1966
Written by George Harrison who later turned his
attention from things material to things mystical,
including support for the Natural Law Party (see p203)

Regional development policy

"My name is little Chrissy Wright
and I know what's wrong and I know what's right
And the wife said Chrissy go to London town
And if they won't give us a couple of bob
Won't even give you a decent job
Then Chrissy with my blessings burn them down."

Jarrow Song, Alan Price 1974 (see also p215)

Revolution

"Poor people going to rise up
And get their share."

Talkin' 'bout a Revolution, Tracey Chapman, 1988

Trade unionism

"So though I'm a working man
I can ruin the government's plan
Though I'm not too hard
The sight of my card
Makes me some kind of superman."

Part of the Union, The Strawbs, 1973

Unemployment

"Government leaving the youth on the shelf
This place, is coming like a ghost town
No job to be found in this country
Can't go on no more
The people getting angry."

Ghost Town, The Specials, 1981
in response to Margaret Thatcher's employment policy.

Speakers of the House of Commons

A concise chronology of Parliament's Officer of Order

The Speaker (together with three deputies) is responsible for the smooth running of debates in the House of Commons and represents the Commons to the outside world. It is he or she who calls an MP to speak, who ensures that minorities within the House are not ignored and who exerts discipline when necessary.

MPs elect a new Speaker from among their number when an incumbent retires or dies. The Speaker always comes from the ranks of one of the two main parties but to ensure impartiality he or she renounces old party allegiances and even avoids contact with former colleagues by not using the bars and restaurants in the Palace of Westminster.

The Speaker represents a constituency like any other MP but by convention the other parties do not contest it at a general election.

Post-War Speakers

Douglas Clifton Brown	1943-1951	Con.	139th speaker, veteran of the First Dragoon Guards
William Morrison	1951-1959	Con.	Subsequently governor-general of Australia
Harry Hylton-Foster	1959-1965	Con.	One of the few Speakers to die while still in office
Dr Horace King	1965-71	Lab.	The first Labour MP to be speaker
Selwyn Lloyd	1971-76	Con.	Previously Chancellor of the Exchequer in Macmillan's government
George Thomas	1976-1983	Lab.	The son of a Welsh miner, one of the few people to be made a hereditary peer in the latter part of the 20th century although he died without heir.

Bernard Weatherill	1983-1992	Con.	Former tailor working for his family's Savile Row firm
Betty Boothroyd	1992-2000	Lab.	First female speaker
Michael Martin	From 2000	Lab.	Former sheet metal worker and trade union organiser; first Catholic to hold the post of Speaker since the Reformation

Violent ends of Speakers

These days the Speaker is a respected, impartial individual whose conduct is expected to be unimpeachable. In the 14th, 15th and16th centuries, however, it could be a dangerous post to occupy:

Speaker	Term	Fate
Sir John Bussy	1394-8	Beheaded in 1399
William Tresham	1439-42, 1447 1449-50	Murdered in 1450
Thomas Thorpe	1453-54	Beheaded in1461
Sir John Wenlock	1455-6	Killed at the Battle of Tewkesbury 1471
Sir Thomas Tresham (William's son)	1459	Beheaded in 1471
William Catesby	1484	Beheaded in 1485
Sir Richard Empson	1491-2	Beheaded in 1510
Edmond Dudley	1504	Beheaded in 1510 (On same day as Empson)
Sir Thomas More	1523	Beheaded in 1535

Speeches

10 works of outstanding, oral political performance art

"Three things matter in a speech – who says it, how he says it and what he says – and of the three, the last matters the least."
John Morley

All politicians deliver speeches – some can't help doing it even when they're in a small room with one other person. A few political speeches are worth listening to but most are a predictable melange of platitude, hyperbole, praise for the speaker's own party and damnation for his opponents. Rare is the speech that is remembered even one day after being delivered, but a select bunch lodge for immortality in the national consciousness. Not all of the orations listed below are great speeches when judged by eloquence and content, but all are historic because they were delivered at crucial moments of crisis or change.

Elizabeth I in the summer of 1588 at Tilbury

The Queen's troops were preparing to repel the Spanish Armada. Her speech was a forerunner of Churchill's "fight them on the beaches" speech in which she said "I know I have the body but of a weak and feeble woman; but I have the heart and stomach of a king." The Armada never showed – it was beaten by the weather rather than English military prowess.

Charles I from the scaffold on 30 January 1649

Not the world's most brilliant speech but he can be forgiven for any shortcomings in the circumstances. Having been unable to speak freely at his trial, the king now addressed the crowds, declaring himself innocent of starting the civil war. He became the last saint to be canonized by the Church of England.

Edmund Burke to the voters of Bristol, 1774 (see 'Burke's Brief' p27)

Winston Churchill to the House of Commons on 4 June 1940

Several of Churchill's speeches to parliament contain famous quotations. This was his rallying "we shall fight them on the beaches..." war cry. Three weeks before he had offered his "blood, toil, tears and sweat." Two weeks later he used the phrase "finest hour" and on 20 August praised aircrews with the words "Never in the field of human conflict was so much owed by so many to so few."

His contemporaries did not always see him as the heroic war leader of historical record: "Winston has devoted the best years of his life to preparing his impromptu speeches," F.E. Smith, a fellow Conservative and himself a skilled orator, is supposed to have commented. "The mediocrity of his thinking is concealed by the majesty of his language," his great adversary Aneurin Bevan waspishly remarked.

Harold Macmillan to the South African parliament on 3 Feb 1960
"The wind of change is blowing through this continent, and, whether we like it or not, this growth of national consciousness is a political fact", Macmillan announced.

Enoch Powell in Birmingham on 20 April 1968
This speech – and Enoch Powell himself – is remembered for the phrase "rivers of blood" as a prophecy of where immigration would lead Britain. He was sacked from the Shadow Cabinet for exacerbating racial tensions. He was actually quoting Virgil's Aeneid but the majority of the audience and of the press didn't get the allusion. He later said that he should have used the original Latin.

Roy Jenkins in the Richard Dimbleby Lecture of 1979
In this speech Jenkins presaged the formation of the SDP (see page 201) and could be said to have taken the first step in the development of New Labour.

Margaret Thatcher to the Conservative Party Conference on 10 Oct 1980
Thatcher is not generally regarded as a great speaker but her absolute conviction made up for other deficiencies and it is agreed that she spoke with a cold passion which made people listen. This "the lady's not for turning" speech summed up her Dunkirk spirit. When she gave it she was only a short way into her premiership, things were going wrong and she was not popular, but she refused to cede an inch of ground to her critics.

Neil Kinnock to the Labour Party Conference in 1985

Although a much better orator than his rival Margaret Thatcher, Kinnock eventually had to accept that history was not on his side. But he did leave some great speeches, especially this one which summed up his party's dilemma at the time with the words "power without principles is ruthless, sour, empty, vicious. We also know that principle without power is idle sterility."

David Cameron to the Centre for Social Justice in London on 10 July 2006

Trying to show that he, like Tony Blair, could be compassionate and care about the causes behind crime, Cameron made what became known as his 'Hug-a-Hoodie' speech. In it he suggested that juvenile delinquents should he understood as well as punished. It pleased no one: the hanging and flogging right wing of his party thought he'd gone soft on crime if not soft in the head, and the left considered it a cynical vote-catching tactic.

Speaking about Speaking

10 words of advice for would-be orators

"If half the people who make speeches would make concrete floors they would be doing more good."

Lord Darling, 1917

"No I was not asleep, but I wish to God I had been."

Lord North, on being woken during
a debate in the House of Commons

"I have nothing to say to the nothing that has been said."

Perceval, during a debate on corrupt electoral practices

"I take the view, and always have done, that if you cannot say what you have to say in twenty minutes you should go away and write a book about it."

Lord Brabazon, 1955

"The human brain starts working the moment you are born and never stops until you stand up to speak in public."

Sir George Jessel, 1949

"I do not object to people looking at their watches when I am speaking. But I strongly object when they start shaking them to make certain they are still going."

Lord Birkett, 1960

"There are three golden rules for Parliamentary speakers: Stand up. Speak Up. Shut up."

JW Lowther, Speaker of the House of Commons 1919

"A good speech will not be remembered; a bad one will never be forgotten — or forgiven."

Bernard Weatherill

"The art of making deep sounds from the stomach sound like important messages from the brain."

Winston Churchill, on public speaking

"Dinna put too much meat in your pie."

Jimmy Maxton, Scottish Labour MP
advice on public speaking

Spies

11 cardinal rules for a successful espionage operation

"Military intelligence is a contradiction in terms."

Groucho Marx

Everything changes. Even spying changes. Once you could count on an organization like MI5 ('Military Intelligence 5') to do what spies are supposed to do: plot, intrigue and double-deal for Britain in complete anonymity. But now MI5 adheres to the principles of open and accountable government. Or is it all an elaborate bluff?

Below, in bold, are some rules of secret intelligence which in former times would have been regarded as axiomatic. Underneath them are the new rules of engagement.

Never give your address to strangers.

MI5's headquarters is Thames House, a Grade II listed building at the corner of Millbank and Horseferry Road SW1 in central London. It overlooks Lambeth Bridge, and is not far from the Houses of Parliament. It's not very convenient for the tube but it's a pleasant stroll from Westminster station.

Never say who you are working for.

The current director general is Jonathan Evans who went to Bristol University where he studied the classics.

Never openly recruit new spies.

See www.mi5careers.gov.uk for current opportunities to work for MI5. On your application, don't forget to specify 'intelligence officer', not 'spy'.

Never dispel rumours which could be useful as disinformation.

MI5 says all the following are myths:

- *MI5 is the 'Secret Police'*
- *MI5 only works in the UK*
- *MI5 carries out assassinations*
- *MI5 'vets' ministers and MPs*

- *MI5 monitors the private lives of ministers and other public figures*
- *MI5 'vets' every public sector employee*
- *MI5 investigates Whitehall 'leaks'*
- *MI5 investigates trade unions and pressure groups*
- *MI5 taps telephones and eavesdrops illegally*
- *MI5 has access to all official computers*
- *MI5 spies on Muslims*
- *MI5 plotted to undermine Harold Wilson*
- *MI5's Head in the 1960s was a Russian spy*
- *MI5 only recruits a certain type of individual*
- *MI5 does not recruit tall people*
- *MI5 staff are prohibited from saying anything about the Service*

☞ **Never publish operational details, least of all how much money you get through.**

The annual budget for all three of Britain's security services (MI5, MI6 and GCHQ) is currently £1,553 million.

☞ **Never offer your enemies a means of comeback.**

MI5 has a complaints procedure administered by the Investigatory Powers Tribunal.

☞ **Never subscribe to a fixed set of ethics which could get in the way when you're faced with agents who don't share your scruples.**

According to its 'Statement of Purpose and Values', the Security Service is committed to operating with:

- legality
- integrity
- objectivity
- a sense of proportion about our work; and
- respect and consideration for each other and for those with whom we work outside the Service.

☞ **Never talk about what you do: you never know who may be listening.**

On 12 June 1994 Dame Stella Rimington, director general of

the Security Service, gave the Richard Dimbleby lecture on the subject, 'Security and Democracy – Is there a Conflict?' This was two years after publishing her autobiography, *Open Secret*.

◉ **Never set up a website with all this information and more on it.**

See www.mi5.gov.uk for FAQs about spies and spying.

◉ **Don't mention other spying organisations that should also remain secret in existence and operation.**

The MI5 website has a handy link to the website for MI6 (www.sis.gov.uk), officially the Secret Intelligence Service, which concentrates on oversees intelligence gathering. James Bond is not on the payroll.

◉ **Final instruction** (listen very carefully; I shall say this only once):

Eat this page after you have read it and forget everything you have been told.

Stabs in the Front

5 well-aimed thrusts on departure

> *"It's probably better to have him inside the tent pissing out, than outside pissing in."*
>
> Lyndon B. Johnson giving his reasons
> for not sacking J. Edgar Hoover

Whatever you think about your colleagues in private, there is an unspoken rule that you don't criticise them in public; but sometimes the temptation is too great. When you realise that your career has peaked; when you can't help flouncing out of the government on a point of pride or principle; when you know you are headed for obscurity anyway – then you can claim the right to break the rules for once and say what you think about those who have hurt you.

It's a risky strategy. What you'd like to do is dictate your side of the story directly to history but as soon as you have finished your speech you will have to contend with reality. You will be momentarily courted by the media but then damned by them, as your brief flirtation with honesty is compared with your past duplicity and viewers, listeners and readers are reminded that you are still "one of them".

Your erstwhile colleagues will naturally loathe you for eternity for breaking ranks. The target of your spite – usually the prime minister – will pluck the dagger from his chest with an infuriating but feigned nonchalance, and all the other greasy careerists and double-crossers you leave behind will either seethe in bitter resentment or envy because they didn't have the guts to join you.

But it will be worth it for those brief minutes of satisfaction; because the main objective is not to make yourself feel better, and usually has nothing to do with enlightening the public. The point is to fatally wound your bully: get the words right and he or she will never recover from the blow.

On the following pages are some famous stabs in the front of recent vintage.

Michael Heseltine Defence Secretary

Date of departure: 9 January 1986

Resigned over: being ignored in Cabinet. He felt his views about the Westland Affair were not being heard.

Swansong: Heseltine dramatically left a Cabinet meeting and made a statement to the press almost immediately, rather than writing a resignation letter to the prime minister as is customary. In it he said, "If the basis of trust between the Prime Minister and her Defence Secretary no longer exists, there is no place for me with honour in such a Cabinet."

Aftermath: Margaret Thatcher stayed in power, although weakened by Heseltine's departure and the resignation of Trade and Industry Secretary Leon Brittan two weeks later.

Nigel Lawson

Date of departure: October 1989

Resigned over: Margaret Thatcher taking economic advice from her personal adviser, dubbed 'part-time Chancellor', Sir Alan Walters.

Swansong: "The prime minister of the day must appoint ministers whom he or she trusts and then leave them to carry out the policy. When differences of view emerge, as they are bound to do from time to time, they should be resolved privately and, whenever appropriate, collectively."

Aftermath: Again, Margaret Thatcher continued in power. Lawson's resignation left bitterness in the Conservative Party and, in hindsight, could be seen as an omen of the fatal split to come a year later.

Sir Geoffrey Howe, Deputy prime minister

Date of departure: 1 November 1990

Resigned over: Margaret Thatcher's attitude to Europe.

Swansong: Speaking to the House of Commons he described "the nightmare image sometimes conjured up by my Right Hon. Friend [Mrs Thatcher], who seems sometimes to look out upon a continent that is positively teeming with ill-intentioned people, scheming, in her words, to 'extinguish democracy', to 'dissolve our national identities' and to lead us 'through the back-door into a federal Europe'. What kind of vision is that for our business people, who trade there each day, for our financiers, who seek to make London the money capital of Europe or for all the young people of today?"

Margaret Thatcher had earlier dismissed his resignation as unimportant with the words: "I am still at the crease, though the bowling has been pretty hostile of late. And in case anyone doubted it, can I assure you there will be no ducking the bouncers, no stonewalling, no playing for time. The bowling's going to get hit all round the ground. That is my style." Howe concluded his attack by picking up the same metaphor, declaring that her obstinate stance over Europe "is rather like sending your opening batsmen to the crease, only for them to find, as the first balls are being bowled, that their bats have been broken before the game by the team captain."

Aftermath: Howe was Margaret Thatcher's longest-serving ally having been with her in government since the start in 1979 (Edward Pearce described him as "a late-developing assassin"). Without him, she suddenly looked isolated, a divisive and confrontational figure at the head of an unpopular government. Within a week of Howe's speech, Michael Heseltine had challenged her for the leadership and she was forced to resign.

Norman Lamont, Chancellor of the Exchequer

Date of departure: 9 June 1993

Resigned over: John Major's attempt to move him from the Treasury to another Cabinet post. He felt unjustly blamed for a recession and the government's humiliating withdrawal from the Exchange Rate Mechanism the previous autumn.

Swansong: Norman Lamont may as well have uttered only one phrase in his political career. In the penultimate paragraph of a considered speech to the House of Commons he complained that John Major's government gave "the impression of being in office but not in power". "The Government listen too much to the pollsters and the party managers," he explained. "The trouble is that they are not even very good at politics, and they are entering too much into policy decisions. As a result, there is too much short-termism, too much reacting to events, and not enough shaping of events.... Far too many important decisions are made for 36 hours' publicity. Yes, we are politicians as well as policy-makers; but we are also the trustees of the nation. I believe that in politics one should decide what is right and then decide the presentation, not the other way round. Unless this approach is changed, the Government will not survive, and will not deserve to survive."

Aftermath: the Major government survived the loss of the Chancellor; but Lamont's political career effectively ended with his resignation from government. He lost his seat due to boundary changes and failed to get elected for the hitherto safe Conservative seat of Harrogate in 1997.

Robin Cook, Leader of the House of Commons

Date of departure: 17 March 2003

Resigned over: Tony Blair's decision to go to war against Iraq with the USA without having achieved a United Nations mandate.

Swansong: Immediately after his resignation, Robin Cook delivered a brilliant speech to the House of Commons setting out his reservations about how Britain had become embroiled in an unpopular war. He stressed his continuing support for Tony Blair but was severely critical of his actions: "Only a year ago, we and the United States were part of a coalition against terrorism that was wider and more diverse than I would ever have imagined possible. History will be astonished at the diplomatic miscalculations that led so quickly to the disintegration of that powerful coalition." He argued that the House of Commons should have the right to decide on whether Britain should go to war.

Aftermath: Clare Short followed Robin Cook in resigning over the war on 12 May. She was even more critical of the prime minister. The two resignations added to Tony Blair's unpopularity and they may have hastened his decision to retire before completing his third term in office. Robin Cook died suddenly two years later of a heart attack. The words "I may not have succeeded in halting the war, but I did secure the right of parliament to decide on war," were carved on his gravestone.

Strikes

6 memorable moments in the history of the trade unions

Trade unions in Britain have played a highly influential role in politics for the last 100 years with varying degrees of success in achieving their objectives. Their power only began to wane during the era of Margaret Thatcher when radical changes were made to the laws governing industrial relations.

Tonypandy, 8 November 1910

A strike in this Rhondda Valley mining town, in response to heavy-handed management, degenerated into a riot which is remembered today, mainly in union mythology, because the Home Secretary Winston Churchill "sent the troops in."

General Strike, 3-10 May 1926

At the time, it was feared by some that this showdown between organised labour and the government, in which 2 million workers walked out, would turn into a Communist revolution. It began with mine-owners proposing to cut wages and make miners work longer hours, and ended with these conditions being forcibly imposed and the unions cowed. The labour movement was split by the last great flexing of its muscles which killed off debate within it as to whether it should – or even could – work through parliamentary democracy to achieve its aims.

The 'Battle of Downing Street', The Seamen's Strike of 1966

The Seamen's Strike of 1966 blocked Britain's import and export trade for six weeks, and was a graphic illustration of the dilemma facing any Labour government: the party relied on union funding for its election campaigns but could not afford to let unions dictate government policy. Harold Wilson and his Employment Secretary Barbara Castle realised that they had to impose a solution on the unions leading to the White Paper, *In Place of Strife*, published in 1969, which only succeeded in splitting the Cabinet. The Home Secretary and trade unionist, James Callaghan, was implacably opposed to trade union legislation and his views prevailed. With cruel irony, it was a failure to curb union power which would bring down the Callaghan government in 1979, leaving Margaret Thatcher to pass legislation to end closed shops, demarcation disputes and the calling of strikes without prior ballots.

Three-Day Week, 1974

A miners' strike compounded the effect of a hike in oil prices in 1973 and on 1 January 1974 the Heath government instructed the country to work a three-day week. As a consequence, he lost the February general election.

Winter of Discontent, 1978–9

The Sun newspaper borrowed the phrase from Shakespeare's Richard III and it has since come to sound like an official historical period. Mrs Thatcher, of course, profited from it by winning the election which was presented to the public as a vote on 'who governs Britain'. As public service unions stuck out for pay increases, rubbish piled up in the streets, accident and emergency departments closed and the dead went unburied.

Miners' Strike, March 1984 to March 1985

There was a first wave of miners' strikes in 1981 when the National Coal Board attempted to close pits but found it wasn't prepared for full-scale confrontation with the miner's union, the NUM. By March 1984, however, the NCB, backed by the government, had stockpiled enough coal to last out a strike and had planned strategies for maintaining law and order in the face of civil unrest. The announcement of new pit closures, especially in Yorkshire, sparked a widespread strike which became the defining episode of Margaret Thatcher's avowed policy of weakening union power in Britain. Humiliated, the miners were forced back to work with nothing to show for their protest.

Wapping, January 1986 to February 1987

The printers' strike at Rupert Murdoch's News International – over redundancies, the introduction of new technology and the ending of collective bargaining – was a testament to the shift in the balance of industrial power away from the unions during the Thatcher years. *The Times* had been closed for almost a year by the unions in 1978/9 but its new owner, Rupert Murdoch, was prepared for battle in 1986. He had secretly built and equipped a new printing plant at 'Fortress Wapping'. When the print unions announced a strike, Murdoch sacked 6,000 on the spot, and activated the Wapping presses with the co-operation of electrical union (EETPU) workers. Despite violent picketing, support from the railway unions who refused to distribute Murdoch titles, and some public sympathy, the print union's actions were unsuccessful, with not a single day's production being lost during the year-long dispute. (see also 'Pilgrimages' p215-219).

Suffrage: One Person One Vote
9 steps from the street to the polling booth

> *"I do not consider the exclusion of the working classes from effectual representation a defect in THIS aspect of our Parliamentary representation. The working classes contribute almost nothing to our corporate public opinion, and therefore, the fact of their want of influence in Parliament does not impair the coincidence of Parliament with public opinion."*
>
> Walter Bagehot the English Constitution 1867

'One adult: One vote', or universal suffrage, seems incontestably the only fair way to choose representatives in a democracy but it took many years and many acts of parliament to achieve.

Before the first reform act, there was little democracy to be had in Britain. Only men with a certain amount of property were eligible to vote and wealthy individuals could vote in several constituencies at the same time – there was no residency requirement. Britain was riddled with 'rotten boroughs' where, because of population shifts, few people were entitled to vote and in some cases the entire electorate lived elsewhere.

Many rural constituencies were openly known to be 'pocket boroughs' because they were in the pockets of the landed gentry and the nobility: they nominated the MP and he did what he was told by his patron. Some dukes and earls controlled several such constituencies. It was not unusual for a seat to be uncontested for decades and simply treated as the personal fief of the local lord.

When no one owned a constituency, it was likely to be rife with corruption. Electors were bribed individually or even collectively and, in one borough, a syndicate of influential local dignitaries simply sold the seat to the highest bidder. Even if a constituency was free from outright corruption, there was no secret ballot to prevent bullying and intimidation.

Pressure for reform built up during the 18th century but the shockwaves of the French Revolution set progress back as campaigns for increased representation took fright at the violent turn of events across the Channel.

Act	Step forward
Representation of the People Act 1832, normally called the First Reform Act	By taking votes away from depopulated 'rotten boroughs' and giving votes to the cities created by the Industrial Revolution, it doubled the electorate but specifically disenfranchised women.
Second Reform Act (Representation of the People Act) 1867	Enfranchised all male householders.
Parliamentary and Municipal Elections Act Ballot Act 1872	Introduced the secret ballot.
Third Reform Act (Representation of the People Act) 1884	Enfranchised more men but still left 40% of them without the vote. An act the following year made most constituencies single member.
Representation of the People Act (sometimes called the Fourth Reform Act) of 1918	Gave votes to all men over 21 and to women over 30.
Representation of the People Act 1928	Made men and women equal, both being eligible to vote at 21.
Representation of the People Act 1949	Abolished plural voting (which allowed university graduates to vote twice.)
Representation of the People Act 1969	Lowered the voting age from 21 to 18.
Representation of the People Act 1985	Enabled Britons living abroad to vote by proxy or by post.

Further improvements?

Giving people the right to vote is one thing; getting them to use it is another. Ironically, as the franchise has extended, turnout has declined. Two solutions proposed are a) to make voting compulsory; b) to offer an incentive to vote (a cash payment or a lottery ticket).

Sun Headlines

7 sensational solar scoops

"The only way with newspaper attacks is, as the Irish say, 'to keep never minding'. This has been my practice through life." Earl Grey

The tabloid press is the modern equivalent of the fishwife screaming her version of the news across the forum, having heard it in a game of Chinese whispers from the local gossip and reduced the story in her head to what she thinks should be its essence. If people's attentions spans are getting shorter because of television and the internet, historians of tomorrow will always be able to skim through the headlines of *The Sun* for a instant guide to what happened when and why it seemed to matter at the time.

"Gotcha!" 4 May 1982
On the sinking of the Argentine warship, the General Belgrano, during the Falklands Conflict. In later editions the headline was toned down to something more respectful.

"Crisis? What Crisis?" 11 January 1979
The headline which helped scupper Jim Callaghan (see p298).

"Up Yours Delors: At midday tomorrow Sun readers are urged to tell the French Fool where to stuff his ECU." 1 November 1990
A verbal and visual two-finger salute to Jacques Delors who then seemed to represent the embryonic single European currency.

"If Kinnock wins today will the last person to leave Britain please turn out the lights" 9 April 1992
The last nail in Neil Kinnock's electoral campaign.

"It's The Sun Wot Won It" 11 April 1992
The paper claims victory for John Major's general election win.

"The Sun backs Blair" 18 March 1997
The next prime minister is anointed by the people's paper.

"Oh No. They've elected Kenny! Blair's Worst Nightmare" 5 May 2000
London gets its first elected mayor without the approval of *The Sun*.

Systems of Government

10 mots justes for funny ways to run a country

Ergatocracy: rule by the workers

Gerontocracy: rule by elderly people

Gynaecocracy or gynarchy: rule by women

Hierocracy or theocracy: rule by priests

Isocracy or pantisocracy: rule by people who have equal power

Krytocracy: rule by judges

Mobocracy or ochlocracy: rule by the mob

Polyarchy: rule by competing interest groups in which government acts as broker

Stratocracy: rule by the military

Timocracy: rule by citizens possessing property

Thatcherism

11 memorable remarks by her and 15 comments by her critics

Like the founder of any religion, Thatcher has left us a body of folklore: a legacy of things she said, almost said or which we think she should have said which amount to a philosophy for the faithful. Strangely, it is her left-wing opponents who miss her most: her rule was a time when the divisions in British politics were starkly clear.

Memorable Thatcherisms

"I speak as a very young Tory and we are entitled to speak, for it is the people of my generation who will bear the brunt of the change from the trials of the past into calmer channels." As Miss Roberts, her first recorded speech, at a Conservative meeting in Sleaford, Lincolnshire, 25 June 1945

"It will be years before a woman either leads the Conservative Party or becomes prime minister. I don't see it happening in my time." 1970

"If your only opportunity is to be equal, then it is not equality." 1976

"I would just like to remember some words of St. Francis of Assisi which I think are really just particularly apt at the moment. 'Where there is discord, may we bring harmony. Where there is error, may we bring truth. Where there is doubt, may we bring faith. And where there is despair, may we bring hope." 4 May 1979, outside 10 Downing Street

"Oh Lord, teach me to learn that occasionally I make mistakes." quoting a favourite poem on Today 1982

"I am extraordinarily patient, provided I get my own way in the end."

"I don't know what I would do without Whitelaw. Everyone should have a Willy."

"If you want anything said, ask a man. If you want anything done, ask a woman."

"I owe nothing to women's lib." (To which one feminist retorted: "She may be a woman but she isn't a sister.")

"I think we've been through a period where too many people have been given to understand that if they have a problem, it's the government's job to cope with it. 'I have a problem, I'll get a grant.' 'I'm homeless, the government must house me.' They're casting their problem on society. And, you know, there is no such thing as society. There are individual men and women, and there are families. And no government can do anything except through people, and people must look to themselves first. It's our duty to look after ourselves and then also to look after our neighbour. People have got the entitlements too much in mind, without the obligations. There's no such thing as entitlement, unless someone has first met an obligation." 1987

"I fight on, I fight to win", when challenged for the leadership battle which she was to lose, 1990

Judgements of her critics

"She is democratic enough to talk down to anyone."
Austin Mitchell, Westminster Man 1982

"She has the eyes of Caligula, and the mouth of Marilyn Monroe."
François Mitterand

"She will insist on treating other heads of government as if they were members of her cabinet."
Ian Gilmour

"Trying to tell her anything is like making an important phone call and getting an answering machine."
David Steel

"The plutonium blonde."
Arthur Scargill

"A brilliant tyrant surrounded by mediocrities."
Harold Macmillan

"A cross between Isadora Duncan and Lawrence of Arabia."
Daily Telegraph

"She sounded like the Book of Revelations read out over a railway public address system by a headmistress of a certain age wearing calico knickers."
Clive James

"Margaret Thatcher plays, I suspect, to an unseen gallery of headmistresses, economists and the Madame Tussaud version of Winston Churchill."

Katharine Whitehorn

"If you want to change her mind you don't use argument – you look for a transplant surgeon."

John Edmonds (GMB Union Leader)

"Paddy Ashdown is the first trained killer to be a party leader... Mrs Thatcher being self-taught."

Gilbert Archer, President of the
Edinburgh Chamber of Commerce, 1992

"Crocodile tears with crocodile teeth."

Neil Kinnock

"Clearly the best man among them."

Barbara Cartland

"The Enid Blyton of economics."

Richard Holme

"Mrs Thatcher is doing for monetarism what the Boston Strangler did for door-to-door salesmen."

Denis Healey

Theory – Some Footnotes to Plato

8 essential texts reduced to rudiments

There are only three things anyone needs to know about political theory:

1. Only insecure and worried men with no experience of exercising authority over anyone else ever bother to lecture others on how to do it (and no one takes their advice anyway).

2. No one has had a big new idea since 1850 (see p310).

3. No one will ever have another political idea worth hearing because we live in a postmodern age (see 'Postmodern Politics' p253).

All political theory is therefore out of date and, having been written by neurotics, inapplicable to the real world. But if you still want to know what has got so many people worked up for the last 2,400 years, here is a summary of who wrote what and why.

Books marked (S) are short enough to read; all others will put you to sleep before you finish them. The strapline provided for each author tells you all you need to know.

Plato (4th century BC)
Occupation: Aristocrat
Chip on shoulder: democrats executed his hero Socrates
Bestseller: The Republic
Strapline: Mistrust democracy and let yourselves be ruled by an intellectual elite of 'philosopher kings'.
Note: for footnotes to Plato, see Aristotle's *The Politics*. For footnotes to Aristotle, see St Thomas Aquinas' *Libros Politicorum Expositio* etc.

St. Augustine (354-430)
Occupation: Bishop
Chip on shoulder: guilty conscience to atone for. In his *Confessions* he says: "Give me chastity and continency, but not yet."
Bestseller: City of God
Strapline: Do what you're told but keep your mind on higher things.

Machiavelli (1469–1527)
Occupation: Civil servant
Chip on shoulder: Couldn't trust his fellow Italians to sort out the mess they were in; and he didn't want to upset the Borgias.
Bestseller: The Prince (S)
Strapline: You can't afford to be nice to everyone when you've got a country to run.

Thomas Hobbes (1588–1679)
Occupation: Thinking secretary
Chip on shoulder: Unprocessed childhood trauma: his mother's fear of the Spanish Armada induced his premature birth.
Bestseller: Leviathan
Strapline: The only good fanatic is a dumb one.

John Locke (1632–1704)
Occupation: Doctor
Chip on shoulder: Exiled when his boss died in disgrace.
Bestseller: Second Treatise of Civil Government
Strapline: Don't trust the government: it doesn't trust you.

John Stuart Mill (1806–1873)
Occupation: Examiner (letter writer) for the East India Company and later MP
Chip on shoulder: Had to live up to the expectations of his father who gave him an education meant to make him the perfect rational man with 25 years' start over his contemporaries.
Bestseller: On Liberty (S)
Strapline: People have the right to ruin their own lives without help from the government.

Alexis de Toqueville (1805-1859)
Occupation: Lawyer and MP
Chip on shoulder: Six members of his aristocratic family were executed during the French Revolution, turning his father's hair white at the age of 21.
Bestseller: Democracy in America
Strapline: Let's work together – selfishness doesn't get us anywhere. (This offer does not apply to women and slaves.)

Karl Marx (1818-1883)

Occupation: Revolutionary bookworm

Chip on shoulder: Chronic inability to earn a living except by drawing an income from the Engels' (capitalist) family business.

Bestseller: Communist Manifesto (S, written with Engels). Other catchy titles in the series are are Grundrisse, Capital and Criticism of the Gotha Programme.

Strapline: Don't worry/do worry (depending who you are and what you own): you'll get what you deserve.

Theory – Contemporary Thinkers

10 thinkers who've tried to make sense of the modern world

All the fathers of political philosophy – and they are all men – lived and died before 1900. It has been said that the 20th century killed off the possibility of, or the need for any more brave new theories because of its horrific wars, totalitarian experiments, creeping bureaucracies, globalisation and all-pervasive mass media. How do you theorise about the average democratic state which takes responsibility for everything from economic growth and healthcare to sporting fixtures?

Bertrand Russell (1872–1970)
A prolific writer and highly influential thinker, Russell was a lifelong believer in pacifism – he actively opposed the deployment of nuclear weapons – and world government. In 1948 he gave the first Reith lecture on *Authority and the Individual:* how the need for social cohesion could be balanced with encouraging human initiative.

Martin Heidegger (1889-1976)
One of the most influential philosophers of the 20th century and the mentor of both Hannah Arendt (his sometime lover) and Leo Strauss. He is remembered, politically speaking, not for any theory he came up with but for a controversial career decision. In 1933, three months after Hitler's rise to power, he was appointed to the rectorate of the University of Freiburg and soon after joined the Nazi party. He remained a member until after the war.

Herbert Marcuse (1898-1979)
A Marxist critic of capitalism (essentially saying that consumerism won't make us happy) which made him the darling of the 1960s 'new' left. Best-known book: *One-Dimensional Man* (1964).

Leo Strauss (1899-1973)
German-born Jew and professor at the University of Chicago who is often described as the guru of the neoconservatism that has driven the White House of George W. Bush.

Karl Popper (1902-94)

An Austrian philosopher who found a home in the London School of Economics after World War II. In *The Open Society and its Enemies* (1945) and *The Poverty of Historicism* he seeks to show that authoritarianism and totalitarianism are based on the belief that human development moves in a set, predictable direction.

Hannah Arendt (1906-1975)

The only woman to have made a mark on the history of political theory. Most of her work is an explanation of how totalitarianism arises and how it operates. She famously and controversially coined the phrase "banality of evil" to describe the methodology of the Holocaust: a neat bureaucratic solution to a social problem carried out not by amoral psychopaths but ordinary people interested in furthering their own careers.

Isaiah Berlin (1909-1997)

Celebrated by intellectuals for his emphasis on pluralism and toleration and his distinction between positive and negative liberty. Celebrated by the rest of us for dividing people into foxes and hedgehogs, based on a formulation by the Ancient Greek poet Archilochus: "The fox knows many things, but the hedgehog knows one big thing." Or to be blunt: foxes "relate everything to a single central vision, one system ... a single, universal, organizing principle," and hedgehogs are "centrifugal rather than centripetal, their thought scattered or diffused, moving on many levels, seizing on the essence of a vast variety of experiences and objects for what they are in themselves."

Anthony Crosland (1918-77)

A politician who held various posts in the Wilson government but whose main contribution to the Labour Party was a book, *The Future of Socialism* (1956), which Tony Blair has cited as an inspiration. In it Crosland laid down the principle of 'revisionism' or social democracy, by which socialism needed to be less ideologically driven and more adapted to the conditions of a modern, changing world.

John Rawls (1921-2002)

A Liberal Harvard professor who reformulated the old idea of the social contract in his *Theory of Justice* (1971) and other books. His basic notion was that everyone should have the same rights and liberties and that inequalities in society should only be tolerated if they work to the benefit of people at the bottom of the social heap.

Noam Chomsky (b 1928)

A linguist turned left-wing political theorist and activist who has classed himself as a libertarian socialist. The onus is on authority to prove that it is legitimate, he argues, otherwise it should be assumed that it is illegitimate.

Theory – Two Cows

Various versions of the laws of bi-bovinology circulate on the internet but here, for the first time, is the definitive pastoral political philosophy for anyone who has trouble sorting sheep from goats.

DEMOCRACY

You have two cows. Your neighbours pick someone to tell you who gets the milk.

SOCIAL DEMOCRACY

You have two cows. Your neighbours have none. You secretly think it is because they don't work hard enough but you feel guilty for not having anything to complain about so you vote people into office who tax your cows so heavily that you are forced to sell one to raise the money to pay the tax. The people you voted for vote themselves a four-fold increase in expense allowances and buy half a cow to give to your neighbours, who look after it so badly that it has to be taken into care. You feel righteous: the system may not be perfect, but at least it works.

THEORETICAL COMMUNISM APPLIED

You have two cows which you care for according to your abilities and which yield milk according to your needs. The state moves your cows to poorer pastures to graze with the cows of 500 other people in order to increase productivity. They all die during the first winter and everyone goes hungry. The government is re-elected with a majority of 100%.

REVOLUTIONARY COMMUNISM (EXPORT MODEL)

Cows are symbols of bourgeois property and the power of the Church. You round them up and shoot them. The peasants starve but at least they are free. You generously assist grateful neighbouring countries to adopt your economic model.

BASIC STALINISM

You have two cows. The government seizes both but makes you take care of them. It takes all the milk and provides you with as much of it as it thinks you need. You wait in line for hours to get it. It is expensive and sour.

ADVANCED STALINISM

You have two cows. The government takes them both and denies they ever existed. You are drafted into the army. Milk is banned.

CONSERVATISM

You have two cows. Your neighbour has none. So what?

FREE MARKET CAPITALISM

You have two cows. You sell one and buy a bull. Your herd multiplies, and the economy grows thanks to you – although no one, least of all the pinkos in state television, appreciates your hard work. You get a tip that mad cow disease is coming so you sell your herd to someone who isn't as good at business as you and retire on the income.

ARISTOCRACY

You inherited two cows from your father who inherited them from his father whose father's-father's-father was given cows in the 14th century for some reason that no one can remember or doesn't want to own up to. You call your cows 'rare breeds' and charge common people to come and see them so they can have a day out from their drab lives. You complain that you never have enough money to fix the leaking stable roof. You used to own all the cows around here and part of you thinks you still should.

MONARCHY

You have never seen a cow but you believe you own a few hundred herds somewhere which are nominally yours although on permanent loan to the state (which happens to be yours in name as well). The Ming Dynasty milk jug, however, is definitely yours.

EUROPEAN FEDERALISM

You have two cows which cost more money to care for than you earn. This is because supermarkets can import their milk from eastern Europe at a cheaper price. You sell your milk at an elevated price to a state-owned distributor which sells it for less than it paid for it to a company which makes winter feed for dairy cows. This ensures that Europe is competitive. You take advantage of a government-subsidised job creation scheme to employ a farm hand to look after your cows so that you can go on demonstrations to Brussels to complain that European farm policy is driving you out of a job.

FEMINISM

There are two sisters in your workplace who, through no fault of their own, happen to be cows. They spend a lot of time complaining about their lot without producing any milk – but why should they conform to stereotypes just because they are cows? You give them a pay rise, fresh straw and preferential treatment on the lower rungs of the job ladder which they don't take advantage of. You apply for the job of farmer but say that you will only be able to do it as a part-time job-share with nine month's leave a year so that you can do an MBA in Female Empowerment in the Workplace. You are rejected because of your gender (whatever they say) but you are secretly relieved to keep your old job – after all, who is going to clean the cowshed floor if you don't?

ANIMAL LIBERATION

There are two cows in a field. You release them into the wild. You live in a city and eat raw grass.

POLITICAL CORRECTNESS

Your next-door neighbours happen to be two non-gender specific quadrupeds who don't like to be referred to as 'cows' because of the discriminatory associations of that word. They have a different lifestyle to yours which you do not understand but which contributes to the richness of society – you know because you once saw a documentary about it. You respect their customs such as eating grass and defecating in the open air. You wouldn't dream of imposing such a loaded, ethno-centric, historically-biased, exploitative demand as 'milking' on them.

ENVIRONMENTALISM

You have two cows living on organic pasture. The state bans you from milking or killing them. You convert your car to run on liquified cow-pats but are taxed for carbon emissions.

ANARCHISM

There are two cows in a field which everyone and no one 'owns'. Whoever wants to can milk them and have the pleasure of sharing the contents of the buckets with everyone else. You believe everyone should take it in turns to do their bit but, hey, it's yet another nice day and you don't feel like doing any work …

Think Tanks
15 celebrated cauldrons of concentrated cerebralism

A think tank is an organization that exists to collect, generate and disseminate information and ideas about political, economic and social issues. Typically it will undertake research, hold seminars, produce publications and seek to influence politicians and civil servants. Most think tanks have a distinctive political bent although many are coy about where they stand and most claim to be independent and objective.

Adam Smith Institute
www.adamsmith.org
"The Free-Market Think Tank". Founded in 1977 "to inject choice and competition into public services, extend personal freedom, reduce taxes, prune back regulation, and cut government waste."

Bow Group
www.bowgroup.org
"The oldest... centre-right think-tank in Britain which exists to ... stimulate debate within the Conservative Party." Founded in 1951, it originally met in Bow, East London. Geoffrey Howe, William Rees-Mogg and Norman St John Stevas attended the first meeting. Michael Howard, Norman Lamont and Peter Lilley have all been chairman in the past.

Bruges Group
www.brugesgroup.com
"An independent all-party think tank" founded in 1989 "to promote the idea of a less centralised European structure". Its inspiration was Margaret Thatcher's Bruges speech in September 1988, in which she remarked that, "We have not successfully rolled back the frontiers of the state in Britain, only to see them re-imposed at a European level".

Centre for Policy Studies (CPS)
www.cps.org.uk
Founded by Sir Keith Joseph and Margaret Thatcher in 1974 to champion economic liberalism in Britain. Its policy proposals are based on a set of core principles, including individual choice and responsibility, and the concepts of duty, family, liberty, and the rule of law." It is also "the champion of the Small State."

Chatham House

www.chathamhouse.org.uk

Founded in 1920 and now "one of the world's leading organizations for the analysis of international issues". It is also the originator of the Chatham House Rule which states 'When a meeting, or part thereof, is held under the Chatham House Rule, participants are free to use the information received, but neither the identity nor the affiliation of the speaker(s), nor that of any other participant, may be revealed'.

Civitas

www.civitas.org.uk

The Institute for the Study of Civil Society, founded in 2000 "to deepen public understanding of the legal, institutional and moral framework that makes a free and democratic society possible." And to achieve "a better division of responsibilities between government and civil society."

Demos

www.demos.co.uk

'The Think Tank for Everyday Democracy'. Founded in 1993 "to help reinvigorate public policy and political thinking and to develop radical solutions to long term problems."

Fabian Society

www.fabian-society.org.uk

Left-of-centre. Founded in 1884 "as a socialist society committed to gradual rather than revolutionary social reform. The name comes from the Roman general Quintus Fabius, known as Cunctator (meaning 'delayer') from his strategy of delaying battle until the right moment. The Society's early members included George Bernard Shaw (later described by Lenin as 'a good man fallen among Fabians'), Sidney and Beatrice Webb, Emmeline Pankhurst and H.G. Wells."

Foreign Policy Centre

fpc.org.uk

"Launched [in 1998] under the patronage of the British Prime Minister Tony Blair to develop a vision of a fair and rule-based world order."

Hansard Society

www.hansardsociety.org.uk

Founded in 1944 "to promote the ideals of parliamentary government when it was seen to be threatened by fascist and communist dictatorship. Its first subscribers were Churchill and Attlee, the then Prime Minister and Deputy Prime Minister. From that time, the Prime Minister of the day and leaders of the main opposition parties have publicly supported the work of the Society, and the Speaker of the House of Commons is our President."

Institute for Public Policy Research
www.ippr.org.uk
Independent, centre-left and "progressive". Founded in 1988 "to build a fairer, more democratic and environmentally sustainable world."

Institute of Economic Affairs
www.iea.org.uk
Founded in 1955. "Without the IEA, Britain could have been overcome by socialism in the 1970s. And the organisation is still there, putting the case for free markets, property rights and individual responsibility and turning cosy assumptions on their heads. The IEA's goal is to explain free-market ideas to the public, including politicians, students, journalists, businessmen, academics and anyone interested in public policy. Society's problems and challenges are best dealt with by people and companies interacting with each other freely without interference from politicians and the State."

International Institute for Strategic Studies
www.iiss.org
Founded in 1958 "by a number of individuals interested in how to maintain civilised international relations in the nuclear age." It claims to be "the world's leading authority on political-military conflict."

Smith Institute
www.smith-institute.org.uk
Founded in memory of the Labour leader John Smith who died in 1994 to research and discuss "issues that flow from the changing relationship between social values and economic imperatives."

Social Affairs Unit
www.socialaffairsunit.org.uk
Founded in 1980 to address " social, economic and cultural issues with an emphasis on the value of personal responsibility ... and the individual's obligations."

The Today Programme

10 facts about Britain's national alarm clock

"I'm only really off-duty if I leave the country and cannot hear the Today programme." Virginia Bottomley

The BBC regards *Today* (broadcast each morning on Radio 4) as its flagship political programme and one former government minister has described it as "a sort of organ of our constitution". No other programme has quite the same ability, in the words of Tom Phillips, "to attract pyjama'd politicians to its radio car to pontificate on the issues of the day" knowing they will be insolently grilled by presenters frequently accused of being macho-mannered. Another word often used for *Today's* hammering interview technique is 'gladiatorial'. An invitation to appear is like a challenge to go ten rounds with the neighbourhood bully. If you stay standing your friends and enemies will respect you and the public may just listen to what you have to say.

1. *Today* was the idea of Sir Robin Day. It was launched on 28 October 1957, on the Home Service, and was going to be called *Morning Miscellany* before the snappier title was decided on.

2. The average audience between 7.30am and 8.00am is 2.4 million.

3. Although many listeners rely on *Today* to schedule their morning, one of the programme's first presenters, Jack de Manio, regularly had trouble telling the time on the studio clock.

4. Every prime minister since Harold Macmillan has been interviewed by the presenters of *Today*.

5. Many leading politicians listen to the programme and some have even contributed to it. Margaret Thatcher phoned the studio from Downing Street while Today was on the air on Thursday 8 December 1988 to comment on a cancelled state visit by Mikhail Gorbachev. She said it took several minutes to get through because staff weren't sure whether or not it was a hoax call. On another occasion, Deputy Prime Minister John Prescott telephoned to correct a story as it was being broadcast.

6. Both main parties have accused *Today* of bias. The former Conservative minister, Jonathan Aitken, complained that the

presenter John Humphrys had interrupted the Chancellor of the Exchequer Kenneth Clarke 32 times during an interview.

7. Small wonder that it was Kenneth Clarke who posed the question that all politicians would like to ask of *Today*: "Why are we always brought in to talk about what is going to happen, and not about all the virtuous and distinguished things we've done the day before." John Humphrys replied: "We set the agenda. That is the purpose of the *Today* programme."

8. *Today* has been embroiled in serious controversy twice in recent years. The first, in 2002, was over an article entitled 'Marching back to Labour' which the programme's editor, Rod Liddle, wrote for the *Guardian*. In it, Liddle said that readers who had forgotten why they voted Labour would remember when they saw pictures of the people campaigning to save hunting. This was considered unacceptably partisan and Liddle was forced to resign (see p17). A year later, presenter John Humphrys was interviewing correspondent Andrew Gillighan live just after 6 am when the latter asserted that, on the basis of an anonymous source, the government had made a misleading claim in its dossier justifying war against Saddam Hussein's Iraq. The Labour government was merciless in its revenge on the BBC for this slur and both the chairman and the director-general of the corporation resigned.

9. It has been claimed that *Today* used to form a key element in Britain's 'defence'. If the commander of a nuclear submarine noticed that a certain number of days had passed without the programme being broadcast he was to assume that Britain had been annihilated by Soviet missiles and that it was time to open his sealed orders and carry out a retaliatory strike. The story is almost certainly apocryphal – no official source has confirmed it – but there is a reassuring ring of British improvisation about it.

10. *Today* holds an annual poll to name the 'Personality of the Year'. Periodically it asks for nominations for other unofficial titles. In 2004 it held a vote to find someone worthy of a peerage, a 'Listeners' Lord'. In 2005 listeners were asked 'Who Runs Britain?' Other straw polls have asked for a 'Listeners' Law' for an MP to put before parliament, and for the audience's choice of an existing law which most deserved to be repealed.

Truth

10 ways of telling the political truth

> "A lie travels round the world while the truth is putting on her boots."
>
> *Rev. CH Spurgeon, 19th century Baptist preacher*

Nothing could be more fundamental in politics, or more slippery, than truth and falsehood. MPs must assume that their colleagues tell nothing but the truth in the House of Commons, or rather they must find devious ways of accusing other honorable members of lying without using that word. The rest of us assume that most politicians sometimes tell us the truth when they want to, but it's like the old riddle of meeting two men at a crossroads and asking them for directions. One always tells the truth; one always lies, and you have to find out which is which. The following is a guide to the vocabulary of political veracity.

"It is perhaps being economical with the truth."

> *Sir Robert Armstrong*, a British Cabinet Secretary, admitted during the Spycatcher trial before the Supreme Court of New South Wales in Australia on 18 November 1986. The remark made headlines as exactly the sort of thing a dissembling senior civil servant would say as a way of avoiding blunt facts. In fact, the phrase was previously used by Samuel Pepys, Mark Twain and many others.

"Something unpleasant is coming when men are anxious to speak the truth."

> *Disraeli*

"Never believe anything in politics until it has been officially denied."

> *Bismarck*

"When you want to fool the world, tell the truth."

> *Bismarck*

"It has always been desirable to tell the truth, but seldom possible (if ever necessary) to tell the whole truth."

> *Balfour*

"You'll never get mixed up if you simply tell the truth. Then you don't have to remember what you have said, and you never forget what you said."

Sam Rayburn

"This is the operative statement. The others are inoperative."

> *Ronald Ziegler*, Nixon's press secretary explaining why previous denials in the White House's Watergate scandal had been misleading, 17 April 1973

"It depends on what the meaning of the word 'is' is. If the – if he – if 'is' means is and never has been, that is not – that is one thing. If it means there is none, that was a completely true statement. . . . Now, if someone had asked me on that day, are you having any kind of sexual relations with Ms. Lewinsky, that is, asked me a question in the present tense, I would have said no. And it would have been completely true."

> *Bill Clinton* quoted in the Starr Report, footnote 1,128

"In exceptional cases it is necessary to say something that is untrue to the House of Commons. The House of Commons understands that and has always accepted that."

> *William Waldegrave*, Minister of Agriculture to a select committee 1994

Dodgy digits

In politics, numbers are no more reliable than words. Many politicians either don't understand numbers or understand them too well and hope that voters don't. The classic decoder is *How to Lie with Statistics* by Darrell Huff (1953 and later editions). *Damned Lies and Statistics: Untangling Numbers from the Media, Politicians and Activists* by Joel Best (2001) is also useful.

Tumbril Remarks

7 indiscreet remarks by members of the elite

It's not certain that Marie Antoinette was the first person to suggest that the peasants eat cake when she heard they had run out of bread, but it's the thought that counts. Hers will always be the most famous 'tumbril remark' – a comment which indicates that the speaker has little idea how his or her social inferiors live.

It was the writer Joyce Carey who invented the phrase, a tumbril being a kind of cart designed for the carrying away of excrement which was used as an improvised means of transport during the French Revolution to convey aristocratics to the guillotine.

A true tumbril mark is delivered without irony; upper class politicians playing up their foppishness for effect don't count.

"I've been meeting the working class and I simply must say that it's absolutely the nicest class I've met so far."

> Humphry Berkeley explaining his switch from the Conservative Party to the Labour Party in 1970.

"Most people have to part with their cooks and live in hotels."

> Margot Asquith, widow of the prime minister Herbert Asquith, c1940 on the privations caused by the Second World War, as reported by George Orwell.

"But this is terrible – they've elected a Labour Government, and the country will never stand for that!"

> An unidentified lady hearing about Attlee's victory while dining in the Savoy in 1945.

"You have your own company, your own temperature control, your own music – and don't have to put up with dreadful human beings sitting alongside you."

> Steven Norris, Minister of State for Transport, explaining the advantages of private over public transport to a select committee in 1995.

"Is it a book that you would have lying around in your own house? Is it a book that you would even wish your wife or your servants to read?"

> Mervyn Griffith-Jones prosecuting counsel in the Lady Chatterley trial.

"I think you have done right by backing a colt when you know the stable he was trained in."

> Lady Honor Guinness to the local Conservative association which had selected her son, Paul Channon, to 'inherit' her father's seat of Southend West.

"... one of the most depressed towns in Southern England, a place that is arguably too full of drugs, obesity, underachievement and Labour MPs."

> The Eton-educated MP Boris Johnson describing Portsmouth in an article in *GQ*, April 2007. He had previously offended the people of Papua New Guinea by implying that they had 'orgies of cannibalism and chief-killing' and had later had to admit that modern Papua New Guineans 'lived lives of blameless bourgeois domesticity like the rest of us'.

"Goodness, can there be such poverty?"

> Lord Curzon, after seeing a silver napkin ring in a Bond Street shop window, and being told that it was used by people who could not afford to use fresh linen at every meal.

Turning Points

9 counterfactual conundrums

Speculating on the different turns which history might have taken is only really illuminating where an outcome depends on a decision made by an individual. Useful or not, it is always entertaining to speculate what might have happened if…

1. **General de Gaulle had not said no** to Britain's earliest application to join the Common Market in 1963. Would the eurosceptic tradition still have sunk such firm roots, particularly in the Conservative Party?

2. **Healey had won the leadership election instead of Callaghan in 1976** (or beaten Michael Foot in 1979). Would he have taken on the unions and beaten them thus making Mrs Thatcher redundant before she had got into her stride?

3. **Callaghan had called an election immediately** after taking over from Wilson in 1976, or at least in October 1978, before the "winter of discontent" set in. Would Labour have found its feet and been forced to face down the unions while Margaret Thatcher languished in opposition?

4. **General Galtieri, the president of Argentina, had quietly occupied the Falklands a month or two later** than he did, making it too late for the British to send a task force before the onset of winter. Instead of an armed conflict with a winner and loser, the Falklands crisis of 1982 might have become a messy, protracted diplomatic incident. In which case, it is doubtful whether Margaret Thatcher would have been popular enough to win the 1983 election.

5. **Mrs Thatcher had resigned over the Westland affair in 1986.** Would she still be talked about today as a political reformer or just be remembered as another prime minister who failed to implement a radical agenda?

6. **Neil Kinnock had found the right campaigning tone** to beat John Major in 1992. Major's majority was only 22 which meant that everything depended on a handful of marginal seats and under 2,000 individual voters. Had Kinnock done better there might

have been a hung parliament in which Labour could have formed a coalition with the Liberal Democrats. And then "New" Labour would have been stillborn.

7. **John Smith hadn't died in 1994.** Would the Labour Party have won an election without 'modernising' (scrapping Clause 4)? Would Smith have modernized anyway? Either way, again there would have been no 'New' Labour and perhaps British politics wouldn't have become enthralled to spin doctors and appointed advisers.

8. **Michael Portillo hadn't lost his seat in 1997,** or had stood in a different, safe seat. He was probably the Conservatives' best choice of candidate to succeed Major and might have united the party, playing the media as well as Blair, and won the 2001 election.

9. **Florida had gone to Al Gore in 2000,** instead of losing it by 537 votes to Bush. Would Tony Blair have been spared the Iraq dilemma, kept his popularity and sailed on to a fourth and fifth term?

UK Personality Problems

Why you may be confused about where you live

The Disunited Kingdom

There is a country whose name confuses even its own inhabitants. Officially the British live in the 'United Kingdom of Great Britain and Northern Ireland', or the United Kingdom for short. This is either a tautology (any kingdom which isn't united would no longer be a kingdom) or a spelling mistake: the name should be the United Kingdoms (as in the United States, United Nations, United Arab Emirates, the Federated States of Micronesia etc).

The name is also a rather dismissive simplification because it really means a union of two kingdoms, England and Scotland. Far from being an equal union, the latter, northern partner has always been treated as a province of London. The identity of Wales (let alone Cornwall) is not even mentioned in the full title of the United Kingdom. A more accurate description of the nation state would be the United Kingdoms, Principality, Duchies other Aristocratic Estates and Sundry Territories Covering Most of the British Isles but admittedly that wouldn't look good on the scoreboard of the Eurovision Song Contest.

Little Britons

Another problem is the name we give ourselves as citizens of this country. We are Britons and our affairs are British, but that comes from Great Britain (not to be confused with Little Britain or Brittany), which is only a part of the territory (England, Scotland and Wales). Shouldn't we have a name that corresponds to our nationality, perhaps unitedkingdomians, or ukians for short (adjective *ukish*, not to be pronounced 'yuckish')?

To complicate matters, most other nationalities don't bother calling us by our official name. They either call us (incorrectly) Great Britain or, more usually and wholly offensively to 10% of the population, England (Angleterre in French, Inglaterra in Spanish etc).

Location, location

And where is this country exactly? Other countries you can draw a border around on the map but ours has a rather diffused geographical layout. The United Kingdom is not synonymous with the British Isles, that small archpelago separated from 'the continent' only recently by a fluke of glaciation as if by geomorphic afterthought. To make geography and politics match, first you have to take away the country of (southern) Ireland but you also have to remove the Isle of Man which is not part of Great Britain (even though its people are British), not part of the United Kingdom, not a full member of the EU (unlike every last rock and gannet colony in the British Isles) and yet not an independent country either.

The fortunate French

Don't you envy the French who live in France – a clear-thinking people in a clearly identified territory who have the same number of letters in their name as they have sides to their country, and who only have to change two letters to get from the name of the state to their nationality? Wouldn't it be simpler to rebaptise our country Britain (neither greater nor lesser)? As an added bonus, we'd come near the top of internet drop-down menus instead of near the bottom.

Brusselsification

All of which might make you wish for greater European integration to simplify our political geography by reducing us to a province ruled from Brussels (lumped in with Ireland; and with the Isle of Man brought into the fold) known by a national ID number instead of a name.

Unparliamentary Language

*10 words that have been objected to in debates
(including a discourse on sweet FA)*

> *"Mr Speaker, I said the honourable member was a liar it is true
> and I am sorry for it. The honourable member may place the
> punctuation where he pleases."*

> Richard Brinslay Sheridan, on being asked to
> apologise for calling a fellow MP a liar

MPs are expected to talk in a respectful way to each other. According
to the guide book for parliamentary procedure, *Erskine May*, tone,
context and intent matter in the choice of language but in general
insulting, coarse, or abusive words or phrases, accusations of lying
and dark motives, of being drunk and misrepresenting what another
member has said are prohibited.

The Speaker can ask a member to withdraw an unacceptable remark
and an adept orator is sometimes able to make a retraction more
wounding than the original insult. When Disraeli was told to
apologise for his allegation that half the Cabinet were asses (or
knaves, depending on which version of the story you hear) he
pronounced, "Mr Speaker, I withdraw. Half the Cabinet are not
asses."

Among the words to which Speakers have objected over the years
have been:

blackguard
coward
git
guttersnipe
hooligan
rat
swine
stoolpigeon
traitor
fuck

The last of these is the final taboo and hardly a useful word for
debating new laws. It was first used in 1982 by an MP quoting a

sign in a sex shop and has appeared more and more frequently in Hansard in recent years, always as a quotation, never as an insult.

For instance, in 2006 one Labour MP told the house, "I was told just a few days ago by someone no less than a bishop – I apologise for putting it in this way, but it is the only way I can do it – that the French now refer routinely to the English as 'les fuck-offs'."

The Speaker remarked soon after, "The fact that I missed one of the expressions used by the Hon. Gentleman does not mean that there is open house for such words."

Utopias

10 places you might want to move to

> *"If you create utopia, what do you do next day?"*
> Brian Redhead (Plato to Nato, Radio 4)

> *"You cannot ask one Utopian to live in another's Utopia."*
> G.K. Chesterton (1924)

> *"A map of the world that does not include Utopia is not even worth glancing at."*
> Oscar Wilde

Unlike heaven, paradise, the Garden of Eden, Arcadia and the Land of Milk and Honey, utopias are genuine attempts to work out the practicalities of running a perfect world but they cannot, by definition, ever exist. Some are mere entertaining flights of fancy but others are meant to be serious blueprints. To design your own utopia see www.achievingutopia.org.

1. *The Republic* by **Plato (400 BC)**
   Plato portrays a model polity ruled over by an elite of philosopher kings who know what's best for everyone beneath them. Plato was also responsible for introducing the world to the mythical lost world of Atlantis (described in his Timaeus and Critias dialogues) which inspired Francis Bacon to write his utopian novel, *New Atlantis* (1626).

2. *Utopia* by **Thomas More (1516)**
   More's classic describes a journey to a fictional crescent-shaped island in the New World which is strikingly different to the chaotic, myopic Europe of the time. There is no private ownership in Utopia and no locks on the doors. Chamber pots are made out of gold to give people a dislike for riches. Women enjoy high status (though they are not equal to men) but there are still slaves in every household.

3. *Gulliver's Travels* by **Jonathan Swift (1726)**
   On his fourth and final voyage, Gulliver visits a country where intelligent horses, the Houyhnhnms, rule over brute human

beings, the Yahoos. The horses, however, see Gulliver as just another Yahoo, but with a disquieting sense of reason which might upset their social order and he is expelled so that he doesn't cause trouble.

4. *Candide* by Voltaire (1759)
   The whole of *Candide* could be interpreted as a satirical combination of utopia and reality since its purpose is to test the proposition that we already live in the best of all possible worlds, even if we don't know it. In the novel, Candide visits the utopian country of El Dorado where there is no need for courts or prisons. "When one is reasonably content in a place, one ought to stay there," remarks the king, but Candide and his companion are determined to leave El Dorado carrying away with them more gold than in Europe, Asia and Africa combined. Through accident, misfortune and trickery they lose the lot but Candide's mentor still persuades him everything is for the best.

5. *News from Nowhere* by William Morris (1890)
   In Morris' vision of socialism the protagonist falls asleep and wakes up in a society built on common ownership and democracy. Life, art and work are treated as inseparable and people work not because they have to but because they find it creative and pleasurable. The book was partly written in response to Edward Bellamy's Looking Backward (1888), another socialist utopian novel.

6. *The Glass Bead Game* by Hermann Hesse (1943)
   Hesse's book is set in a fictional central European province of the 23rd century, a utopian society for the intellectual elite in which time is dedicated to education and the playing of the eponymous game (the details of which are never fully explained).

7. *Walden Two* by B. F. Skinner (1948)
   This book depicts a society organized according to psychology or "the science of human behavior". Life in Walden Two is so good that no one needs to compete with anyone else or cause conflict, and the inhabitants are taught techniques to deal constructively with their jealousy. The original *Walden* (1854)

was Thoreau's account of simple, solitary living in the woods by a pond – a community based on good psychology.

8. *Island* **by Aldous Huxley (1962)**
   The author's last novel is an antidote to his more famous dystopia, *Brave New World*. The island utopia in question, Pala, is thought to be modelled on Sri Lanka or an Indonesian island. Palanese culture combines what Huxley saw as the best of western science with eastern mysticism. The book has become the inspiration for the Island Foundation (www.island.org).

9. *Lost Horizon* **by James Hilton (1933, filmed in 1937 and 1973)**
   The book which popularized the name Shangri-La, a utopian spiritual community in the Himalayas based on the concept of Shambhala, a mystical lamasery in the Tibetan Buddhist tradition. The inhabitants in this mountain hideout, which is cut off from the world, are well fed and have many modern conveniences but their greatest luxury is longevity.

10. *Shikasta* **by Doris Lessing (1979)**
    Part of the *Canopus in Argos* series, which passes from utopia to dystopia to utopia again. Shikasta is the Earth and the history of human civilisation on it is seen from the point of view of a benign planet far away. 'Prehistoric' peace and harmony is disrupted by evil forces but agents are sent to restore cosmic order.

Wars involving Britain

"The people of England have been led in Mesopotamia into a trap from which it will be hard to escape with dignity and honour. They have been tricked into it by a steady withholding of information. The Baghdad communiques are belated, insincere, incomplete. Things have been far worse than we have been told, our administration more bloody and inefficient than the public knows . . . We are not today far from disaster." A comment on the Iraq War?*

"War is hell, and all that, but it has a good deal to recommend it. It wipes out all the small nuisances of peacetime." Ian Hay

Although the Prussian general Clausewitz famously wrote that "war is nothing more than the continuation of politics by other means", and the Chinese premier Zhou Enlai reversed the same thought to read "all diplomacy is a continuation of war by other means", it could be argued that war and politics are incompatible human activities: a trial of strength takes over where negotiating fails.

The institutional use of force by a country in pursuit of its political goals – otherwise known as warfare – is understood in a different way today than it was a hundred years ago. At the beginning of the last century, soldiers were mostly dispatched to maintain imperial interests with no further justification necessary; by the end of it, they were more likely to be deployed in 'humanitarian' or peace-keeping missions sponsored or approved by 'the international community'.

Some things have not changed, however. It has always been accepted that soldiers must sometimes die in order to defend a point of political principle or national pride which may seem trivial to the next generation. A country's military leaders never believe they have enough resources to do their job effectively – either in manpower or materials – and there is always animosity between generals and politicians over the costs of weaponry in peacetime and who should decide what in times of war. There is a tacit assumption that the opposition can berate the government for not spending enough on defence during peacetime but that it should not try to win votes by challenging the government's conduct of a campaign in time of war.

---

* Answer: T.E. Lawrence, August 1920

War	Dates	Enemy	Battlefield	War aim	Allies
Boer Wars (1st and 2nd)	1899-1902	Transvaal Boers	Southern Africa	Absorption of two breakaway Boer republics into British Empire	Canada, Australia, New Zealand
Boxer Rebellion	1899-1901	The Society of Right Harmonious Fists (a.k.a. the Boxers)	China, incl. Peking (Bejiing)	To protect European interests, trade and religion, in China	7 other nations in the 'Eight-Nation Alliance'
War of the Golden Stool	1900	Ashanti Kingdom	Gold Coast (modern Ghana)	Bring the Ashanti kingdom into the colony of the Gold Coast	Yoruba warriors from Nigeria
First World War	1914-1918	Germany	France Belgium	Defeat Germany	US Common-wealth
Irish War of Indep-endence	1919-1921	Irish nationalists	Ireland	To prevent Ireland from separating from the UK	
Second World War	1939-1945	Germany, Italy, Japan	Germany, Italy, Japan, Europe Far East	Defeat Nazi Germany, Italy Japan; liberate Europe	US, Common-wealth
Palestine	1944-1948	Zionist groups	Palestine (modern Israel)	Fufilment of British Mandate (under the League of Nations) to administer Palestine	

War	Dates	Enemy	Battlefield	War aim	Allies
Malayan Emergency	1948-1957	Malayan National Liberation Army	Malaya	Retain colonial control over Malaya	Australia New Zeland Fiji
Mau Mau Rebellion	1952-1954	The Mau Mau (secret society of Kikuyu tribesmen)	Kenya	Suppression of the Mau Mau	
Korean War	1950-1953	North Korea	Korea	To prevent communist forces in the north taking over the whole of Korea	US
Suez Crisis	1956	Egypt	Egypt	To take control of the Suez Canal which Nasser's Egypt had nationalised	France Israel
Aden	1965-1967	Yemeni republicans	Port of Aden (Red Sea)	Maintain Britain's presence in the Red Sea	
Falklands Conflict*	1982	Argentina	Falklands /Malvinas	Recapture of South Georgia and the Falkland Islands	US (in non-military role)
Bosnia (Operation Deliberate Force)	1995	Bosnia Serb Army	Bosnia and Herzegovina	Bombing campaign to protect UN safe areas in Bosnia	Other Nato members

* Not officially a war as neither side's mainland was invaded

War	Dates	Enemy	Battlefield	War aim	Allies
Kosovo War	1999	Yugoslavia (Serbia)	Kosovo	"humanitarian bombing" to drive the Serbs out of Kosovo, allow peacekeeping troops in and allow refugees to return	Other Nato members
First Gulf War: Recapture of Kuwait	1991	Iraq	Kuwait	Liberation of Kuwait	US and others
Sierra Leone Civil War	2000	West Side Boys and Armed Forces Revolutionary Council	Sierra Leone	Restore peace and rescue British hostages	Other United Nations members
Invasion of Aghanistan (Operation Enduring Freedom)	2001	Taliban	Afghanistan	Elimination of terrorist training camps as part of the 'War on Terror'	US and others
Second Gulf War: Invasion of Iraq	2003–	Saddam Hussein	Iraq	Overthrow of Saddam Hussein and elimination of his supposed arsenal of WMDs	US and others

We are all ...

6 summings up of unwanted solidarity

All you have to do to start disagreement is to say, "we are all...", add your favourite plural noun and conclude the phrase with a damning "now" – implying that some terrifying homogenising process has been completed and that humanity has a new default setting.

"We are all socialists now."
Often attributed to that egalitarian Edward VII but now believed to be the formulation of the Liberal Chancellor of the Exchequer, Sir William Harcourt, in 1888.

"We are all minorities now."
Jeremy Thorpe's appraisal of the situation in March 1974 when no party could muster a majority in the House of Commons.

"We are all Social Democrats now."
A remark of John Biffen at the Conservative Party conference in 1981 when the SDP (see page 201) seemed to be in the ascendancy.

"We are all middle class now."
Supposedly said by Deputy Prime Minister John Prescott in 1996. He probably meant it at least half ironically but it articulated a widespread view that the importance of class in British society had diminished since the Thatcher revolution. The upper class made no comment about it, presumably because they had no need to challenge the assumption – they know they're not middle class. Members of the working class, however, were indignant with John Prescott, one of their own made good, who seemed to be forgetting his roots.

"We are all Europeans now."
Said by too many people every day to be able to attribute it to anyone in particular. Eurosceptics say it to imply that the British are in danger of losing their identity in pursuit of a fictitious European one. Europhiles say it more timidly to remind their compatriots that they belong to a continent as well as a country.

Westminster, The Palace of

Some vital statistics for the mother of parliaments

The building in which Parliament sits is called a 'palace' because the royal family had a residence on the site until a fire in 1512 obliged it to move out.

Another fire on 16th October 1834 caused by a stove overheating virtually obliterated the medieval palace and a new neo-Gothic building was completed by 1870. (C. Northcote Parkinson impishly observed that the date for finishing the new Palace of Westminster coincides with the date around which power shifted from Parliament to the Cabinet.)

On 10th May 1941 a German bomb destroyed the Commons chamber and a new steel-framed, air-conditioned block was built to replace it.

UK residents can arrange a tour of the Palace through their MP. Overseas visitors can take a guided tour during the summer recess.

Plan of the Palace of Westminster

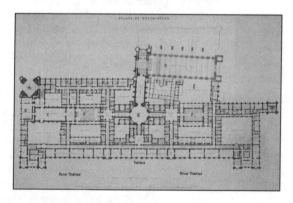

A: Sovereign's entrance
B: Sovereign's robing room
C: Royal gallery
D: Chamber of the House of Lords

E: Central lobby
F: Chamber of the House of Commons
G: Westminster Hall
H: Clock Tower (containing Big Ben)

(source: Wikimedia Commons)

The Palace of Westminster in Figures

Levels: 4 principally. The ground floor has offices, private dining rooms, bars and meeting rooms. The chambers are on the first floor along with libraries and more dining rooms. The top two floors are mainly given over to committee rooms.

Length of river front	265.8m (872ft)
Area of site	3.24 hectares (approx 8 acres)
Lawns	4 acres
Staircases	100
Length of passageways	about 3 miles (4.8km)
Rooms:	1,100
Victoria Tower	Height 98.5m (323 ft)
Clock Tower (popularly, but mistakenly called Big Ben)	Height 96.3m (316 ft). The real Big Ben is a bell inside the tower which weighs 13.8 tonnes (13,760 kg). The hour hand of the clock is made of gunmetal and is 2.7m (9 ft) long; the minute hand is of copper and measures 4.3m (14 ft). There are 32.1 panes of glass in the clock.
Central Tower (over Central Lobby)	Height 91.4m (300 ft)
Population	Fluctuating. As well as the 659 MPs there are 1,000 permanent staff, 8,000 passholders and varying numbers of MPs' guests. It is not just an office block open 9-5 but has a large resident community of employees. It is literally 'the Westminster Village' made up of social clubs, living quarters, places to eat, and recreational spaces.
Overspill buildings	7 Millbank, Parliament Street Building, Portcullis House (built 2000 so that all MPs have their own office).

Westminster Hall

The oldest part of the building is Westminster Hall, whose walls date from 1097. It is one of the largest mediaeval halls with an unsupported (hammerbeam) roof in Europe. It was used for several historic state trials including those of:

- the Scottish rebel William Wallace (1305)
- Thomas More (1535)
- the Gunpowder Plot conspirators (1606)
- King Charles I (1649)
- the impeachment of Warren Hastings (1788-95) – the only one of five on this list who wasn't found guilty and executed.

Trade Unions recognized in the Palace of Westminster

- Association of First Division Civil Servants (FDA)
- Prospect
- Public and Commercial Services Union (PCS)
- General Municipal and Boilermakers Union: Britain's General Union (GMB)
- Consortium of Craft Unions

Works of Art in the Palace of Westminster

- Modern bronzes of Churchill, Lloyd George and Attlee in the Members' Lobby
- A marble statue of Gladstone in the Central Lobby
- Frescoes and murals
- A large collection of paintings illustrating parliamentary history
- Reconstructions of paintings found in the old St Stephen's Chapel in the early 19th century, displayed on the Terrace Stairs
- Furniture and fittings designed or influenced by Augustus W. Pugin
- Medieval statues of kings at the south end of Westminster Hall
- An analemmatic sundial – one which uses the shape of a person to cast a shadow to tell the time – in Old Palace Yard
- A larger-than-life bronze statue of Margaret Thatcher unveiled in 2007, the first of a living prime minister installed in the palace

Westminster Restaurants and Bars

Where to do your drinking between divisions

> *"There are 11 bars in the House of Commons, no crèche and no shop. It would be an ideal place for a small Waitrose. It could replace the rifle range."* Barbara Follett MP

If it was a shopping centre, it might be called a 'food village': the palace offers a variety of places to eat and drink. All are for the exclusive use of MPs and staff who work in the Palace of Westminster, and their guests. The general public is expected to find its own food village.

MPs are traditional British eaters and the menus are not all that different from the average pub: fish and chips, steaks, roast beef, Yorkshire pudding, meat pies, curries etc. Hot puddings are the most popular desserts. The bars serve a weekly-changing guest ale from a small independent or regional British brewery but lager is the preferred long drink. Two other big sellers in the bars of the Palace are House of Commons red wine (a claret), and House of Commons whisky.

If the names of the bars and restaurants are disappointingly staid, then at least in the Palace's annex, Portcullis House, MPs can eat and drink in *The Debate*, *The Adjournment* and *Despatch Box*.

Dining Rooms

* Members' Dining Room.
* Strangers' Dining Room - although Strangers (you and me) can't wander in.
* Churchill Room and Bar.
* Terrace Pavilion, open from Easter to July on the terrace which extends along the whole river front.
* Press Dining Room for lobby journalists, as the name suggests.

Cafeterias

* Terrace Cafeteria self service.
* Members' Tea Room, an inner sanctum of British civility, where

Margaret Thatcher is reported to gone after a backbench rebellion on a 'search and destroy mission'.

- Press Cafeteria, again for journalists.
- The Staff Hall.
- Jubilee Cafe, the most recent catering addition, opened in 2002.

Bars

- The Pugin Room bar lounge, also serving morning coffees and afternoon teas.
- Members' Smoking Room.
- Strangers' Bar.
- Terrace Bar.
- Annie's Bar.
- Press Bar.

Banqueting halls

- Terrace Dining Rooms: four rooms on Centre Curtain Corridor which are available to Members, Officers and all-Party groups when they want to hold a private function.
- The State Apartments, the State Dining Room and the State Bedroom are used for Speakers' functions.

What's Wrong with Government?

8 epigrams of universal applicability

"A government big enough to give you everything you want is a government big enough to take from you everything you have."

Gerald Ford, 1974

"The government solution to a problem is usually as bad as the problem."

Milton Friedman (attrib.)

"Whichever party is in office, the Treasury is in power."

Harold Wilson

"The most terrifying words in the English language are: I'm from the government and I'm here to help."

Ronald Reagan

"Whenever you have an efficient government you have a dictatorship."

Harry S. Truman, 1959

"This Government will soon be in the position of Rabelais, whose will consisted of this sentence: 'I have nothing, I owe much, and the rest I leave to the poor.'"

Herbert Samuel 1919

"The Chancellor is not like Robin Hood, taking wealth from the rich and giving it to the poor. He is taking it from the rich and giving it to the sheriff."

John Pardoe 1975

"Giving money and power to government is like giving whisky and car keys to teenage boys."

PJ O'Rourke, 'Parliament of Whores'

Who Runs Britain?

10 suggested culprits

The answer may seem obvious but give yourself a mark if you ticked any or all of the following:

1. The **government,** or more specifically...

2. the **Cabinet,** which takes collective responsibility for what is done; but these days it is almost by-passed by...

3. the **Prime Minister** with the advice of his appointed spin doctors and special advisers. But...

4. he only acts, by convention, through **crown privilege.** The monarch is ultimately responsible for appointing the PM and the government of the day (she appoints ministers on the PM's recommendation) and, by convention, she has to choose the leader who can command...

5. **a majority** in the House of Commons which only acts with one swarm-mind because of the sadistic manipulation of the whips and in any case owes its existence to...

6. the **electorate.** That's a laugh! You wish. Voters can only choose once every five years between manifestos which are dictated by...

7. the **two main political parties** but they are beholden to...

8. the various **vested interest groups and sponsors** who keep them going. And influenced by...

9. the **mass media** (aided by opinion pollsters) who like to think they interpret 'public opinion' and can make or break politicians on the public's behalf.

    but all this is meaningless if policies cannot be put into practice, which means that ultimately we rely on...

10. the **civil service** which is the power behind the throne. If they don't want to do it, it doesn't get done. What's the point of ordering goods if no one wants to deliver them?

Women in Parliament

"In politics if you want something said, ask a man. If you want something done, ask a woman."

Margaret Thatcher

"In the last Parliament, the House of Commons had more MPs called John than all the women MPs put together."

Tessa Jowell

The first woman MP to win a seat at Westminster was Countess Constance Markievicz who won the St Patrick's division of Dublin in 1918. However, she did not take her seat.

The first woman to *enter* Parliament therefore was Viscountess Nancy Astor (1879-1964) who took her seat on the 1 December 1919 as Conservative MP for Plymouth, after a by-election.

Of the 4,533 members of parliament elected between 1918 and 2001, 252 or 6%, were women. The number of female MPs doubled overnight in 1997: the Labour landslide victory contributed 101 of the 120 women elected. This was also the year in which the first woman speaker, Betty Boothroyd, was appointed.

If it's difficult for a woman to make it in any male-dominated profession, it is even harder in politics. Normally, she has to devote the years between her mid-20s and mid-30s to furthering her political career; she will have to 'blood' herself on a no-hope constituency, which means spending lots of time away from her family, before standing a chance of getting elected. Once in parliament the really anti-social hours begin if she is to get any further up the career ladder.

Table of female MPs

Year	Con	Lab	Lib	Other	All f.	All seats	% f.
1918	0	0	0	1	1	707	0.1%
1922	1	0	1	0	2	615	0.3%
1923	3	3	2	0	8	615	1.3%
1924	3	1	0	0	4	615	0.7%
1929	3	9	1	1	14	615	2.3%
1931	13	0	1	1	15	615	2.4%
1935	6	1	1	1	9	615	1.5%
1945	1	21	1	1	24	640	3.8%
1950	6	14	1	0	21	625	3.4%
1951	6	11	0	0	17	625	2.7%
1955	10	14	0	0	24	630	3.8%
1959	12	13	0	0	25	630	4.0%
1964	11	18	0	0	29	630	4.6%
1966	7	19	0	0	26	630	4.1%
1970	15	10	0	1	26	630	4.1%
1974 Feb	9	13	0	1	23	635	3.6%
1974 Oct	7	18	0	2	27	635	4.3%
1979	8	11	0	0	19	635	3.0%
1983	13	10	0	0	23	650	3.5%
1987	17	21	1	2	41	650	6.3%
1992	20	37	2	1	60	651	9.2%
1997	13	101	3	3	120	659	18.2%
2001	14	95	5	4	118	659	17.9%
2007	17	95	9	5	126	646	19.5%

Writers Turned Politician

10 men and women who both voted while they wroted
- or vice versa

> *"Men of power have no time to read; yet the men who do not read are unfit for power."*
>
> Michael Foot

Plenty of politicians have written diaries and memoirs which are of more or less merit (see p90). Some politicians have also tried to establish a sideline or new career as novelists. Conversely, some writers have tried to become politicians. Only a few men and women, though, have successfully combined literaturising with legislating.

- **Andrew Marvell** (1621-1678) poet was MP for Hull from 1659 to the end of his life. He was a strong supporter of religious toleration and this informed both his poetry and his work as a parliamentarian.

- **Richard Brinsley Sheridan** (1751–1816), the playwright author of *The Rivals* and *School for Scandal* and manager of Drury Lane Theatre was MP for Stafford from 1780. He was a distinguished orator and spoke for five hours in support of the impeachment of Warren Hastings.

- **Benjamin Disraeli** (1804-1881) Although his consuming passion was politics he was also a prolific writer. "When I want to read a novel, I write one." he supposedly remarked. Which he did. His first novel was *Vivian Grey* (1826-7) but his best two are considered to be *Coningsby* or *The New Generation* (1844) and *Sybil* or *The Two Nations* (1845). He is said to have corrected the proofs of Hansard as he lay dying with the words, "I will not go down to posterity talking bad grammar."

- **Anthony Trollope** (1815-82) stood unsuccessfully as a Liberal candidate for parliament in 1868 at Beverley and described the experience as "the most wretched fortnight of my manhood". He came last, with 740 votes. Politics feature in many of his novels.

- **WB Yeats** (1865-1939) was elected as senator in the Irish Free State in 1922 and served 6 years until retiring due to ill health. He described himself at this time as "a sixty-year-old smiling public man". He expressed admiration for Mussolini but supported the Spanish republic against fascism.

- **HG Wells** (1866-1946), the science fiction writer and seer, was also an "undisciplined Fabian Socialist" and "a tireless and constantly frustrated working reformer". He twice stood unsuccessfully as Labour candidate for the London University constituency in the 1920s. His main political proposals were to create a world state that would advance science, make nationalism redundant and make it possible for people to succeed through merit alone, not through advantages of birth.

- **Hilaire Belloc** (1870-1953), the essayist, novelist and poet, best remembered for his light verse, was Liberal MP for Salford South from 1906–1910. He was a rival of George Bernard Shaw and Wells, with ideas markedly in opposition to their socialism. As a Catholic he was an advocate of distributism which maintained that owership of the means of production should be spread widely, not confined to a few bureaucrats as in socialism or to a few wealthy individuals as in capitalism.

- **Winston Churchill** (1874-1965) Few people have had more intensively active political careers than Churchill who was Home Secretary, president of the Board of Trade, First Lord of the Admiralty, Chancellor of the Exchequer and Prime Minister for two terms, amongst other posts. While out of office he wrote biographies and works of contemporary history but he was also the author of a youthful novel *Savrola* (1898).

- **John Buchan** (1875-1940). The confirmed imperialist and author of *The Thirty-Nine Steps* (1915, filmed by Hitchcock in 1935) was a Tory (Scottish Unionist) MP from 1927 for the Scottish Universities, and in 1935 was made Governor General of Canada.

- **Douglas Hurd** (b1930) A gentlemanly Conservative politician who served both Margaret Thatcher and John Major between 1979 and 1995, when he retired. Before, during and after being in office he has had a parallel career writing political thrillers.

X-Factor: Making Your Vote Count
8 recommendations to avoid wasting your time

Despite endless campaigning and party research, newspaper and media discussions, opinion polls, and focus groups, communication between the voted and the voter in British elections is in one direction – the latter barely get a say. It is hard to register a protest vote through the ballot box under a first-past-the-post system which makes it surprising that there is so little civil disturbance (not to say so few revolutions) in Britain. Before you make a trip to the polling station, you might like to consider the following:

1. Whether you think you are voting for your local candidate, the party, its leader or its current manifesto, no one will be able to distinguish your intentions from where you place your cross.

2. You can't vote for just one policy – it is the whole manifesto or nothing and then it is not binding. The party can ignore any 'promise' it finds inconvenient to implement in practice.

3. Unless you are a party member, you cannot dictate the choice laid before you: the candidates are selected by party machines.

4. If you live in a safe seat, your vote is almost certainly wasted. You will have no chance even of voting 'tactically' i.e. voting for a candidate you don't particularly like in order to stop a candidate you dislike even more from winning. In the watershed 1997 election, the only votes that mattered were those of around 168,000 people in crucial marginal constituencies.

5. If you vote for a minor party, even if you live in a marginal seat, your vote will almost certainly be wasted. There are rare instances where an independent takes a seat, but he or she does not usually hold it for long.

6. If you abstain no one cares. You become part of a statistic – one which should worry anyone concerned about democracy. No one can distinguish between positive abstention and negative abstention.

7. If you deliberately spoil your ballot paper to show your contempt for the choice you are being offered – e.g. write a

political slogan on it – it is merely recorded as a wasted vote. Spoiled ballot papers have only been counted since 1964. The record year for them was 1979 when 117,848 papers were spoiled (out of 31 million people who voted). 72,000 of them were counted as invalid because they expressed votes for more than one candidate. The average of spoiled papers was 186 per constituency.

8. Stand for election yourself and you will at least have an opportunity to make your grievance public (you can even write it on the ballot paper next to your name) but you are almost certain to lose your deposit and achieve nothing in practice: policy makers pay little attention to 'fringe candidates'.

Yes Minister

9 quotes to make you laugh or cry or both

"This is not political satire, this is political documentary."
Margaret Thatcher, quoted by Andrew Neil

There are rules for writing television situation comedy and the main one is to choose a situation familiar to most viewers. A suite of offices behind the closed doors of Whitehall should be the ultimate turn-off, and yet this is the setting for one of the greatest comedy series ever made.

Antony Jay and Jonathan Lynn's *Yes Minister* works because it pits together a government minister and his senior civil servant, the Right Hon. Jim Hacker MP and Sir Humphrey Appleby, two people who must work together but whose vested interests are constantly forcing them apart.

To anyone interested in politics, the programmes have the added dimension of reality. The writers were fed material directly from contacts in Whitehall, and you could almost believe they have done nothing with it except put it in the mouths of their principal characters. Several former ministers have commented on how disturbingly true it all looks and sounds and for this reason it was Margaret Thatcher's favourite TV programme. In the absence of a written constitution (except that of Bagehot, see p58), a curious Martian visitor could easily mistake the scripts of *Yes Minister* for the missing manual to British politics.

The Constitution
"It is unthinkable that politicians should be allowed to remove civil servants on grounds of incompetence. Of course some civil servants are incompetent but not incompetent enough for a politician to notice. And if civil servants could remove politicians on grounds of incompetence it would empty the House of Commons, remove the Cabinet, and be the end of democracy and the beginning of responsible government."

The Monarch
"The Queen is inseparable from the Church of England. God is an optional extra."

Parliament
James Hacker (the minister): "I don't want the truth. I want something I can tell Parliament!"

The House of Lords
"Going from the Commons to the Lords is like being moved from the animals to the vegetables."

The Civil Service
"'The matter is under consideration' means we have lost the file. 'The matter is under active consideration' means we are trying to find the file."

The Government
"There are only 630 MPs and a party with just over 300 MPs forms a government and of these 300, 100 are too old and too silly to be ministers and 100 too young and too callow. Therefore there are about 100 MPs to fill 100 government posts. Effectively no choice at all."

The People
"MPs are not chosen by 'the people' – they are chosen by their local constituency parties: thirty-five men in grubby raincoats or thirty-five women in silly hats."

Prognostic
"Diplomacy is about surviving until the next century – politics is about surviving until Friday afternoon."

Zoo

10 rare species of fauna that inhabit the wilderness of Westminster

If man is a political animal, a parliament must be akin to a zoo – its members certainly make zoo-like noises when they get excited. In the French national assembly, the analogy is taken as given: the place from which the president addresses the hemisphere of seated deputies is called the *perchoir*, literally a perch from which a caged bird can crow at those below him on the pecking order.

Cuckoo, cloud *(Cuculus fantasia)*

- Unlike the more familiar cuckoo which steals other birds nests, the cloud cuckoo tries to lure innocent birds to its own unstable habitat, cloud cuckoo land. The idea is thought to have been invented by Aristophanes but Margaret Thatcher was an expert in recognising the species at 250km (in Brussels from London) without binoculars.

Dogs, assorted *(Canis backbenchicus)*

- "Every dog is allowed one bite," Harold Wilson told his pack of MPs, the Parliamentary Labour Party in 1967, "but a different view is taken of a dog that goes on biting all the time. He may not get his licence returned when it falls due."

- Lloyd George described the House of Lords as 'Mr Balfour's Poodle' in 1907.

- Running dogs were traditionally the lackeys of capitalism in Maoist rhetoric.

Duck, Lame *(Anas disadvantagean)*

- A 19th century stock exchange term for a debtor and now applied to anyone or anything that can't stand up by itself (metaphorically), let alone fly.

- Edward Heath used it of nationalised industries that depended on inputs of government money; although genetically improbable, a lame duck, in this sense, is related to a white elephant.

- It is also used in the US sense of an office holder who has been discredited (or announced that he will be announcing his resignation without specifying a date for either announcement or resignation) and therefore lost his power.

Elephant, Rogue *(Elephas insensitus)*

- An animate version of a loose cannon but essentially the same thing: a large, lumbering creature which has a mind of its own and goes around knocking over things.

Horse, Stalking *(Equus subterfugis)*

- A politico-zoological version of a kamikaze or forlorn hope, being a challenger for a post (usually that of party leader) who hasn't a hope of winning, and knows it. The idea – if this isn't a metaphor too far – is to test the water for someone more serious.

  The most famous such horse in recent history was Sir Anthony Meyer who, in 1989, undertook the unthinkable in challenging Margaret Thatcher for the leadership of the Conservative Party to see whether the time was ripe for a pro-European such as Michael Heseltine to openly declare himself. Meyer was, as expected, soundly defeated in his challenge and thus committed political suicide but his action revealed that around a sixth of the parliamentary party was having doubts about Thatcher as leader.

  A year later, she was successfully removed from office.

Monkey, Rear-flashing *(Simia exhibitionisticus)*

- An animal observed in the wild by Lloyd George's son, Gwilym (who may have been adapting an existing proverb): "Politicians are like monkeys; the higher they get up the tree, the more revolting are the parts they expose."

Polecat, Semi-house-trained *(Mustela semipissidomestican)*

- The species identified by Michael Foot in the House of Commons in 1977. He was referring to Norman Tebbit.

Sheep, dead *(Ovis mortuus)*

- As in, "that part of his speech was rather like being savaged by a dead sheep": Denis Healey's remark in the House of Commons on Sir Geoffrey Howe, 14 June 1978.

  Dead animals crop up quite a lot in politics. George Orwell said that Clement Attlee "… reminds me of nothing so much as a dead fish before it has had time to stiffen." And Denis Thatcher made a rare public comment during the 1979 election campaign when his wife picked up a calf in a cattle market for the press to take a photograph of her. "Unless she's careful," he said within the earshot of reporters. "we're going to have a dead calf on our hands."

Boa constrictor *(Boa wetestrangulae)*

- Tony Banks described Margaret Thatcher as acting "with the sensitivity of a sex-starved boa-constrictor".

Turkeys voting for an early Christmas *(Maleagris autocondemnis)*

- Jim Callaghan's famous verdict on the Scottish Nationalist MPs who were frustrated with his government's failure to deliver devolution and who sought the no-confidence motion on 28 March 1979 which would bring his government down. He was pointing out that they might lose their own seats in the forthcoming general election and certainly wouldn't get devolution from Margaret Thatcher, a prognostic which was proved right.

Bibliography

10 texts for understanding politics

This list is at once an acknowledgement of some of the best sources used to compile this book and a recommendation for further reading.

There is no shortage of political reading matter in circulation; the problem is choosing something to match your mood and interest. In other parts of this book there are recommendations for choosing political fiction, plays and poetry; political theory texts; economics tracts; politicians' diaries; and even a politico's selection from the works of Shakespeare. The Bible and the Koran can also be mined for their political content.

The books below are arranged in descending somniferous order – that is according to the suitability of the contents for bedtime reading – from one that will keep you awake all night until you finish it, to one that will cure the worse insomnia (and particularly if you read it in a public reference library).

All the books mentioned are informative and point to yet more universes of political reading.

'The Political Animal: An Anatomy' by Jeremy Paxman (2002)

Not only is this a readable and even, in places, funny book but it is also strong on facts and figures. It is probably as good an answer as we will get to the question of why anyone would want to go into politics when almost every political career involves years of struggle at the outset and ends in scandal, disappointment or failure by another name.

'Great Parliamentary Scandals' by Matthew Parris (1995)

Despite the title this is not at all a prurient book. Rather it is an insight into the humanity that underpins all politics. Parris was himself an MP and what stands out is his empathy for the people he writes about, some of who were personal friends and acquaintances. Although the book is ostensibly a series of cautionary tales about individual foibles and bad luck leading to disaster, it could be better thought of as a humane history of British democracy.

'The Oxford Dictionary of Political Quotations' edited by Antony Jay (2005)

There are many dictionaries of political quotations around, and several websites on the same subject, but most of the rest are either drearily arranged or lacking in essential source details. This book compiled by one of the writers of *Yes Minister* (see p352) and *Yes Prime Minister* is browsable, dippable and authoritatively consultable at the same time.

'Brewer's Politics' by Nicholas Comfort (1993, revised 1995)

An extraordinary compendium of all things political – most serious but some not so – presented with a lightness which makes it as good to flick through as it is to consult as a dictionary. Covering British and US politics mainly, although with some entries on other countries of the world, it includes an extraordinary number of quotes, nicknames and details that might otherwise get forgotten. Its one minor drawback which could just as easily be seen as its charm is the "mildly whimsical approach" to selection and organisation characteristic of Brewer's, so that, for instance, the main entry on Margaret Thatcher is under I, for Iron Lady.

'The Time of My Life' by Denis Healey (1990)

Many retiring politicians write their memoirs but most range from dull to dire. This is widely regarded as the best autobiography by someone who has held high office (Chancellor of the Exchequer), regardless of political views of writer or reader. Another minister in the same governments as Healey, a junior one, was Gerald Kaufman (before that, a contributor to *That Was the Week That Was*); just out of office he wrote the readable 'How to be a Minister' (1980, revised 1997). The Conservative minister and twice candidate for the mayoralty of London, Steve Norris, also wrote a much praised book about his career, 'Changing Trains' (1996). Another good book is 'A Bag of Boiled Sweets' (1994) by the veteran Conservative MP Julian Critchley. For more intimate confessions, see Diaries (p90).

'Chronicle of the 20th Century' edited by Derrik Mercer (1995)

A large book which gives the news for the 20th century year by year and almost day by day, along with lots of photographs and maps. It is particularly good at showing how issues that are mere history to us must have seemed to people at the time, and how political events related to all other aspects of contemporary life.

'The New Fontana Dictionary of Modern Thought' edited by Alan Bullock and Stephen Trombley (originally published in 1977 but much revised)

As it says in the title, this book is an A–Z guide to ideas. Not all of them are to do with politics but many of them have an indirect bearing to the subject. It's strength is in tackling slippery concepts that other books might skirt around. There is, therefore, an entry on 'prime ministerial government' rather than on the post of prime minister.

'The Oxford Companion to Twentieth-Century British Politics' edited by John Ramsden (2002 and later editions)

A scholarly encyclopedia written by over 100 experts in their fields, with the added advantage of suggested further reading at the end of each main article. It has a useful classified contents list at the beginning – so that you can see quickly, say, which individual communists have got a mention – and a summary of the composition of governments and of election results at the end.

'British Political Facts since 1979' by David Butler and Gareth Butler (2005)

This is not a relaxing read but that's not the point, which is to deliver hard facts on ministries, parliaments, parties, elections, the civil service. In a similar vein is 'The Almanac of British Politics' by Byron Criddle and Robert Waller (2007).

UK The Official Yearbook of Great Britain and Northern Ireland (published annually)

All statistics are out of date and most should be treated with suspicion, but this is as reliable as they get. The book, available in reference libraries if you don't think you'll be reading it regularly, is a dry but detailed read with plenty of tables and maps. Alternatively, the whole thing can be downloaded from www.statistics.gov.uk – but, then, there are usually more up-to-date statistics available on this same site.

Webography

10 sites for political sleuths

Politics is complicated enough without having to tunnel into some distant server to find the information you need. Some websites seem to challenge the visitor to dive into a maze of archival dead ends and unlinked pages in search of even the most innocuous fact. The websites below, however, honour the spirit of the web in making things easy: they offer substantial amounts of reliable content, use graphics to clarify not to dazzle, are easily searchable (usually in more than one way, including intuitively) and have abundant, well-placed links to other good sites.

Some political information – especially much detail relating to affairs before the mid-1990s – is not on the web, but if it is there, the chances are you will get to it using one of these 10 sites as a starting point. They are arranged in order of scope: from the most wide-ranging to the most specific to a particular subject.

Wikipedia
en.wikipedia.org
An almost bottomless resource on all subjects, and extremely detailed on British and world politics. Wikipedia articles are generally open to anyone to correct or add to, and hence mistakes in the information are possible although surprisingly rare. If nothing else, the site provides a good starting point through its external links. Usually its main drawback is that you will get side-tracked from your original search through some nugget of curiosity you can't resist following up.

BBC
www.bbc.co.uk
This site can be seen either as a huge public resource or a huge public resource which is also a huge waste of public money. It has vast layers of information, including an archive of the news going back several years and an excellent set of links to all things political. Many television and radio programmes have their own sub-sites within the labyrinth.

Politics Studies Association
www.psa.ac.uk

Principally a resource to encourage people to study politics – this is a good way to find out about university courses available – but also a portal into a vast universe of political information with links to 12,000 sites in Britain and around the world.

Richard Kimber's Political Science Resources
www.psr.keele.ac.uk

A set of links to an extraordinary number of useful sites in Britain and abroad, including many organizations you never knew existed, all arranged in clear menus. It includes its own pages on elections, breaking the results down into statistics.

Directgov
www.direct.gov.uk

In the interests of making government as open as possible, this portal is intended to be a simplified, one-stop access for the citizen to any branch of the poltical system. It includes a sketchy outline to the constitution but works best as a starting point for finding other official websites.

Parliament
www.parliament.uk

A comprehensive source of facts about the Palace of Westminster, its history and everything that goes on inside it. Particularly useful is its series of downloadable (in pdf format) factsheets about aspects of parliament past and present. It connects to Hansard (see page 142), the official record of debates in the House of Commons and House of Lords.

Ask Aristotle
politics.guardian.co.uk/aristotle/

Part of the *Guardian* website, this is a searchable database of information about MPs and their constituencies. It can be searched via a blue, red and yellow map, an A to Z list or a keyword search engine.

Theyworkforyou.com
www.theyworkforyou.com
This is "a non-partisan website run by a charity which aims to make it easy for people to keep tabs on their elected and unelected representatives in Parliament, and other assemblies." Search for your MP or any other and it instantly returns a detailed list of what he or she has or hasn't been up to in parliament.

Downing Street
www.number-10.gov.uk
The official website for the office of the prime minister. It is primarily about the current incumbent but also has useful information about all past prime ministers and about the house which is their official residence.

Margaret Thatcher Foundation
www.margaretthatcher.org
A work of hagiography rather than a critical assessment, this site has almost every last detail of the great lady's life, making it an invaluable resource for finding out anything about her, or for getting at least a one-sided view on any event between 1979 and 1990. If only there was such a site for every past prime minister.